A MOST UNSETTLING PERSON

A MOST UNSETTLING PERSON

The Life and Ideas of Patrick Geddes,
Founding Father of City Planning
and Environmentalism

by
Paddy Kitchen

Saturday Review Press / E. P. Dutton & Co., Inc.

Copyright © 1975 by Paddy Kitchen
All rights reserved. Printed in the U.S.A.
First American edition published by Saturday Review Press.

10 9 8 7 6 5 4 3 2 1

ISBN: 0-8415-0409-1
Library of Congress Catalog Number: 75-33591

Each individual is at best unique, and the great man
is a culminating product of past tendencies and forces,
all hard to unravel, and perhaps harder to estimate
at their respective importance, whether for him or
the world. Such in fact is the many-sidedness of every
full life, every developing and varied career, that we
may have as many biographies as there chance to be
biographers, perhaps as many fresh interpretations
of these as they find reflective readers.   (Geddes)

CONTENTS

Illustrations follow page 176

ACKNOWLEDGEMENTS

My sincere thanks to Mrs Jeannie Geddes for her co-operation and permission to use copyright material.

The main collections of Patrick Geddes's papers are kept in the National Library of Scotland, and the Department of Urban & Regional Planning, University of Strathclyde. I thank both institutions for their assistance.

My stays in Edinburgh were made extremely happy by the helpfulness of the staff at the National Library, the kindness of the many people whom I met, and by Frank Thomas who provided me with a home.

My task was made much easier by the existence of two earlier biographies: *Patrick Geddes, Maker of the Future*, by Philip Boardman, and *Pioneer of Sociology, the Life and Letters of Patrick Geddes*, by Philip Mairet, and I am grateful to those authors—both of whom knew Geddes.

I thank the R.I.B.A. for permission to use their library, and would like also to mention the London Library. Although this is a subscription library, its vast stocks and its civil atmosphere combine to make membership a privilege and a bargain.

I thank all the people I have written to and talked to about Geddes, and who have so readily supplied me with help and information; particularly David Pearce, editor of *Built Environment*, and Peter Redgrove. Also Fred Mann of the Carnegie Dunfermline Trust, Kitty Michaelson and Giles Playfair.

I am most grateful to the Arts Council for financial assistance, and to my sympathetic bank manager.

Doris E. Kitchen, my mother, and Dulan Barber, my husband, respectively typed and criticized my manuscript, and welcomed Geddes's presence into our home. To have outstanding (and willing) secretarial skill and critical perception on the premises are benefits beyond value.

P. K.

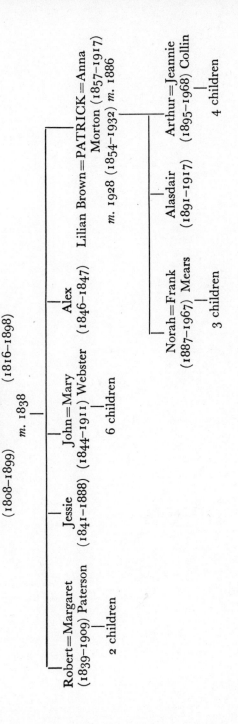

Alexander Geddes=Janet Stivenson
(1808–1899)   (1816–1898)
m. 1838

Robert=Margaret
(1839–1909) Paterson
2 children

Jessie
(1841–1888)

John=Mary
(1844–1911) Webster
6 children

Alex
(1846–1847)

Lilian Brown=PATRICK=Anna
                              Morton (1857–1917)
m. 1928 (1854–1932) m. 1886

Norah=Frank
(1887–1967) Mears
3 children

Alasdair
(1891–1917)

Arthur=Jeannie
(1895–1968) Collin
4 children

INTRODUCTION

PATRICK GEDDES BELIEVED passionately that, given reasonable social conditions, man is a co-operative animal. He also believed that, treated properly, the earth is fundamentally a co-operative planet on which to live. He aimed to find out how to achieve those "reasonable social conditions" and to teach people how their environment might be "treated properly". He was the most comprehensive, if least acknowledged, father of civic renewal and bio-social ecology as we are beginning to understand them today.

Born in 1854, his influence is directly felt by only a handful of people. He saw western thought become pessimistic, introspective and hair-splitting; yet to the end of his life in 1932, by his actions even more than by his words, he demonstrated his conviction that education, participatory citizenship, and appreciation of the natural world, would save industrial society. Like the morally-earnest Victorian which he partially was, he had his own Latin motto: *vivendo discimus*—by living we learn; or, fieldwork and civic action are better than indoor study and book-writing. Besides the motto he also had a symbol, and this was more characteristic of the twentieth century (though both were appropriated during the 1880's). The symbol was the three doves that appear on the title page of this book. Geddes called them the three S's, and they stand for Sympathy, Synthesis and Synergy. Sympathy for the people and environment affected by any social remedy; synthesis of all the factors relevant to the case; and synergy—the combined, co-operative action of everyone involved—in order to achieve the best result. The doves also represent peace. One of the most evocative sentences Geddes ever wrote is: "People volunteer for war; and it is a strange and a dark superstition that they will not volunteer for peace."

By training he was a biologist (like H. G. Wells he studied under T. H. Huxley), and this influenced his whole approach to society. He saw man as an integral part of nature, and nature as a combination of forces, predominantly benevolent, working towards species-maintaining ends. The "struggle for survival, weakest-to-the-wall" ethic that fuelled the *laissez-faire* economists and industrialists was an anathema to him (though he was a loving admirer of Darwin himself as a naturalist). The strong element of international co-operation and communication that exists between scientists, involving travel and correspondence, taught him to continue a similar mode of operation when considering broader issues. He travelled extensively throughout his life, meeting and corresponding with people as diverse as Haeckel, Ruskin, Kropotkin, William James, Annie Besant, Charles Booth, Jane Addams, John Dewey, Thorstein Veblen, Tagore, Gandhi and Bergson.

His first major step towards practical civic renewal was taken in 1886 when, as a university lecturer of thirty-two, he took his new wife, Anna, to live in the tenement slums of old Edinburgh in order to teach the impoverished community how to renew their environment. He persuaded neighbours to put colour washes on the walls of the old dank closes, to brighten the tenement façades with window boxes, and while he organized the installation of bathrooms, he pointed out to the authorities the follies of demolition when it left the native citizens of a town with nowhere to live. At the same time he and a group of friends and business-men bought up nearby properties and converted them into the first self-governing student hostels in Britain. Collegiate life and urban working life were to develop together, side-by-side, to their mutual benefit. He never denied the evils that existed in cities, but he always believed they could be diagnosed, and steps taken towards their cure.

This belief in the capability of man to solve his own social problems was encouraged by his study of the early French sociologists Comte and Le Play, and as a young man he strove to fuse what he learned from them with his convictions as a biologist. He was one of the first men to see that economics should be a matter of resources, not money, and he tried to work out structures which could formulate supply and need on an international basis. The driving intensity which made him synthesize his knowledge, to open people's eyes to the world as a co-ordinated, functioning organism which must not be abused, meant that he was never accepted into the higher realms of the academic establishment, with its specialisms and moderate behaviour.

In 1897, when a Turkish massacre caused Armenian refugees to flee into surrounding countries, he and Anna organized an expedition to aid the 500 or so who had landed in Cyprus. This expedition was in many ways a model for the types of relief and aid which, through costly trial-and-error, we have now learned are most beneficial for areas under stress. Geddes emphasized the establishment of work-operations congenial to the refugees and their new habitat, and thoroughly surveyed the island in order to recommend agricultural initiatives.

By the time this event occurred, he had been responsible for the founding in Edinburgh of several student houses, a publishing company, a small art school, a yearly international summer school, and a museum called the Outlook Tower in which he tried to précis his synoptic view of the universe in order to educate people towards sharing his vision. As well as the sheer hard work involved in these activities, the financial jugglings to bring them about were extremely complex, and so as to relieve him of some of the pressures and responsibilities, friends and colleagues formed a company called the Town & Gown Association Limited to take over most of the practical administration.

However, projects tended to founder when Geddes himself was no longer totally involved, vitalizing them with his energy. He in turn expected others to be capable of initiative similar to his own, thus leaving him free to develop new ventures, and he grew impatient when his friends and followers lacked his superhuman stamina. A clue to the kind of vitality he had can be found in William James's essay "The Energies of Men". Lewis Mumford has suggested that the essay may have been prompted by James's meetings with Geddes, and in it he explores the phenomenon whereby a few people seem able to tap sources of energy beyond the normal fatigue barrier. If they continue to repeat the experience, they do not, as might be expected, become cumulatively tired, but rather they seem to "energize" their systems and grow capable of prolonged mental or physical activity, way beyond the habits of most men.

Geddes was certainly like this. In childhood he had formed the habit of waking very early and reading for two or three hours before it was time to get up. Then, once the day was under way, he was unstoppable. This made him both inspiring and exhausting, and accounted for his impatience when other people could not stand the pace, for to him it was quite natural. This concept of "energized" man has been fully explored by Colin Wilson, and much of what he has written on Abraham Maslow's psychological explanation of "self-actualizing" people is applicable to Geddes. Maslow had recognized that "we are living in a low-synergy society . . . and that it would be healthier if it was a high-synergy society", and he devoted much of his work to studying people of high achievement. A "high-synergy society" is a concept Geddes would have applauded; and it is also reminiscent of ideas developed by Buckminster Fuller. There are indeed many parallels between Geddes and Fuller—not least their ability to talk out their all-embracing theories at prodigious length.

Long before he was entitled to the designation, Geddes was known in Edinburgh as "the Professor". Slight, untidy, always hurrying, with a shock of wiry hair parted in the middle and a thick, reddish beard, he was the traditional storybook professor. And he was invariably talking. Not gossip or chatter, but a continuous, life-long monologue as he strove to inspire others with his vision of a combined knowledge, where the arts and sciences harmonized for the benefit of society. (Tagore wrote of him: "He has the precision of a scientist and the vision of a prophet.") In short bursts his company was exhilarating —an elixir. Impossibly, he wanted his companions to remain in that state of exhilaration for a lifetime. When he did pause for breath, it was usually to savour the intricacies and beauty of the natural world—which had provided the background to his extremely happy childhood; and his rather large hands were once described as "hands that seem like roots that have not quite shaken off the earth".

He never did "shake off the earth" in his approach to any subject, and his most urgent appeal to planners and architects was that they should physically survey in every possible aspect (geographical, historical, cultural, economic, social) all areas that they were asked to develop or restore. Only then would they be equipped to find humane, practical and comely solutions. The displays which he instigated at the Outlook Tower during the 1890's included a survey of Edinburgh made with this thoroughness, and it foreshadowed the city exhibitions which he organized in Britain, Europe and India between 1910 and 1920. The first, held at the Royal Academy, was part of

the great Town Planning Exhibition and Conference promoted
by John Burns whose Town and Country Planning Act had
been passed the previous year. A group of architects, including
Raymond Unwin, Patrick Abercrombie and H. V. Lanchester,
were involved in the establishment of town planning as an
organized profession, and all three of them were closely associated with Geddes at various times. It is from Abercrombie's
description of Geddes at the Royal Academy exhibition that
I have taken the title of this book. He recalled the "nightmare
complexity" of Geddes's exhibit, "a torture-chamber to those
simple souls that had been ravished by the glorious perspectives . . . shown in those other ample galleries. Within this den
sat Geddes, a most unsettling person, talking, talking, talking
. . .". But Abercrombie also claimed that Geddes's inclusion in
the exhibition was a major factor in some people's realization
that a new approach, which must include more than just a
grandiose aesthetic solution, was needed to town planning.
Because Unwin and others were heavily involved in the garden
city type of development, history has tended to treat Geddes as
though this were his prime concern also. He certainly was in
favour of creating new, balanced communities, but never at the
expense of the old high-density urban ones—and it is his principle of "conservative surgery" in relation to the latter that we
have at last come to realize is so relevant.

This principle, along with many others, is outlined in his
book *Cities in Evolution*, which has never gone totally out of
favour with enlightened architects and planners. Recently it
was recommended in a planning journal by one architect
"because every time I read it, it seems to have been written
yesterday". A caveat should perhaps be added to that: many
of the ideas are up-to-date, but the prose style is not. One of
Geddes's early influences was Carlyle, and he also had an
inability to settle down for sustained periods to create planned
volumes. Most of his books were written in collaboration
(J. Arthur Thomson, his scientific collaborator, claimed that
working with Geddes bled him of his last ounce of energy),
and *Cities in Evolution* probably only saw the light of day
because he had an excellent stenographer at the time who
could capture the rapid rhetorical flow. There is, however,
another work for which he was also totally responsible, and
which has equal relevance with *Cities in Evolution*. This is the

report he presented to the Carnegie Dunfermline Trust when asked to make design proposals for a substantial area of land bequeathed to the City of Dunfermline by Andrew Carnegie. It is a stunning report (happily reprinted in 1974 by the Irish University Press), showing Geddes's grasp of minute detail, which then blossoms out to create a philosophical and humane vision for virtually the whole city. It is a tragedy that such vision was obliterated for two generations.

Over the last twenty years we have seen what happens when Planner-Economist Gullivers push over old town centres and their peripheral acres of terrace housing without properly respecting the history, folk-lore and community-sense inlaid into the old fabric. The urban haemorrhage created as bull-dozers and pile-drivers move in on run-down city-landscapes has been painted and filmed by artists who recognize the horror of the images, the implications of treating cumulative evidence of life as though it were so much excrement. One ex-resident returning to visit Stepney, declared: "It was a ghost town. I was shocked. This is the gospel truth. They killed it. They annihilated the area." We are gradually coming to understand, as Geddes had always understood, that demolition and recon-struction can only be successful when the majority of the com-munity affected by the changes favourably understands them, and is included in the rehabilitation plan.

We realize now that instant environment can no longer be slapped down on to cities with impunity by power élites whose expertise and ambition lie mainly in the field of economics. Occasionally these environments have been designed by men of vision, and are exciting for those who understand and share that vision. Rarely does that encompass the less sophisticated, yet extremely complex, subconsciously-formed instinctive vision of the people who will use the environment. In saying this, I do not wish to join in the current obloquy of architects and planners. Blame for our mistakes cannot suddenly be heaped wholesale at their doors. These mistakes have grown from an undiscerning refusal on the part of so-called "developed" nations to cultivate the synoptic vision every man needs if he is to keep his balance. They have grown from a blind belief that it is money, and not its own resources, that makes the world go round. Now we are starting to recognize some of the faults of our system and to seek remedies. But we grossly mis-

lead ourselves if we think that our present imbroglios were un-
foreseeable, and that they were the inevitable result of the run-
away "progress" of the twentieth-century as it snowballed in
front of our eyes, apparently leaving us no time to assess each
of its stages of growth. Many of them *were* foreseen, and many
of those were foreseen by Patrick Geddes.

His Dunfermline report proved too much for the Trust's
committee, and they turned down both it and a more conventional one which had been commissioned from the architect, T. H. Mawson. But very many of Geddes's practical
proposals for Pittencrieff Park have in fact seeped through
over the years, and anyone walking through the boldly landscaped and intricately planted Glen will experience both the
kind of wild beauty he loved and a diversity of plants that
would have delighted his botanist's eye. Botany, indeed, was
perhaps his fundamental love. He was part-time Professor of
Botany at University College Dundee for over thirty years—a
Chair endowed for him by a wealthy friend after he had
repeatedly failed in his applications for other posts. The
appointment entailed his attendance for only the summer term,
and the small botanical garden which he developed there was
copied both by himself and others in many places. This garden
had evolved from his childhood love of nature, in which he was
encouraged by his father—a retired soldier who had a profound
but benign effect on his life. Living in a modest cottage on the
outskirts of Perth, Alexander Geddes had reared his youngest
child in a way which unconsciously embodied most of the basic
principles of what we now consider to be enlightened education.
It instilled in Geddes a deep disdain for all dry academic
drudgery, and he adamantly refused to take degree examinations—another contributory factor to his rejection by the
educational establishment. Indeed he always deplored the
whole examination system, and used to claim that the three
H's—heart, hand and head—should be substituted for the
three R's. He tried to rear his own three children in this way,
so that love and care of plants and animals, the enjoyment of
painting, singing and dancing, were as important as reading
and numeracy. And everyone, he felt, should have practical
experience of as many crafts as possible.

This practical emphasis did not mean that he had little time
for intellectual cultural pursuits. As a teenager his early

morning reading had encompassed philosophy, novels, poetry, and later sociology and psychology, and it was a practice which he kept up until his death. As well as reading, he used these early hours to limber up his own thoughts, making endless charts, notes and outlines which he seldom threw away, and which encumbered his travels in the vain hope that one day he would find someone who would help him synthesize them into definitive volumes. No field of knowledge failed to excite him, and nothing was ever so foreign that he would put up a defensive wall and refuse to try to understand it.

Conventional politics, however, were virtually irrelevant to his life, since the whole structure of opposing parties was quite contrary to his belief in co-operation, and could not, in his view, lead to anything abidingly useful for the community. As a young man he wrote a paper in favour of the co-operative movement rather than socialism, and he was close friends with anarchists such as Peter Kropotkin and the brothers Elisée and Elie Reclus. He utterly opposed violence for political ends, but anarchism of the kind developed in Kropotkin's *Mutual Aid* he understood.

He denounced the war-like, jingoist spirit which pervaded Britain towards the end of the nineteenth century, and tried to show how the technical advances of the industrial revolution should be used for homes and peace, not armed forces and war. But his eldest son, Alasdair, was killed in the first world war, a son on whom he had imprinted his vision and his ideals, but whom he had failed to convince that he was not morally bound to go to the aid of their friends and allies in France and Belgium. Geddes was in India at the time, and he remained there for the better part of several years, making suggestions for the re-planning of over fifty towns with the same care for detail and understanding of the Indian people as he had shown for the Scots in Edinburgh and Dunfermline. His wife, who had lovingly and practically supported all his plans and ideals, and never despaired at his failures, died there shortly after Alasdair was killed.

In 1919 he was commissioned by the Zionist Federation to suggest improvements to the Military Government's extension plan for Jerusalem, and to design a new university for the city. Helped by his architect son-in-law, Frank Mears, he floated a dream at the Zionists, an outline of his own dream for a truly international university—though it was a dream with concrete shape. The buildings were designed on an hexagonal plan (Star of David), with the faculties radiating from a great domed central hall. Town and gown elements were to be united by a garden village in which student accommodation stood alongside workers' homes, both elements sharing the responsibility for self-supporting market-gardens. Geddes quickly grasped the need for extremely sensitive urban renewal proposals, in which the old Arab quarter would be respected and integrated with the new additions, but once again his vision was too wide. As one of the Zionist authorities put it afterwards, when Geddes's design plans had been frustrated and his social integration proposals ignored: "Suffice it to say there are few who could rise to the lofty heights of his imagination and practical knowledge."

He returned to India, where his supporters had created a part-time Chair of Sociology and Civics at Bombay University which he filled for five years. He continued to travel, keeping up contacts in Europe, Britain and America, and observing with hope the work of the League of Nations, while judging that it was doomed to failure through bureaucracy. In the winter of 1923 he became extremely ill, and doctors advised him that he would not survive the Indian climate any longer.

He settled in the South of France near Montpellier, whose University he had often visited, and where he had old friends. The Mediterranean climate suited him, he loved France, and as an old man in his seventies he began to create his own college on the stony slopes outside the old medieval town. Called the Collège des Ecossais, it was to be the culmination of his ideals— an international college, where everyone gardened, made the buildings, surveyed the countryside, created festivals, paintings and music, and studied all the writers whose images and words hummed in his own brain in a resounding symphony of ideas. Thus equipped, his students would then be able to return to regenerate their own parts of the world.

The practicalities never really worked out, and when, in 1931, he was offered a knighthood for the second time ("for services to education"), he decided to quell his republican ideals and accept the honour. As he wrote to his daughter, the offer "does not stir or touch my pulse . . . but it might do both for my purse"—in other words help to bring in financial support for the college. In fact the winter stay in London for the investiture (the King was ill so the ceremony had to be delayed), damaged his already fragile health, and he died, at the age of seventy-seven, not very long after returning to Montpellier.

His tangible legacy is hard to catalogue. He left thousands of letters, papers, charts and manuscripts, the bulk of which have fairly recently been presented to the National Library of Scotland and Strathclyde University. The Sociological Society, founded by his close friend and colleague Victor Branford partly in order to promulgate the Geddesian approach to social studies, initiated the *Sociological Review*—which is still published from Keele University. One of this century's most profound writers on cities and civilization, Lewis Mumford, was initially set on that particular course through the work of Geddes—with whom he corresponded as a young man and met for the first time in 1923. In *The Condition of Man* (1944) he named Geddes as the example of the type of man that hopefully would evolve to defeat the recessive forces which had been pervading society: "Geddes was on the side of life. . . . He challenged every success that was bought at the expense of further growth, further self-renewal."

Of the several words coined by Geddes, it is unfortunate that only one with unpleasant connotations—"conurbation"—should have been accepted into the English language, whereas his more positive "geotechnics"—the science of making the earth more habitable and restoring its resources—has not. Above all, almost the whole foundation of our current regional, environmental and ecological thinking is there in his ideas and actions, but that foundation was swept aside by society's preoccupation with war, power and money.

Geddes's intimate family life and public work are inseparable, and they interweave in this study. I do not claim mastery of the various disciplines with which he was familiar, and other people will write on aspects of his work more thoroughly. Indeed, during my researches I discovered there is an awakening interest in his ideas, and other studies are in preparation. One of the reasons why he has been neglected is, I believe, that people distrust active polymaths. Few of us can judge their multifarious ideas with any certainty, so we tend to dismiss them as charlatans or wool-gatherers. Also, as Lewis

Mumford has pointed out, "the very self-absorption that sustains their work, along with a god-like self-confidence, corrodes normal social relations". But once such men are dead, one can wander through their complicated, intersecting paths of thought without harassment. Geddes, I am sure, partly kept his correspondence and papers for posterity. (Unfortunately, due no doubt to his peripatetic life, there are tantalizing gaps, even though the two collections contain literally tens of thousands of items.) He did not keep these papers out of self-importance, but because he felt his ideas were useful. He did not mind if his name was not attached to them, as long as the ideas were disseminated.

Many of the advances of this century have been inward-looking, affecting the private individual: the development of psychology, more freedom in emotional behaviour, more comfort inside dwellings, weather-proof containers to travel about in, press-button entertainment. While these were taking place (and I do not wish to denigrate them), exteriors were being neglected. Not just the exteriors of buildings and all kinds of urban and rural environments, but also our external behaviour as part of a community, part of society. The balance is being righted now. We are recovering from national myopia, individual self-absorption. I hope it is an appropriate time, therefore, to write about Patrick Geddes. He tried to synthesize inward and outward needs, saying that life should be nurtured "both by the objective work of reconstructing the environment and by subjective expression of the individual . . . in other words this simply means that agriculturalist, architect and politician will be working out the visions of a Ruskin, a Tolstoy, a Walt Whitman".

A MOST UNSETTLING PERSON

Chapter 1

MOUNT TABOR

THE "DOUBLE VISION which sees with both eyes—the scientific eye of actuality, and the illumined eye of imagination and dream"—the words are Lewis Mumford's, and he used them to describe Melville, but he could also have used them to describe Patrick Geddes, his more immediate mentor. For Geddes possessed and practised this "double vision" from his earliest days.

He was born in Ballater, West Aberdeenshire, on 2nd October 1854, and proved an archetypal Libran in his life-long attempt to synthesize and balance the resources and forces he found in the world. His baptismal name was Peter, but this was soon superseded by Patrick, and throughout his life his family and close friends called him Pat.

By 1857 the Geddes family had moved fifty miles south to a cottage on the slopes of Kinnoull Hill, overlooking the small city of Perth. This cottage was to remain the permanent centre of his childhood, and its atmosphere of family love, practical learning, and spiritual faith, leavened with an appreciation of both created and natural beauty, held until the death of his parents some forty years later.

It is an ordinary-looking stone cottage, but Alexander Geddes, Patrick's father, gave it an extra-ordinary name—Mount Tabor. This mountain which lies near Nazareth, is mentioned in the Old Testament, and is claimed by some to have been the site of the Transfiguration. As an elder of the local kirk, Alexander Geddes would have been well aware of these references, but he may also have actually climbed the mountain during his itinerant thirty years with the Royal Highland Regiment. If so, he would have discovered, as did another traveller, Lord Nugent, that the view "was the most splendid sight he could recollect ever having seen from a natural height". As far as Patrick was concerned, it was the exceptional view of Perth, with its setting of hills and riverside which lay before him like a perfect relief model, that was to be influential, rather than the biblical connection.

From the seat at the top of the garden, he could gaze down on Perth and imbibe without realizing it the concept of relationship between city and geographical region. The "scientific eye of actuality" noted the shape of the River Tay as it wound in front of the town, and around the shoulder of Kinnoull Hill. It saw how much prettier Perth looked on a Sunday, when the factories were not belching smoke. When the river flooded, it knew that the houses nearby would become dank and smelly. And in the nearby village of Scone it could glimpse the monument to Douglas the botanist who "brought home so many of those North American pines, Californian cypresses and the like". At the same time "the illumined eye of imagination and dream" could see the low pass between Strathearn and Strathtay where the Romans were traditionally supposed to have exclaimed: "Ecce Tiber; ecce Campus Martius!" because they thought the Tay and its bordering meadows were so beautiful; and it learned to imagine "the procession of fateful boughs" from *Macbeth* in the distant views of Dunsinane and Birnam. It would also treasure the days when a river mist lay over the city in a long, grey-white lake, with just the spires of the churches rising through like so many Excaliburs.

Geddes once described himself as "a *visuel* (learning by eye-gate rather than ear)" and deplored the fact that

> nine people out of ten . . . understand print better than pictures, and pictures better than reality . . . a few well-chosen picture postcards will produce more effect upon most people's minds than does the actual vision of . . . beauty.[1]

He was in fact a precocious learner by book as well as by experience, but experience always came first. Even the act of learning to spell he traced back to watching insects in a pool.

> Over the surface the little water-measurers were always scudding about, sending strange rippling shadows from around their moving feet upon the bottom. The creature's thin nimble-jointed legs, his spotted, jewel-dotted back were

endlessly interesting; and I think I partly learned to spell from precisely observing these markings which came somehow to associate themselves with the look of printed words upon the page.

His earliest lesson in mathematics was equally original, this time at the instigation of his father who had invited his son to help in planting a row of potatoes.

And of course at first I put them in too irregularly; but soon saw the sense of not having them too close at one point, and too far away at another. So he showed me how people learned to measure, setting one foot after another; and thus we found the length of the row in feet. Then, cutting a stick a little longer than his foot, he gave me this for a measuring-rod, and now I relaid my potatoes with accuracy as to length. . . . Then I counted them (I think there were 31 or 32 in the row) and he suggested cutting notches on the stick to remember this number by. But this was to be a long operation, so he showed me how to simplify it: with three deep notches for the tens, and little scratches beside the last one for the rest.

A one-time sergeant-major might not normally be expected to have employed such imaginative educational methods, but Alexander Geddes was in many ways an exemplary man. While travelling around the world he had always provided as well as he could for his family's physical and mental well-being, and, in semi-retirement, with a bright and responsive child on his hands, his talents for teaching and simple living flourished unimpeded. Patrick was certainly the most privileged of his children, since he received a great deal of individual attention and grew up when the family was free from financial worries, but he was also the most gifted. A slightly-built boy, he had the energy and stamina that spring from fervent intellectual motivation; a motivation which appears on his part to have been innate, though which of course flourished and developed under the imaginative stimuli it received. With thick, wiry dark hair, and alert eyes that in later years developed a disconcerting, sometimes glittery, stare, his physical presence was always assertive. Alexander appears to have enjoyed having such an apt pupil, and for the rest of his life Patrick never failed to acknowledge his father as his best, and most enduring, mentor.

He was forty-six when Patrick was born, and had himself been orphaned when only eight. He had then lived with an older brother, herding sheep during the summer and attending school during the winter. When he was almost eighteen he had walked to Perth (about 70 miles away) to enlist with the Royal Highland Regiment—the Black Watch. Initially he was taken on as a drummer, being too short for the ranks, and over the years rose to the rank of sergeant-major, working as a quarter-master. During that time he refused three offers of a commission: it would have been impossible for a man with no private means and a growing family to lead the life conventionally expected of an officer. He was put on reserve after nearly thirty years' service with the regiment, and was then commissioned as a Captain in the Perthshire Rifles, a volunteer regiment, a year before the Crimean War broke out and Patrick was born. His duties were not particularly arduous, and thus he was able to spend a good deal of time with his youngest son.

The early loss of his parents reinforced Alexander's sense of the importance of permanence and responsibility within a family, and he always tried to help and keep in touch with various scattered relations. When he was twenty-four, he discovered a young cousin, Isabella, abandoned after her parents' death from cholera, and went to her uncle to arrange for her protection. When the uncle refused to accept this responsibility, Alexander would not spend the night under his roof, and went angrily to an hotel, even though this meant the uncle altered his will which was to have made his nephew his heir. Alexander then found a post for Isabella in the regimental mess.

When he was twenty-nine he married Janet Stivenson,* who was twenty-two and they had four children before Patrick. Robert was born in 1839, Jessie in 1841, John (Jack) in 1843, and Alex in 1846. The latter, however, died on board ship between one army garrison and another when he was only a year old, so Patrick's arrival seven years later no doubt commanded particular rejoicing and concern.

* In some early documents this appears to have been spelled "Stevenson"; but in later years her father called himself "Stivenson".

Janet was a deeply religious woman, whose firm moral attitude had perhaps been partly moulded in reaction to the unsatisfactory behaviour of her father, John Stivenson. (One member of the family wrote: "She owed him little, and admired him less".) It is perhaps worth recounting his story, since in his later years he kept in contact with the Geddes family, and came to spend the last year of his life at Mount Tabor when Patrick was thirteen. There is no record of the latter's feelings towards his grandfather, though his illness and subsequent death apparently left Mrs Geddes and Jessie in a state of exhaustion.

When John Stivenson married Janet's mother, he took on his father-in-law's baking business in Airdrie, not far from Glasgow. They had three daughters and one son, the latter being drowned while sliding on Kirlbirnie Loch when he and Janet were staying with an aunt in Beith. Janet was thirteen at the time and recalled the tragedy as being a "terrible grief" to her. The following year her father's business seems to have failed, and he was only able to pay off his debts at 15s. in the £1. He then "took himself off to America", apparently disappearing out of shame during the period before he left, and "leaving his women folk to fight their own battles". Mrs Stivenson was forced to re-establish the baking business, but two years later she and her eldest daughter—who was about to be married—died of cholera. This left Janet and her younger sister, Elizabeth, to be brought up by their maternal grandmother, Nellie Steel. Mrs Steel's own mother was still alive at the beginning of this period, and was said to be "the finest needlewoman of her day". Both Janet and Elizabeth were brought up to do the very fine traditional Ayrshire embroidery, and the former was also to have been an elocution teacher when she met and married Alexander Geddes. She later taught the children in his regiment, and retained a "schoolmarmly" air throughout her life.

In 1840 John Stivenson became a naturalized citizen of the United States and remarried in Philadelphia. He had two more daughters, and was said to have been divorced by his wife in about 1850 because he struck her, receiving a three-month prison sentence for the offence. By 1857 he was working as a storekeeper in Delaware, and when Janet and Alexander's eldest son Robert left home, it was arranged that he should join his grandfather, hoping that this would be an opportunity for him "to get on in the world". However, it did not work out, as Robert was made to do the chores and did not like his grandfather's "solitary miserly life". He returned to Perth and unwillingly embarked on a banking career, in which he was very successful, but which he never really enjoyed.

John Stivenson still kept in regular touch with the Geddes family. In one letter written during the first year of the Civil War (he was a staunch supporter of Lincoln), it is difficult not to catch fore-echoes of Patrick's later habit of corralling huge social issues, and describing them in patchy, yet dynamic, prose:

The free states of this Union are democracies, in the true sense of the word, wherein there is as much equality and real liberty as man in his present state of intelligence is capable of enjoying (and the masses of the free states exceed in intelligence, and probably, orderly conduct, any people in the world). The slave states never have been democracies, except in name—there are four distinct classes among them— the first is the slave-holder (the *large* slave-holder) who is usually pretty well educated—brought up and bred a tyrant—tyrannizing over the young negroes in youth and the grown-up ones when he grows up—he becomes a despot, and an irresponsible oppressor—these habits he carries into society—which begets duels—broils—street fights—and imperiousness—who always wants to rule, and is impatient . . . of law and order—he usually tyrannizes over the other three classes—the next class is the "poor whites" who are very ignorant (many of them scarcely knowing the name of the County in which they live) they drink whisky and chew tobacco—are lazy, thriftless, and are looked on by the slaveholding class as an inferior race—they are mostly as ignorant as the negroes—and more so than the body servants of the first class—next is the *free negroes*, who like the poor whites are thriftless—poor (not being employed except when the slaves cannot do all the work) they are not very numerous, and are not looked on with favour by the slave-owners—the next and last are the slaves, who are doomed to perpetual bondage, which no human power can legally cancel, except with the consent of the owner—they are

mostly ignorant and marriage among them is a mere form—
the owner having the power to sell husband, wife or children
—when they never meet again—and even Ministers (of
course wolves in sheep's clothing) tell the negroes when
parted that they may marry again without regard to former
wife or husband.

In a letter written early the following year, when Patrick
was seven, he mentions his grandson:

. . . your young son—who I presume needs *mental* rest—as
well as country air—for six months at least he ought not to
go to school or have much to do with school or books—let
his mind for that time become familiar with natural and
sensible objects.

In fact Patrick was deemed strong enough to start school
later that year, but during his early childhood he had not been
very robust. The nature of his illness is not known, but Jessie
once nursed him through a bout from which he was not
expected to recover. Thirteen years older than Patrick, she
shared closely in his upbringing, and as both his brothers had
left home by the time he was six, he had three adults to give
him a good deal of their undivided attention throughout his
childhood. Jessie adored him; when she died in 1888, Jack
wrote to Patrick saying: "I can enter into your feelings at the
bereavement for you were the apple of her eye . . . and in
losing her you have lost a love that few ever experience."
Patrick nicknamed her "Mousie", and enjoyed a confident,
joking relationship with her, writing when she was away on a
visit in 1864: "I have pleasure to enclose a carte and an
epistle from one of your beaux. Never mind though he squints,
he is a goodlooking chap for all that." She did at some point
become engaged, but her fiancé died, and she remained at
home for the rest of her life. Like all the family, apart from
Janet Geddes, she could be quick-tempered, and was apt to
take offence rather easily. But Patrick could usually draw the
best from her, and the foundations of his love of France and
French thought were laid during his early lessons with her.
When the Franco-Prussian war broke out he wrote to Jack:
"What a dreadful war this is! . . . Our sympathies are with the

French, at least mine are very warmly so. The sympathies of the nation are mostly with the Prussians." And there his sympathies remained for the rest of his life, "Prussianism" being the only national-racial phenomenon he consistently decried.

But well before troubles of this kind, or even the lesser evils of school, entered his consciousness, he had long hours of experiencing the peace and drama of garden and countryside. If Perth implanted the embryo concept of city, then Mount Tabor provided the platonic ideal for all the gardens and open spaces with which he was to become involved in later years. There is nothing more magical than a well-stocked garden when one is a child. This one had thirty apple trees, long lines of blackcurrant bushes, many varieties of gooseberry, red currants, potatoes, all the vegetables for daily needs, strawberries, big gean (wild cherry) trees—glorious in spring— and an abundance of flowers. The latter were tended by his mother until she lost her sight in her early fifties (possibly as a result of eyestrain doing embroidery by candlelight as a child— both her grandmother and great-grandmother had become blind, apparently for this reason), and there used to be vases of fresh flowers in the darkish rooms of the cottage during the summer, while in the winter the sills were lined with pots of fuchsias and other frost-shy plants. Bunches of garden flowers, picked by Jessie, were always given to departing summer visitors. Occasionally the horticultural passion was carried a little too far, and in 1864 Patrick wrote somewhat ironically to Jack:

I hung up my stocking on Christmas Eve and Santa Claus generously filled it with potatoes, onions, wizzant [wizened] apples and 2 packages which made me suppose from his partiality to vegetables that they were Carrots, but to my agreeable surprise I found to be Confections, also a fine ball, and an orange.

In between tending the vegetables, his father had time for play, and after emptying loads from their wheel-barrows— Alexander, with memories of coaching days, had named his own large one The Tally-ho, and Patrick's small one The Express—they would race each other back down the garden. One of the huge old gean trees (after which the cottage is now named, Mount Tabor having become the name of the road), which whitened into a snowy mountain of blossom in the spring, provided in its nest of branches a "big natural chair, a horse, an eyrie, all in one".

Not surprisingly Perth Academy, the school to which Patrick was sent, seemed dull by comparison. After his father's practical arithmetic teaching, there were "only rules, and tables, and examples to be worked in an exercise book—paper drudgery with no interest, and thus no sense, meaning, or significance . . . ". The contrast between the real potatoes of his father's garden, the sweet-smelling soil, the sunshine, the birdsong, and the damp, solemn classrooms—they overlooked the North Inch green bordering the river—was the beginning of a lifelong battle against the established pattern of formal education. One of his contemporaries had equally unfavourable memories, this time of the school's discipline:

> I have never forgotten the masters who taught and flagellated us—I fancy I can see old "Poker Steel" now—with his scruffy old bandana, his blackboard and those terrible instruments of torture—his taws* . . .

In fact in some ways Perth Academy was quite a forward-looking school, with an emphasis on science unusual for that time. Patrick did very well indeed at lessons, though it was to be this experience of success (which he gained with no particular effort) that convinced him of the worthlessness of examinations and the titles and certificates that came with them.

On his first day at the Academy he fell into a fight with another seven-year-old, Harry Barker, who beat him, and they were to remain friends for the rest of Geddes's life. Barker recalled Patrick's unparalleled energy as a boy—"I still see his kilt swinging as he hurries along"—and remembered teasing him about how he would need a wheel-barrow to carry home all his book prizes at the end of one academic year. Although an agile child, Patrick never took to the organized games of football and cricket which they were supposed to attend on Saturdays. "Play—to call that play—still less to

* Taws, tawse: an instrument of family or school discipline, used in Scottish and some English schools, consisting of a leathern strap or thong, divided at the end into narrow strips.

stand looking on at it. Once or twice in a lifetime is surely enough for that."

His idea of play, of absorption and adventure, lay in the very varied territory of Kinnoull Hill. Although the slope up from the cottage is quite gentle, the hill falls away in vertical cliffs on the far side, and here Patrick climbed, not without risk, to discover hidden caves. He felt the attraction of danger keenly: precipices, bathing in the swift river, going up paths marked "no road this way" or "prosecution to trespassers". There is also a small quarry in the hill where he found calcite and quartz crystals, while higher up there were agates. Accumulating these gems "soon became a hunger and a passion", and this covetousness led to the stealing of two fragments from a neighbour's garden. The theft was noticed, and Patrick lied, saying he had found the crystals in the quarry. His story was accepted, but he no longer wanted the stones and removed them from the garden, without being courageous enough to give them back to the neighbour. "The experience acted like some illness, expelling the poison [of covetousness] for good and all."

His enthusiasm for egg-collecting died early because he did not like robbing nests, and he never developed a liking for any form of hunting after experiencing "the shock of killing a cock-robin with an idly-thrown stone". He asked his father for a plot in which he could make a botanic garden, and always remembered Alexander's rueful expression when, after duly handing over a small area, he discovered his shrubs had been grubbed up and replaced by ill-arranged groups of weeds. "Here was a life-long lesson; that in seeking science, one need not, one must not, forget the claims of beauty."

While his leaning towards the natural sciences was never thwarted, either at school or at home, Geddes was, of course, growing up at the time when debate over Darwin's *Origin of Species* (published in 1859) was rife. His father was an elder of the local kirk, and his mother harboured a fond but forlorn hope that Patrick would grow up to be a minister. And divinity as well as science was one of the strong points of Perth Academy. Every Sunday the Geddes family would leave their cottage, walk down the hill and over the bridge into Perth to attend the morning service in the rather forbidding-looking Free Kirk. Then, after a sandwich eaten in the kirk sessions room,

they would proceed into the afternoon service. Perhaps it was
not surprising that Patrick decided by the age of eleven that
the dogmas of the church were not for him. He never rejected
religion as a phenomenon in its widest sense, but his mother's
endeavour to instil a love of the Pauline Epistles into his heart
failed completely. He much preferred his father's favourite,
the Book of Proverbs, adopting its adage to "get wisdom, and
with all thy getting get understanding" as a personal creed.
However, it was not until he was in his teens that he admitted
his disenchantment with formal religion and managed occasionally to evade attending Sunday service. It is to his
father's credit that he encouraged Patrick to read as widely
as possible, although this must have been instrumental in
dissolving any hard-and-fast belief. Alexander had introduced
him to the Mechanics' Library in Perth not long after he had
learned to read, and by his mid-teens he had "devoured the
home library and soaked up the public one". Harry Barker
recalled that

> He read as a boy every novel in every library and in ab-
> surdly short time . . . suppose he went to bed sometimes—
> but at 4 a.m. he was reading (not novels but philosophy)
> with a candle—till time to get up, winter and summer.

For Patrick the best part of Sunday occurred after the
church-going was over, when the family would walk around
the garden, and "every flower was scanned anew, every apple-
tree admired and rejoiced in". He must, particularly in the
case of his mother, have experienced the usual guilt at rejecting
the dearest beliefs of loved and respected parents, but at least
it does not seem to have hung albatross-like around his neck
for very long. He never went to extremes of rejection, aware
apparently from an early age that the synthesis of all that was
good and useful was what was needed in the world, rather than
debilitating analytical sparring matches between warring
factions. Even as late as 1889, when his mother had been
blind for years, she appended her husband's letter congratulating Patrick on his thirty-fifth birthday with a shakily-
written hymn:

> .   Oh when without reserve 'tis given
> Wholly surrendered every part

There shines within the dawn of Heaven
Give him thine heart

and he could apparently receive such messages with equanimity and not over-react with impatience or guilt. In 1895, when his third child, Arthur, was born, he wrote to his parents saying he had performed a christening ceremony himself. In an otherwise mild and kindly letter Alexander expressed his distress that his son should have taken it upon himself to go through a form of baptism only authorized for Ministers of the Gospel—and then only to children whose parents attended church. "We should take great care how we interfere with the ordinances of God," he concluded.

At fifteen Patrick went through a phase of jokey troublemaking but managed to avoid police detection and punishment. One Saturday night he organized a group of friends into tying all the bells along one terrace of houses to the door handles, so that when the inhabitants tried to pull their doors open the next morning in order to go to church, they found they could not get out, and the harder they tugged the more the bells jangled. Another trick was to close people's kitchen chimneys with sods of turf, or barricade their back doors. A farmer's field provided large turnips with which to make lantern ghosts to frighten people, and when the farmer complained the gang of boys wrecked a disused cottage on his land. Partly through cunning, and partly because they were not the kind of boys who normally fell under suspicion, the police never caught them. Geddes was to remark years later: "When poor boys do such things and are caught, their state-education, into criminals proper, used to begin."[2] This phase came to an end when a local minister, whom they had been wont to annoy, invited them to chop up a heap of old logs and tree stumps. He supplied them with a big axe, "a compliment which no one had ever paid us before . . . and there was no longer any joy in doing mere mischief like small boys when we felt we had learned to work like men".

His father had a fair inkling of what his son was up to, and unobtrusively guided his energies into other channels. A year or so before, Patrick's eldest brother, Robert, had written from Mexico:

One word tho' about your last letter—you speak of the good-nature of the new French teacher notwithstanding the stupidity of some of his pupils—I've mislaid your letter so I can't quote exactly—the sentence is "priggish"—Now I don't believe you are a "prig"—but you must excuse your big brother giving you the above hint.

He ended more lightheartedly: "Have you made up your mind about whether you are to be a philosopher or a militiaman yet?" Alexander Geddes probably realized that coming from such a precocious child the practical jokes were a welcomely normal sign of adolescent reaction to boredom, and set about finding him something to do.

Chemistry had recently caught Patrick's imagination, and the smells, noises and damage to vessels that accompany its early stages were taking their toll at Mount Tabor. Alexander had a shed built in the garden in which Patrick could conduct his experiments without disturbing anybody. He later arranged for him to take lessons after school from a cabinet-maker, and a carpenter's bench was added to the equipment in the shed. In the holidays he took his son on a long walking tour, visiting friends in Grantown and Ballater, and climbing between the valleys of the Dee, Don and Spey. They also visited Edinburgh together, and Patrick was enchanted and excited by the city.

Indeed, as Perth was an appropriate city for childhood impressions, Edinburgh must be a city in a thousand to show to an adolescent unconsciously developing towards a lifetime involvement with social and architectural problems. Poverty and dilapidation were there, as in all British towns, but the stunningly dramatic effect of the four steep heights (the castle, the war memorial, and Salisbury Crags and Arthur's Seat in Holyrood Park), from which one gets such a variety of city vistas stretching to the Pentland Hills, the Firth of Forth and across to Fife, make the newcomer almost intoxicated by the non-stop visual grandeur and surprise. The surprise element is particularly apparent too in the Old Town, where narrow archways lead to secret closes, unexpected gaps give glimpses across the narrow valley to the New Town, and the engineering feats that connect the Old Town to the New create in part a split-level town with new streets raised above the old steep cobbled ones, giving a strength and drama that adds to, rather than detracts from, the townscape. With the clear yet soft Scottish light, and quickly-changing weather, it is both a kaleidoscope city in the sense that perspective and illumination vary from one minute to the next, and also a strong, coherent capital, whose main centres are easy to locate, and whose blackened buildings impress but do not intimidate.

It is pointless to speculate what differences there might have been if Geddes's first introduction to a city had been other than Edinburgh, but given his innate need to try to grasp and understand whole entities, it was perhaps fortuitous that this first major-city-experience was so comprehensible. The sprawl, dingy excitement and sporadic splendour of London would undoubtedly have affected him, but would not have provided the visionary clarity of that initial awareness.

Patrick left Perth Academy when he was nearly sixteen and spent the following year continuing his lessons in cabinet-making in the mornings, and attending Perth School of Art some afternoons. Part of the remaining time he spent in his chemistry workshop, and his usual athletic programme of reading was undiminished. It was about this time that he was discovering Carlyle, and also Ruskin—who was strongly to influence his early economic and ethical thinking. This original and varied timetable was at the instigation of his father who did not attempt to hurry his son into choosing a specific career.

The art school's drawing books had printed firmly on the cover:

DIRECTIONS: Keep your pencil well pointed; stretch your fingers on it; before drawing a line, mark points at beginning and end; draw from left to right, and from above downward; press very gently on your pencil when you are sketching, and lean firmly on it when lining in your drawing; you are not allowed to measure or rule the lines.

Patrick found this style of teaching mechanical and unrewarding, and was unimpressed by his success in a national drawing competition. In fact it is doubtful whether he would have developed along particularly outstanding lines as an artist. He was a neat draughtsman and appeared to enjoy lettering, but his few surviving drawings lack real originality or sensitivity, and later on his aesthetic sense in wider spheres was somewhat eccentric. He became interested in all forms of graphic presentation, and what he might have benefited from, had it existed at that time, is a well-run and sophisticated course in graphic design and communication as we know them today.

By this time his eldest brother Robert was managing the Land Bank of Mexico in Mexico City—at first receiving £900 p.a. and ending up with £3,000 p.a. when he retired at forty-two. He and his wife Margaret (daughter of General Paterson "who thought the Geddes family very small beer") had to endure considerable dangers and upheavals to achieve those rewards, as it was the period when the Napoleonic troops were withdrawing and Juárez, the constitutional president, was being reinstated. Nevertheless, by contemporary financial standards, they were certainly doing very well. Jack's trading attempts in New Zealand had not, however, by that time been particularly successful—though later on, aided by his partially-Maori wife Mary, they were to flourish.

It is not therefore surprising that Alexander should have decided, since Patrick still had no specific choice for a career, that his son should do a trial year in banking. They came to a gentleman's agreement that if, after the year, he wished to go into another profession, he would be free to do so. He accordingly started, in September 1871, in the Perth branch of the National Bank of Scotland.

Superficially, the eighteen months which he spent in the bank would seem to have been irrelevant to the subsequent development of his life. Certainly he was anxious to leave, although the Manager, Mr D. M. Jolly, wrote a reference declaring:

> . . . he is quick and expert at his work and has been most attentive to all his duties. I have never had a more promising Apprentice and am sorry to lose him. I wish him every success and trust he will prove an Ornament to the Profession he may choose.

However, during that time he had acquired a knowledge of the grammar of finance (loans, mortgages, interest rates, company affairs and the like) which is not normally vouchsafed to academics from modest backgrounds. Given his excellent mathematical brain it was not surprising that he had a facility for money-dealing, and so the way was paved for his extra-ordinarily fecund manner of property-buying and company-starting later on. To have a facility with money may also teach people not to be afraid of it, or to over-value it, but to treat it simply as a means to oil the wheels of practical and social projects. Or, from the point of view of people whose money is being borrowed in order that wheels may be oiled— not always with overwhelming success—to have a somewhat cavalier attitude towards it. Apart from the natural sciences, economics was one of the first subjects he wrote about, and it remained always a real thorn in the flesh of his thought. At 4 a.m. on his seventy-seventh, and last, birthday, he wrote to his daughter, Norah:

> Here's my birthday—and good early start—and vivid waking—with jottings of great vision of History—the Masque of Mammon . . . I've seen inside Pilgrim's burden . . . and how stupid never to have realised its weight of sins was weighted essentially in Gold.

While he had honoured his agreement with his father by giving banking a fair trial, he still had not narrowed his choice of an alternative career to anything more specific than "science". It was agreed that he should attend classes in chemistry and geology—the latter under James Geikie, whose teaching was so vivid Patrick was almost persuaded to become a geologist. At the time Geikie was a member of the Geological Survey, an enthusiastic worker in the field and very sympathetic teacher, later becoming Professor of Geology at Edinburgh University. After a year, however, Patrick decided that biology was more important to him, and elected to go to the Department of Botany at Edinburgh.

This was a proud moment for his parents. When he returned home after a mere week, apparently because he did not like the University's teaching methods, they must have doubted both their previous leniency and understanding, and Patrick's capacity for perseverance. In fact it was a crucial decision, sprung from his instinctive loathing of all methods that took the excitement out of learning. He had experienced boredom at Perth Academy, but he had never dreamed that the atmosphere in university laboratories and lecture-halls could be monotonous and dreary too. Botany, which to him meant living plants, was treated as a dry-as-dust process of analysis— "a mere farrago of dog-latin labels upon mouldering hay".

However, to make a wholly negative move was out of character. Patrick had not rushed home simply because he hated the Department of Botany. His apparently rash decision was powered by inspiration rather than disgust, and he now knew exactly where he wanted to go.

Chapter 2

HUXLEY ONWARDS

THAT ONE WEEK in Edinburgh provides an image of Geddes's later long and uncompliant relationship with the educational establishment in the Scottish capital. However, for the moment he would simply appear to be an impatient country student, brighter than most, who was not willing to submit to the normal step-by-step procedure of an academic course. But it was not disgust at the "mouldering hay" approach which was uppermost in his mind when he arrived back at Mount Tabor. During that week he had been reading Thomas Huxley's *Lay Sermons*, and as a result had formed a burning desire to go and study under Huxley in London. Nor is the cliché "burning desire" too strong a phrase: there was something wilful and comet-like about Geddes once any ambition took hold of him.

Bearing in mind that he would need his father's continued financial, as well as moral, support, and that Huxley was at that time the most outspoken scientific opponent of the Bible's account of man's genesis, it was not the easiest piece of news to break in a loving but strict Nonconformist home. Patrick's mother had lost her sight a year before, and she must have felt that her youngest son was plunging into an even more menacing darkness. That he obtained his parents' permission and blessing within a few days speaks both for their affection and for Geddes's compelling powers of persuasion.

At that time Huxley was teaching at the Royal School of Mines which had recently moved to South Kensington. Later this amalgamated with the new Normal School of Science, of which he was made Dean, and from 1907 it became the Imperial College of Science. During the period Geddes was there, however, Huxley mainly taught mining students and science teachers, his class being merely one of several which they had to attend for their professional qualifications.

Even in those days, qualifications, as Geddes was soon to

discover, were uppermost in the minds of academic administrators. Because, during his years of private study, he had never
obtained any official certificates, he was not allowed to go
straight into Huxley's class, but had to do a probationary
year with the first-year students. "The only way of getting any
mental activity out of the School of Mines men is to run down
their occupation," he remarked derisively. It was during this
marking-time preliminary year that he sat the only official
examination of his adult life—as a wager. He bet some of the
engineering students that he could pass the elementary
examination in mining after only one week's study. He crammed
the requisite text books for seven days and duly passed, eventually receiving a certificate which entitled him to become a
sub-inspector of mines—although by then he had forgotten
virtually all his ill-digested mining knowledge.

At least the untaxing nature of this first year left him free
to explore London and make frequent visits to the museums
and theatres. He also had time to reflect on the physical
character of the city as a whole—which in many ways shocked
him. A London handbook published a decade later remarked
on the deterioration of the area around Gray's Inn from "the
playing-ground and promenade of many a pretty school miss"
to "a wretched, sooty forsaken place" and commented on "the
monster Metropolis, which is still swelling every year . . . in a
way which makes it bewildering to contemplate".[1] Geddes
had taken lodgings in Ovington Street, Chelsea, not just
because it was within short walking distance of South Kensington, but also because one of his heroes, Thomas Carlyle, lived
half a mile away in Cheyne Row. He sometimes saw him, now
eighty years old, slightly stooped and grey-bearded, walking
along the Embankment, but never found the courage to approach him. It must have been almost the only time in his life
that he was too nervous to speak out, and perhaps it was as
well. Although Carlyle retained some of his old fire, he was by
then a somewhat cantankerous and repetitive conversationalist,
who in his later writings had apparently renegued on some of
the radical beliefs expressed in *Sartor Resartus*—which had stirred
Geddes's adolescent imagination. In fact he still quite enjoyed
visits from young disciples as long as they did not challenge
him, but it is difficult to envisage Geddes in a passive, respect-
ful role for very long. In some ways the two had much in

common, with their encyclopaedic thirst for knowledge, their desire for change, their attempts to tackle universal themes, their gifts for rhetoric, and their Scottish Nonconformist backgrounds. But Carlyle was primarily an artist and a pessimist, regretting his lack of practical deeds, while Geddes was a man of action and an optimist, who never managed to complete a popular major work. Because Carlyle can be quickly identified by the titles of two of his books his name is better known than that of Geddes. Yet his contribution and relevance are arguably smaller.

During that first autumn in London, so soon after the Edinburgh University débâcle, Geddes must particularly have remembered the description of university students in *Sartor Resartus*: "The hungry young looked up to their spiritual nurses, and for food were bidden to eat the east wind." And whether consciously or not, the development of his prose-style seems increasingly to have leaned on that of Carlyle, so that by the end of his life his letters are bespattered with proper nouns, oddly-constructed sentences, quirky exclamations. But whereas Carlyle's style was deliberate artifice, Geddes's was at times an unchecked torrent.

While waiting for admission to Huxley's class, he re-read *Lay Sermons* at a more leisurely speed. In it Huxley attacked those who saw Nature only as

> a sort of comfort-grinding machine . . . a sort of fairy god-mother, ready to furnish her pets with shoes of swiftness, swords of sharpness, and omnipotent Aladdin's lamps so that they may have telegraphs to Saturn, and see the other side of the moon . . .

His claim for natural knowledge was that it alone could assuage spiritual cravings, reveal laws of conduct and lay the foundations of a new morality. He also attacked the education system for teaching nothing of relevance to the practical world of business, manufacturing and government, or to the world of art.

> In explaining to a child the general phenomena of Nature, you must, as far as possible, give reality to your teaching by object-lessons; in teaching him botany, he must handle the

plants and dissect the flowers for himself. . . . People talk of the difficulty of teaching young children such matters, and in the same breath insist upon their learning their Catechism, which contains propositions far harder to comprehend than anything in the educational course I have proposed.

It was expressions of this kind that had brought Geddes to London. What he then thought of Huxley's views on Negroes and women, as stated in the book, is not recorded, but they represent the side of Huxley he later rejected. According to Huxley, no rational man could believe that "the average negro is the equal . . . of the average white man" or that he would ever "be able to compete successfully with his bigger-brained and smaller-jawed rival, in a contest which is to be carried on by thoughts and not by bites". And "the big chests, the massive brains, the vigorous muscles and stout frames, of the best men will carry the day, whenever it is worth their while to contest the prizes of life with the best women". Geddes, himself not a large person, soon realized that intelligence and capability had little to do with measurement. He was much more in sympathy with Ruskin's ethos of co-operation instead of competition, and a few years later a letter to him from Ruskin gives a small anecdote which demonstrates what they both regarded as Huxley's rigidity:

When Huxley gave his lecture on the serpent's motion he anatomized the ribs dextrously—I followed him as he left the lecture table, and simply asked—"How many steps does it take a second"—He stood helpless—and began to say—"It depends on the number of ribs!"—Fancy saying that the rate of a regiment's pace depends upon the number of men!

One essay, however, he was in no position to comment on, since it was entitled "The Scientific Aspects of Positivism" and he knew nothing of Auguste Comte or his followers. In the essay, Huxley acknowledged his debt to Comte "for awakening in me, that the organization of society upon a new and purely scientific basis is not only practicable, but is the only political object much worth fighting for", but attacked Positivism, saying he "could not distinguish it from sheer Popery, with

M. Comte in the chair of St Peter . . .". Geddes was intrigued
by what he learned of Positivism from the essay, and not
wholly convinced by Huxley's attack, so he started to visit the
Comtist church in Chapel Street to hear Dr Richard Congreve's
Sunday morning discourses.

Comte postulated that human thought had developed in a
natural sequence of three stages according to its degree of
remoteness from man. Thus primitive man and early society
passed through the theological stage; medieval society developed the metaphysical stage; and modern society, beginning in
the early nineteenth century, had entered the scientific era. As
man came closer to understanding himself and society, so
theology was seen to be an intellectual error, psychologically
necessary for early man, but now to be replaced by a scientific-
ally evolved system of moral philosophy. Although this theory
of the "law of three stages" has been discounted (Durkheim
remarked that it was not only *not* a law, but was not even a
reasonable hypothesis since it could not be tested), and his
claims for an ultimate law of social evolution have been criticized for their totalitarian implications, it is easy to see why
Geddes should have been attracted to Comte.

Geddes did not, as Carlyle did, have a deep inner need to
replace the religion of his upbringing by an equally powerful
moral force, but he did have the outward-looking man's
passionate zeal to discover some morally-based scientific system
that would explain the chaotic state of society and help towards
evolving it on more humane lines. Comte, of course, actually
invented the name "sociology" for the science which he
regarded as the most complex of all, and it was partly his, and
other men's, endeavour to pursue a synoptic approach, that
first raised opposition to the subject; the resulting theories
tended to be unwieldy and dogmatic, and open to attack on
many grounds. Recent opposition has been quite different:
reaction to minutely specialized studies which demonstrate
what many people think is already perfectly obvious. Later
Geddes could perhaps be said to have come somewhere near a
balance between the two, in as much as he always retained a
questing attitude to the minutiae of life, while striving to perfect
a synoptic view.

After one or two visits to Chapel Street, Geddes asked
Richard Congreve some questions on points that had arisen

from his discourse. Congreve was intrigued by the young man who, while being impressed by so many of Huxley's ideas, could nevertheless criticize his master's attack on Comte, and he introduced Geddes to the weekly meetings of the Positivist Society. Here he met John H. Bridges, translator of Comte, who gave him a complete and balanced view of the movement. Congreve, on the other hand, he found had a "touch of pontificalism . . . there was no arguing with him". These meetings provided Geddes with the kind of vivid and wide-ranging discussion that always nourished him, and he met a broader circle of people than hitherto.

He returned to Mount Tabor at the end of the academic year, and as he walked up the lane from Perth "filled with joy and happy memories", he had one of those minor, yet over-whelming, experiences that bring the constancy of a happy childhood to a close.

On coming up the hawthorn den, lo! the ivied wall was gone, and in its place, in trim, regular ugliness stood a new one, at least a rebuilt one, absolutely gaunt and bare. Never before or since have I felt such a shattering of associations; never again so deeply mourned any material change or loss.

But, as he concluded, ". . . it is a fortunate childhood and youth which has known no graver shock of disaster".

When he went back to London in the autumn of 1875, keenly anticipating the forthcoming session under Huxley, he was almost twenty-one. The notebooks in which he took down Huxley's lectures are meticulous, and loosely inserted into one of them, and apparently dating from that time, is a character-istically thorough, and in the last resort hilarious, scheme for designing insect and animal traps. They were obviously devised to earn a little money, being carefully priced (7s. 6d. for flea traps, up to 30s. for ones for pole-cats), and every endeavour is made to produce a veritable palace of a trap.

The two other corners should contain troughs for food and water respectively. Adjacent to the water trough is a spirit lamp with chimney for ventilation and warmth in winter— in the heat of summer its place may be taken by one of our patent pocket refrigerators. . . . During incarceration the lack of society of an individual of the opposite sex might be compensated for by the addition of a looking-glass to the furniture of the trap.

And finally:

A greater difficulty, viz. the means of supplying spiritual consolation to those condemned has engaged our most serious attention; but we can only refer you to the clergyman of the parish in which our traps are first introduced. Doubtless he will be able to make arrangements.

Geddes always disliked wilful destruction of animals, and he was bending over backwards to reconcile the needs of research with humane methods. Like many of his money-making schemes, it did not apparently bear fruit.

Apart from his father, Geddes always maintained that Huxley was the most determining teacher in his life. "Never, of course, had I heard such lectures; or indeed since."[2] William Irvine wrote of Huxley:

He could think, draw, speak, write, inspire, lead, negotiate and wage multifarious war against earth and heaven with the cool professional ease of an acrobat supporting nine people on his shoulders at once.[3]

The lectures took place on winter mornings, usually lasting well over the allotted hour, and were followed by an afternoon of dissection under the demonstrator, T. Jeffery Parker (later Professor of Zoology at Dunedin). During the summer the laboratory was open morning and afternoon, and Huxley would visit the students daily. His own demonstrations and drawings were exceptionally clear and precise. Once, after explaining the construction of a crayfish skeleton, he said to Geddes: "You see, I should have been an engineer." Privately his pupil tended to agree with him since, despite his brilliance, he found Huxley's approach too mechanistic to be wholly satisfying. He was not without a sense of humour, however, and once drew several heads of leading genera of primates, in which the profiles of the big-nosed scientist John Tyndall, Darwin, the Duke of Argyll, and himself, were easily recognizable. Beatrice Potter (later Mrs Sidney Webb) noted in her diary at about this period:

I doubt whether science was pre-eminently the bent of Huxley's mind. He is truthloving, his love of truth finding more satisfaction in demolition than construction.[4]

Geddes became a skilful dissector, and one of his specimens was kept for display in the museum. Huxley indicated that it was time he started some individual research, and asked him to work out the mechanism of the masticatory organs on molluscs such as the limpet and the whelk. The result was that Geddes found himself in disagreement with Huxley's own explanation of the mechanism—and succeeded in proving himself to be right. His teacher was not at all put out, and made Geddes draw three plates and write a paper on his discoveries, which he then presented to the Zoological Society as a pupil's correction of his own work. Geddes "searched Huxley's books and papers to see if there were any other little point I might try again to catch him on, but failed completely . . .".[5]

After this, Huxley was particularly concerned to help Geddes. He arranged a demonstratorship for him during a vacation course, and introduced him to colleagues in Cambridge with the idea that he might work there. However, although Geddes enjoyed the company, he did not like what he saw of the teaching set-up in Cambridge, so Huxley put him up for the Sharpey Physiological Scholarship at University College, London, and he became demonstrator under Professors E. A. Schäfer and J. Burdon Sanderson.

One day when he was working in Sanderson's laboratory, Geddes

was amusing a spare hour by searching a pond-sample with his microscope and had drawn a comparative blank, with only two or three common green Euglenas swimming amid a few motile bacilli. He was about to put this slide away for a fresh dip, when he was gently pushed aside. A big beard came over his shoulder—here was Darwin! who had come in unnoticed. He said nothing, but looked closely into this— to me—barren microscope field: then suddenly broke out, positively shouting for joy: "I say! They're moving, they're *moving*! Sanderson! Sanderson! come and see; they're MOVING! Look at that!"

Was not here a vivid and memorable lesson in biology—this literally Pan-ic intoxication of ecstasy, in our oldest of veterans, greatest of masters, before this simplest spectacle of life![6]

Writing to Jessie during his first term at University College, he said:

... the work is lighter, and the students much more intelligent than last term at Kensington. I have lots of time, and every facility for doing microscope work for myself, and am able to attend Prof. Schäfer's lectures which are very good.

He moved to lodgings in Oak Village, Hampstead, and these too were congenial. A fellow lodger remembered them nostalgically after he had returned to Edinburgh:

I have often pictured to myself, by way of moral refreshment, the classic arcadian calm of Oak Village, its green umbrageous nooks, and its breezy atmosphere redolent of culture and the breath of the marigold ...

At this time the documentation of one of Jessie's more volcanic bursts of temper arrived to disturb the "arcadian calm". Their brother Robert's wife, Maggie, had come over from Mexico and was staying in Scotland with her children, not far away from Perth. A row, based on a very minor misunderstanding, had erupted between her and Jessie, and the latter immediately dashed off pages and pages of narrative describing the incident to her youngest brother. Alexander Geddes had then attached what amounted to a solemn affidavit certifying that Jessie's letter was a true and just record of events. It would seem that Patrick, with his assurance and incisive mind, had become established as Mount Tabor's arbiter. Certainly his reply to Jessie was a very model of how to pour oil on troubled family waters:

I return herewith as requested your budget of papers, and

am very heartily sorry for you in your troubles. But said troubles are not so serious as they seem to you, child; and I am almost relieved to think the inevitable crash is over, and yet here we are all alive and wonderfully well after it. I have also a letter from Maggie, in reply to one I wrote to her the other day towards the close of which she says "I wrote you a letter this morning, but it was a most unpleasant subject; and acting on my brother's advice have suppressed the letter. I had some unpleasant words with your sister, which I am extremely sorry for." That's all she says about it, and I merely say a word in passing about keeping sweet, and better not bother Bob with such disagreeables. . . . And now I am going to tell you once and for all what to do. Believe me the matter is not so very serious, cannot possibly look so serious to men at a distance, like Robert and myself, who have talked all these things over and know quite well your tempers are incompatible—so just burn all the rubbish here enclosed— (don't think the word hard, for rubbish is what is of no use) and never write one word of it to Robert. He is not a fool— he understands and respects you, and even if Maggie should be unwise enough to write of these matters to him, which I don't think very likely, will quietly smoke and forget the whole affair; unless you make him think there's been something terrible by mentioning it. I assure you, and this is the main point of my letter, the only possible risk of the deep quarrel with Robert, loss of the children, and all those things you are so afraid of, will be if you (or any of us) write an explanatory matter whatsoever or whensoever . . . Least said soonest mended; don't sit moping in the house. I know you won't be sulky, but don't make too premature or pressing attempt at reconciliation. Enough said. Keep up your bit heart, old lady.

There appears to have been no continuance of the affair. Maggie later admitted to have been in a highly nervous state during that visit. She experienced difficulty in adjusting to the northern climate after Mexico, and remembered weeping for days on end.

During the early part of 1878 Geddes had what he described as a "sharp illness", and was advised by his doctor to take a holiday out of London. Hearing of this, Huxley gave him an

introduction to Henri de Lacaze-Duthiers, Professor of Biology
at the Sorbonne, who had founded a marine biological station
at the little fishing port of Roscoff, on the north-west coast of
Brittany. Accordingly, Geddes spent the Easter vacation at
Roscoff, where, under the guidance of three Breton fishermen
attached to the station, the students learned to cast nets and
dredge the sea for their specimens. Lacaze-Duthiers was an
enthusiast for fieldwork, and took fatherly care of his pupils.
The atmosphere he inspired combined hard work with
comradeship in a way that appealed to Geddes very much. Also
the students came from a wide variety of backgrounds, thereby
giving him his first experience of a truly international enterprise.
(It is not known exactly how the group was comprised for
Geddes's visit, but in August the following year there were two
Dutchmen, three Belgians, one Turk, three Roumanians and
an Egyptian working at the station.)

He returned to London for the summer term, but was back
in Roscoff for the vacation. The research which he was doing
concerned a little primitive flatworm whose characteristics
particularly attracted him. Its cells contain minute algae
which colour the animal green, and plant guest and animal
host coexist in biological harmony. Geddes was the first to
demonstrate that these algae are capable of photosynthesis,
taking nutritive carbohydrates from the water during sunlight
and the carbon dioxide produced as waste from the animal cells,
thereby evolving oxygen useful to the animal. His discovery was
later published in a paper by the Royal Society. When the
time came for Lacaze-Duthiers and his pupils to return to the
Sorbonne, Geddes went too. He continued his general biological
studies and also enrolled at the École de Médecine for a course
in histology.*

Paris has provided an intellectual and emotional forum,
and a freedom from the restriction of parochial society, to
generations of young students. Geddes experienced its unique
magnetism with enthusiasm, though apparently it was the
intellectual rather than the fleshly offerings which involved
him. He noted in later years that, despite Paris's notorious
reputation in puritanical circles, he would always recommend
it to serious students so that they might

* The branch of anatomy or biology concerned with the minute
structure of the tissues of animals and plants.

above all . . . be moralized. Does that seem a paradox? What morality does one find there, as compared with Edinburgh, Oxford, Cambridge, London? First and foremost the morality of truth. How so? To see the thing as it is—that is the perpetual quest, the essential atmosphere of French criticism . . . What next beyond this? Morality of action— *to make the thing as it should be!*

In 1878 a World Fair was held in Paris to demonstrate that France had recovered from the Prussian war and subsequent political upheavals, and with her new prosperity was about to make the Third Republic truly republican. The universities were undergoing a process of reform, and meetings and manifestos proliferated. Geddes participated in these, and heard lectures from men as diverse as Renan, Lafitte and Pasteur. The latter he described as having "superman-like intensity, beyond all the men I have ever seen".

But it was a lecture by a young man called Edmond Demolins that initiated what was to be the strongest single influence he discovered in Paris. Demolins was lecturing on the work of Frédéric Le Play, one-time Professor of Metallurgy at the École des Mines, then in semi-retirement due to ill-health (he died in 1882). Le Play applied the methods of scientific field research to society itself, and was one of the most prolific gatherers of facts in the early development of sociology (though he would not use that term himself, being dubious of Comte). Growing up at a time when "the most obvious facts of life were war and technical progress"[7] he was one of the first people to emphasize the gap between technical and moral progress. He longed for social peace, and thought that society should exist for the wellbeing of the family, since he believed the latter, rather than the individual or a larger group, to be the basic social unit. In order to discover the elements that constitute this wellbeing he travelled extensively, claiming that "the time is not far distant when the fact that an author has not moved out of his study will be sufficient refutation of his theory".[8]

Le Play provided Geddes with a strategy that avoided the megalithic structures of Comte and the micrometer-minded approach of Huxley. His biographer, Michael Z. Brooke, sums up his theory of social change as comprising six elements:

a deep pessimism about human nature, a study of the influence of custom and informal leadership, the conflict of security and freedom, the determination of the route of change by technical and economic factors, the concept of cohesion, the cyclical view of history.

It was a pretty all-embracing yet subtle mixture, and after that first lecture Geddes bombarded Demolins with questions.

The concept of Le Play which Geddes seized upon most eagerly is that societies are conditioned first by geography, later by occupation. Thus primitive societies were determined by their situation: people located by the sea developed as fishermen, or those in the valley as horticulturalists; these occupations in their turn moulding the personality types and community structure. But modern man could more easily choose his occupation, thereby exercising influence on his environment. This reversible interaction between man and nature Geddes telescoped to Place→Work→Folk or Folk→Work→Place, and it became a paradigm with a much more fundamental meaning to him than could ever have been apparent to a listener encountering it for the first time. Indeed he must have put off quite a lot of people with his repetition of those three jerky words, which apparently formed some kind of holy trinity that was quite lost on the uninitiated. But they gave him the key to two important aspects of his work.

The first was the necessity of thorough survey—which Le Play demonstrated by huge harvests of facts concerning working-class communities. In other words, a society (Folk) would only be understood when its occupations (Work) and environment (Place) had been thoroughly researched. The other aspect was simply that the paradigm *was* reversible, and that people were not necessarily mechanistically determined by environment in the Darwinian sense, but could exercise their own will and: "Having chosen their work, they can fashion the place; they can mould the environment in harmony with their ideals."

A verse of Alexander Geddes's favourite *Proverbs* says, "Happy is the man that findeth wisdom, and the man that getteth understanding," and this was certainly a happy period for Geddes. His world was expanding, he had many new friends, and was discovering a discipline of social research on human lines to combat both the immediately competitive hell-broth of industrialization, and the eternally competitive concept of life put forward by some of the evolutionists. When wandering around Paris on long, exploratory walks, he often used to cause amusement by wearing his Scots Lowland bonnet—"a little absurd perhaps, but in France it stood for something". And by way of further exercise he took lessons in *la boxe française*, in which a swift kick to the chin is one of the chief forms of attack.

When he left the Sorbonne, he went straight to the zoological station in Naples at the expense of the British Association for the Advancement of Science. He was to stay for a week and gather information in order that he might help organize a similar station for the University of Aberdeen under Professor Cossor Ewart. This station was at Stonehaven, a small town on the coast fifteen miles south of Aberdeen, and the work he did there during the summer of 1879, both organizing and demonstrating to students, was highly praised. But he had more ambitious projects in mind, and was exploring the possibility of a sponsored trip to Mexico, while at the same time applying for the newly-founded Chair of Zoology at Queen's College, Manchester.

Applications for academic posts of that period make our contemporary practice of forms in triplicate or sextuplet look quite informal. The applicant's letter, together with numerous testimonials and lists of publications, were printed and bound into a booklet, copies of which were quite widely circulated. After the event, a Dutch friend wrote to Geddes:

> You never sent me the printed copy of your Manchester application which you promised in your letter; if you have got any still do send it; for us on the continent your English system of applying for vacancies in this way always seems very curious and the printed testimonials are valuable additions to our collections of curiosities.

Among the testimonials was one signed by 69 medical students at Aberdeen University expressing "their regret at the prospect of so soon losing your valued instructions" and praising "your skill in dissections, your excellent qualities as a draughtsman, and the unfailing courtesy and geniality you have always displayed towards us".

One of Geddes's sponsors was James Geikie, who was informed privately by a friend at Manchester University that

Your friend Mr Geddes has given us endless trouble. There are *three* men of whom he is one, whose claims and merits we have canvassed and recanvassed until we are half tempted to settle the matter by the schoolboy's method of tossing up!

On 18th July Geddes was informed that the appointment had in fact been given to Dr A. Milnes Marshall, and after telling a woman friend of this he was commended for "that delightful breezy manly way of being glad to be *worthily* beaten".

It was in fact probably pride as much as humility that inspired Geddes's lack of disgruntlement and positive bursts of energy after failures or disappointments. On this occasion he threw himself into organizing the Mexican trip, for which the British Association gave him £50 in order to conduct palaeontological and zoological research. A friend writing from Roscoff complained that in a four-page letter Geddes had said nothing personal—"c'est une lettre d'homme d'affaires plutôt que d'ami"—but obediently answered his practical queries, including one on the availability of espadrilles, remarking laconically that one could get them in shoeshops and markets all over Paris "et probablement aussi à Perth ou à Edinbourg ou à Londres".

With or without the espadrilles, Geddes sailed from Liverpool for Vera Cruz on 10th September.

Chapter 3

EYELESS IN MEXICO

HE ARRIVED IN Mexico City exactly a month later—10th October 1879. The dry season, with its brilliant, spring-like days and frosty nights, had just begun, and the high plateau, surrounded by the snowy peaks of Popocatepetl, Ixtaccihuatl and Orizaba, was an exhilarating place for a natural scientist. Before setting out, he would no doubt have read Alexander von Humboldt's account of his travels in South America, *Personal Narrative*, and more particularly his treatise on Mexico* which was the first modern regional economic geography of its kind, and unwontedly precipitated the frantic English involvement in the silver mining industry. By 1879 the mines were mainly abandoned, but contained rich deposits of pre-historic remains. Geddes might also have seen Humboldt's novel graphic presentation of plants on Chimborazo where "within the space of a few vertical miles virtually all the climates" were represented "and a correspondingly wide range of vegetation".[1]

The atmosphere in Mexico City at that time was not exactly conducive to peaceful research. One night Geddes had to join his brother Robert in mounting guard over the bank: they had been tipped off about a possible attempt at armed robbery—which did not, in fact, take place. And Robert tried to make his brother carry a revolver when he rode out of the city to look for specimens, since bandits were by no means uncommon. Geddes, however, preferred to carry £5 for possible ransom money, and planned hopefully to rely on his prowess at *la boxe française* if captured.

Sometimes he was accompanied on his expeditions by one or two Indians, but Robert insisted that he return to the city by nightfall. Although a wise precaution, it proved disastrous for research purposes. One day Geddes and his helpers discovered

* *Political Essay on the Kingdom of New Spain.*

a magnificent Edentate skeleton, closely resembling *Mylodon;* but, on returning with my workmen early next morning to continue the excavation, we found our specimen shattered into fragments. Some of the country people, who always watched one's movements with intense suspicion, and who alternately regarded us as treasure-seekers and as magicians, so adding considerably to the danger and discomfort of the undertaking, had done this, and we were able only to rescue a single broken tooth . . .[2]

As if this experience were not discouraging enough, during November Geddes fell ill. The exact nature of his illness remains obscure,* but it is known that the available medical treatment consisted of periodic bleedings and the administration of mercury in some form, and that among other afflictions he temporarily lost his sight. He was ordered to sit in a darkened room, with bandages over his eyes, and remained there for several weeks.

The impact of this disaster cannot be over-emphasized. It has already been mentioned that Geddes received his "learning by eye-gate rather than ear", and to have become blind at the age of twenty-five must have been like having the majority of the tools and raw materials for his thinking processes snatched from his grasp. From Kinnoull Hill to the Sierra Madre, the world had flooded him with riches, and these had been enjoyed, analysed and sorted in the chambers of his mind. No words could ever replace the images, no sense of touch take the place of colour.

However, there was a strand in Geddes's character which might best be labelled by that somewhat pregnant word "hubris". In its meaning of "insolent security" it perhaps prompted his habit of turning disasters on their head in order to make them appear as successes of an innovative kind. Certainly it seems possible that any man who sets out to develop a synthetic, practical vision of a benevolent universe, must possess at least a very virile, if not a positively insolent, strand of security in his nature.

Going blind was almost the worst thing that could happen to Geddes, so, conversely, the gain which he rescued from this

* The health record in Mexico City at that time was poor, largely due to bad drains and sanitation.

disaster, had to be one of his greatest. Indeed, to many of his subsequent close followers, it was his greatest, though to a considerable majority of colleagues and acquaintances it was an unnecessary smokescreen. This invention—be it gain or obfuscation—he later called his "thinking-machines".

He had spent what no doubt seemed an interminable period in darkness, trying to discipline his mind into sorting his thoughts and knowledge into some manipulative whole. (As relief from this solitary concentration, he persuaded Maggie, his sister-in-law, to sit outside the door and read Mill's *Political Economy* to him.) One day when he was standing in the room feeling the objects around him with his fingertips he encountered the window, whose shutters were on the outside. As is customary, the frames around each pane were slightly raised, and he ran his fingers around the connections between each smooth glass rectangle. The tactile sense of connection between each equal area—a connection which could be made horizontally, vertically or diagonally—made him think of the connections between the different, but equally important, fields of knowledge.

It was not long before he was folding pieces of paper, the folds being ascertainable by touch as the window frames had been, into four, six, eight or twelve rectangles. Soon he was mentally allotting subjects to each rectangle, and running his mind around the joyous richness of inter-connection. One of his first diagrams started from the diagonal ascendancy of Comte's four hierarchies of the sciences: Mathematics & Logic, Physics & Chemistry, Biology, Sociology.

			Sociology
		Biology	Anthropology
	Physics and Chemistry	Biochemistry	Ecology
Mathematics and Logic	Mathematics (as applied to Physics)	Biometrics	Statistics

The squares to the right of the diagonal show how individual sciences relate to each of the four hierarchies, while those above were later to be filled by the metaphysical sciences.

From these humble beginnings, proliferated a lifetime of "thinking-machine" production, and it would seem convenient to comment on them here. Those who obtain insight from them will find further information in the 1949 edition of *Cities in Evolution*, and those whose thoughts do not too easily marshall themselves into rectangles will not be troubled by much further thinking-machine discussion in subsequent chapters. It is just possible that part of his initial prompting in the direction of unique graphic representation of facts and ideas came from Humboldt "a lot of" whose "influence in science came from the novel graphic ways in which he represented his results",[3] and who strove, in his huge work *Cosmos*, to describe the physical contents of the entire universe.

The expression of thought processes is a limitless subject. In the thinking-machines Geddes found an image, which satisfied him, for the concepts that developed, collided, merged and clarified in his mind. Jacques Monod has written:

> . . . mental reflection, at the deeper level, is not verbal: it is an *imagined experience*, simulated with the aid of forms, of forces, of interactions which together barely compose an "image" in the visual sense of the term . . . the significance of the simulated experience comes clear . . . only when it has been enunciated symbolically.[4]

The trouble with Geddes's method of symbolical enunciation was that it was so often dealing with such very large concepts, that their reduction to titles in rectangles was too astringent a form of shorthand for most people (particularly strangers to his method) to follow. He could not be accused of biting off more than he could chew, for his brain seemed capable of chewing intelligently almost any subject, but it is, as yet, impossible to find a satisfactory digestive process for such gargantuan mental feasts.

One of his favourite diagrams, which in simplified form had four rectangles and at its most complex thirty-six, represented what he called "the ledger of life". One half represented the outer world, both active and passive; the other the inner world, both passive and active. Both versions, with a written explanation, may be found in Appendix I, from which it will be seen that the "Acts" rectangle was sub-divided into a scheme based on the Le Play Place-Work-Folk paradigm, and this was often used on its own in differing versions when Geddes expounded the relationships between geography and people.

Those readers who are interested in thinking-machines will realize that they have many parallels. Peter Redgrove has written the following comment* after seeing the diagrams illustrated in Appendix I:

> In some form or other they have always been used when people wanted to think completely on a subject—what is nice is that Geddes arrived at these ancient forms and that they have entirely modern reference. . . . The swastika appears—often in fragments to begin with—in modern dreams in a process eventually leading to a complete look round some problem. It has a centre, and four sides: that is, an I, and four faculties: thought, feeling, sensation and intuition in Jungian thought. . . . The game ludo—the word ludo means "the game" since there is no other worth playing, it is the master-game, to make oneself complete— has four cells from which one-sidedness one is released by chance and persistence. There is much of [this kind of] patterning in Ouspensky and Buckminster Fuller' et al., but very little with the tone of responsibility Geddes's has.

Jung's use of mandala symbolism as a means towards realizing man's need to recognize and delineate his complete personality is described thus by Frieda Fordham:[5]

> Jung found that the experience which was ultimately formulated in the mandala pattern was typical of people who were no longer able to project the divine image—i.e. to find God somewhere outside themselves—and so were in danger of inflation. The round or square enclosures seemed to act like magically protective walls, preventing an outburst and a disintegration, and protecting an inward purpose. There was a similarity in them to the sacred places that in ancient times were often made to protect the God, but the

* In a letter to the author.

significant fact about a modern mandala is that it rarely if ever contains a god in the centre, but instead a variety of symbols, or even a human being. A modern mandala is therefore "an involuntary confession of a peculiar mental condition. There is no deity in the mandala, nor is there any submission or reconciliation to a deity. The place of the deity seems to be taken by the wholeness of man." (Jung, *Psychology and Religion*.)

The centre of Geddes's evolved mandala or thinking-machine (Appendix I) was a quartered circle symbolizing the development of the town, through experience and meditation, into the ideal city. Later in life he became very interested in psychoanalysis, but always related any inner journey to the significance it might have to the outer manifestations of society. In this he was, as Redgrove has indicated, truly responsible. Seminal planners have tended to be outgoing, practical thinkers, just as seminal psychologists have tended to concentrate on inner phenomena. In his thinking-machines Geddes achieved the synthesis of the two worlds. But it is a difficult code to crack if one has not already made a little progress along the two paths. Interestingly, Le Corbusier (a many-sided thinker, and infinitely stronger than Geddes in aesthetic vision as well as realization, though weaker in all-round historical "feel" and social understanding), created a *grille* on which he included the chief components of urban activity, in order that the members of the Congrès Internationaux d'Architecture Moderne could develop their programme on the basis of a common analysis.

Perhaps one of the things that most confused bystanders to Geddes's conversations and lectures, was the wide range of variation he produced in his diagrams. It would be untrue to say that no two ever looked quite alike, for he often reproduced the simpler ones, but such a comment would be a true reflection of the spirit of the production. Among his papers are literally hundreds of browning, dusty, often illegible, pieces of paper, either folded or partitioned by lines. Some are complete charts, the majority are not. Their sizes vary from tiny sheets torn from pocket diaries to double-elephant with fancy lettering and decoration. Sometimes there is an expressionist graphic movement about them that impels attention.

Whatever their value to other people, these charts always remained central to Geddes's method of thought, and very precious to him. When he was seventy-two he wrote to a friend:

> I chill people with my diagrams, the coldest looking things imaginable; and though it is *in that way* I turn out so many gardens and buildings, university and city plans; my lectures and books too . . . they just won't believe me!

His conviction of their importance, the impression of a golden structure plucked from the dark fire of blindness, is most clearly expressed in a series of essays published in 1905:[6]

> And were I in prison . . . I would make thinking-ladders of my prison-bars, and so climb away up into the skies of thought, and away down into its strange dim depths, where no jailer, himself a prisoner, could ever follow . . . some day I must tell you how I first learned this, and found out for myself how to make thinking-machines—(inventors will come to these after flying-machines—they are a better sort), in weary months of literal darkness, to which I now look back as the worst yet best experience of life.

The blindness did not last, but Geddes's sight was permanently impaired as far as long periods of microscopic research were concerned. Dispirited, he made arrangements to return home.

While in Mexico he had been in correspondence with William Stirling, a one-time colleague at Aberdeen University. Geddes had been enquiring about employment possibilities on his return, and Stirling stated quite categorically that he would not be offered another place at Aberdeen. This was presumably because Professor Cossor Ewart either did not appreciate Geddes's teaching methods as much as the students did, or because he resented him going off after more ambitious posts so quickly—or both. As soon as Stirling heard of his illness, he wrote: "I cannot tell you how sad I am at the news contained in yours just received. An end to fame and glory for the present . . ." This mention of "fame and glory" gives an indication of the strong impression Geddes's aspirations made on his friends, though they tended to treat them as rather more materialistic and conventional than they actually were. Hugh MacDiarmid once described another Scotsman in a way which seems entirely fitting for Geddes:

> . . . the wayward, antinomian Scottish type—versatile, erudite, filled with wanderlust spiritual and physical, indifferent to or incapable of mere worldly prudence . . .[7]

On his recovery, Geddes gathered together a few more specimens and made his way to Vera Cruz, where he booked a passage home. He sailed on 1st March, spending the intervening days collecting, among other things, crayfish and prawns for Huxley. He also took home with him a small collection of sub-tropical plants to the Royal Botanical Gardens in Edinburgh, and the following collection for the British Museum: Jaws of *Canis*, milar of *Elephas*, fragment of jaw of *Myloden*, three Mammalia, twenty-five reptiles, fifty-two fish, twelve crustaceans and sixteen insects.

He spent much of the voyage playing chess with fellow-passengers, no doubt seeing embryonic thinking-machines among the chequered squares.

Chapter 4

THISTLES OF ACADEME

GEDDES WAS BACK in Britain by the beginning of April 1880, and went straight to Mount Tabor. He made no immediate attempt to see friends, although William Stirling was anxious to advise him on job possibilities. He must have been in a curious state of mind: unnerved by the experience of blindness and the possibility of never again being able to do long periods of close microscope work; yet galvanized by his vision of an integrated social and scientific network of knowledge. Certainly he did not rest for long.

By the third week in April he had sent off an application to teach as an extra-mural lecturer in zoology in the Edinburgh School of Medicine. He had also received a letter from the *Encyclopaedia Britannica* commissioning an article on Insectivorous Plants, and asking if he felt able to undertake one on Instinct. Later he wrote to Charles Darwin asking permission to copy figures from his work on insectivorous plants—which permission was readily granted; and when the article was printed, Darwin pronounced it "wonderfully well done . . . you have managed to give in the one piece a surprising amount of information". This prompted James Geikie to comment: "I hear with very great pleasure what you say as to old Father Darwin. His letters are very precious . . ."

Geddes planned his lectures (which inevitably ranged rather wider than mere zoology) and went ahead with negotiating a lease for some rooms in Edinburgh in which to deliver them and set up his specimens. He had not, however, yet obtained the official blessing of the University Court. Were he to do so, it would guarantee him an audience (and in those days lecturers relied for their fees on the number of students attending); but if he was merely advertising a course of lectures that was outside the curriculum, the chances of success were much more slender. In the meantime Alexander Dickson, the kindly professor of Botany at Edinburgh, invited him to assist in his class of Practical Botany and Vegetable Histology, which was dormant for lack of a demonstrator. Geddes accepted on the condition that this was considered compatible with his zoology teaching. However, when, at the end of May, the University Court rejected his application for recognition, it was on the grounds that there was no precedent for such double employment.

One cannot but suspect that the university was relieved to seize such a practical, impersonal excuse. Geddes's lecture syllabi were never of a format that slotted easily into a curriculum. William Stirling wrote firmly:

> Stick to your Botany. Dickson is a gentleman and will support you and see you through your difficulty. Try and get rid of your lease of your zoology cellars, urge them to free you (why the devil did you do such a foolish thing?). ... Do not attempt to give ambitious special courses, nobody will come and few people care for Morphology or anything else, therefore dismiss these projects and in the meantime stick to Dickson and live. It is a mistake to aspire after advanced men, nothing will pay which is not in the medical curriculum and therefore compulsory.

Geddes ignored Stirling's advice and embarked on the lectures.

Also during 1880 he delivered a paper ("The Phenomena of Variegation and Cell-multiplication in a Species of Enteromorpha") to the Royal Society of Edinburgh which was well-received, but the following year he was not content with a biological offering. Instead he produced a paper called "The Classification of Statistics and its Results", which took three meetings to deliver (21st March, 4th April and 2nd May) and was comprehensive to a degree. It may be remembered that "Statistics" was the subject lurking innocently at the bottom right-hand corner of one of the earliest thinking-machines so that one could visualize all other subjects radiating from it like the rays of an art-deco sun. This paper is discussed in more detail in the following chapter—which gives a general outline of the strands of Geddes's philosophy formed by the mid-1880's. He sent a copy of the paper to Ruskin indicating its links with the latter's expression of politico-economic philosophy in *Munera Pulveris*. Ruskin replied:

I should like to understand, myself, how you mean to bring
—or feel that the evidence will bring—statistics to the conclusions of *Munera Pulveris*. The entire gist of *Munera* is the
sentence "No noble thing is wealth but to a noble person"
and where do your statistics calculate nobility? . . . But I
am sure that a rational classification of statistics will bring
out some truths which will be afterwards demonstrated, as
you deal with them. Only—as I never understood a column
of statistics in my life—you can't expect me to see how!

This did not prevent Geddes, a year later, from again approaching Ruskin, this time asking if he might call on him to seek
advice over some lectures on economics which he had arranged to address "certainly to ladies, and perhaps within the
University as well". He added:

Pray do not ascribe this request—(over which I have long
hesitated)—either to an over-estimate of the value of my
work or to forgetfulness of the value of your time. The simple
reason is that having for the last half of a year been getting
ready for the fray, it would now that I am fairly entering
it, be useful in more ways than I can readily explain to take
counsel with you, from whom I learned to desire that kind
of soldiering.

Ruskin, however, was abroad.
Although Geddes could still present himself as a disciple to
someone he admired as much as Ruskin, he was already beginning to build up a considerable following among his own students, and the numbers in his classes were increasing. His driving
energy and commitment to a humane synthesis of knowledge
attracted those who disliked pettifogging specialism and over-
concern for conventional "getting on". Any student willing to
act as audience and occasional chorus to the flowing mono-
logues was welcome until the small hours at his lodgings in
Princes Street. Sometimes, however, he tried to sweep them
along too far and too fast. One student, Harvey Gibson, had to
dig his toes in firmly when Geddes endeavoured to persuade
him to accompany him to the Naples Zoological Station in the
summer of 1881. Gibson wrote:

It is all very well for you to do as you do, you know pretty well that your brains can get you work at any moment. You, if I mistake not, prefer a roving and absolutely free life—I prefer a settled and methodical one—and a settled and methodical one I mean to lead—I intend to attempt mounting Jacob's ladder rung by rung like an ordinary mortal and not on the brilliant pinions of the revolutionary political economist or the philosophical wings of the sage of Princes Street . . .

But Gibson remained a friend who in later years claimed that his own love for science was engendered by Geddes's teaching: ". . . his enthusiasm and energy arouse a corresponding feeling in those who have the good fortune to work under his direction".

Geddes delayed his journey to Naples because his brother Jack was in London. Robert had not long before returned from Mexico, and the three brothers had an enjoyable reunion. Patrick wrote to Jessie at Mount Tabor:

Jack and I are penitent about having written such short letters home for the last fortnight, but he is worrying himself about not being able to do any business, and I am busy doing all the library work I can instead of doing it in Naples, and Father will be pleased to hear that my essay for the University prize will be finished in a few days more, and will be a good one. I did not know I had so many friends in London, but people never were so kind. I cannot accept all the invitations I get, as two come for the same evening now and then, so that I don't get so very much time with Jack after all. Still we are becoming great friends—and I would have been off, of course, long ago but for wishing to rub noses with him as long as I can get on with my work here. Robert came up from Farnham the other day and stayed two nights with us. We all went and got photographed together, so you will have a lovely trio! Mind you say I am the best looking. Jack made me a very handsome present— of money to buy my pictures of Father and Mother as soon as I can afford it—and to help my Naples expedition at present. And then I am his guest just now. The only thing which makes me dislike staying so long is that I am ashamed of his kindness.

I am glad David Barker has got a job and hope he will keep it. I shall be delighted if you can play off Margaret Barker on Jack. He ought to get married. I've time enough.

The prize to which he referred was the Ellis Physiology Prize—for which he was successful with an essay based on his researches on the presence of chlorophyll in certain animals. It was a particularly fecund few months as far as his scientific work was concerned, and Professor Angelo Andres, with whom he worked in Naples, later suggested that if he could "find time to bring together all your work on protoplasm and the cell . . . it would certainly be a new milestone in the progress of science". However, microscopic work pained his eyes more and more, and this was to be his last prolonged period of original biological research.

He was still in Naples on 26th October when he received a telegram from his father informing him that the Edinburgh chair of natural history had fallen vacant. He wrote home immediately:

I have Father's telegram today, and wrote a lot of letters to start my candidature forthwith. You will, I hope, all clearly understand however at the outset, that the odds against me are very considerable and that it is best to hope for nothing— and so make sure not to be disappointed. I shall, of course, make as good a fight as I can, but shall take my probably ultimate defeat with the greatest composure, and I hope you will also do the same. It won't altogether be lost time and money, as I'll get very thoroughly advertised as a rising young naturalist, which may pay another time, and at any rate enable me to preach my political economy more authoritatively. It is very unfortunate for me that this vacancy has occurred so soon. I have such quantities of paper in the press, and such quantities more in my head and notebooks unfinished. Had some of this been ready, I would have stood a better chance. Of course, I shall hurry a lot of papers out, but they won't be so well finished.

He returned to his teaching duties in Edinburgh with his

candidature for the Chair uppermost in his mind. Early in December James Geikie, whom he had asked to provide him with a testimonial, wrote:

> Enclosed is the letter you ask for. I never could write the kind of letter that is needed on such occasions. It would be so much easier to say: "you had better elect my friend Pat Geddes. He is a damned good fellow. You know—with strong radical tendencies:—hates humbug and all that sort of thing—don't set much store by Mrs Grundy—etc. etc. etc."

and later commented "this canvassing makes a man do much that he would laugh at in others". Among the many others who agreed to support Geddes's candidature were Darwin, Huxley and Alfred Wallace.

Other contenders for the post included Cossor Ewart, the professor under whom he had worked at Aberdeen, and Ray Lankaster, who occupied the Jodrell Chair of Zoology at University College, and was seven years older than Geddes. The behind-the-scenes speculation and manoeuvrings were pretty active. Geddes's supporters were indignant when an anonymous article appeared in *Academy* apparently attacking some of his ideas, and which turned out to have been written by Lankaster. "What a wild bull Lankaster is!" commented one, while another, George Murray,* urged Geddes to put in for the Jodrell Chair, should Lankaster be successful in Edinburgh, reasoning thus:

> . . . as for University College there can be no question about its being the best thing for you to do. I am not slumbering and shall go at once to Poore who I suppose will have a vote and to Marcus Beck. Have only to tell Beck that Schäfer is likely to be influenced by Ewart against you—to enlist Beck's warmest sympathy. Marcus cordially detests Schäfer (and Ewart too!).

Finally, at the end of March 1882, the post was offered to Lankaster. Geddes sent a note congratulating him and asking

* Keeper of Cryptogamia at the Natural History Museum.

if he would be willing to support his own application for the Jodrell Chair. Lankaster declined, explaining that he was to be on the selection committee. Some friends continued to urge Geddes to put himself forward for the London post, while others suggested he should try for one in Manchester. Then, only a fortnight after his appointment, Lankaster resigned and returned to University College. Apparently the conditions of the appointment had turned out to be other than he supposed. The normally benevolent James Geikie was furious. He wrote to Geddes:

> Did he imagine that he was of such everlasting importance that the University in order to retain so brilliant and shining an example of modern scientific culture would be willing to forego the usual winter course? No wonder he was so very anxious to come north. £1,000 a year for 3 months work is not bad. I suppose he would have come for even £500 a year to do the same work. Really it exasperates me as a Scotsman and an old Edinburgh man to think that such a puppy should have had it in his power to behave so badly to us. But it serves them right. We have had quite enough bending of the knee before the pretentious pups and Hosts of Know-ledge whom the English universities provide for the improve-ment of us poor hyperborean savages. D— them and their products.

A month later no alternative appointment had been made. George Murray replied to a letter of Geddes's:

> I return Stirling's letter. I wonder he betrays the fact that he is in the Ewart-Schäfer plot. . . . Did you see in Saturday's *Dundee Advertiser* (or it may have been Friday's) a Ewartian paragraph intended to insult you? He is a low devil!

A few days later Ewart was appointed. As promised, Geddes showed no outward evidence of disappointment. George Murray, however, was still railing against Lankaster three years later, when he reported to Geddes on an address Lankaster gave to the Royal Society:

. . . he said (that) at present the *male of the sole was unknown*!
Let Ray go down to any fish cadger at Billingsgate and repeat
that, and he would probably get one chucked at him before
he knew where he was. Because the said male is small and
escapes the net oftener than the other, he needn't be ruled
out of existence!

(It should perhaps be added that though of impetuous temperament, Ray Lankaster was a distinguished biologist who later
became Director of the Natural History Museum.)

Immediately after the Edinburgh appointment, Geddes tried,
also unsuccessfully, for the Chair of Biology at St Andrew's.
This time he was advised by his one-time teacher Burdon
Sanderson:

> If I might venture to offer you advice which I daresay you
> will think stupid, it is that you should now make your utmost
> effort to fix upon *the* subject of investigation to which you
> will devote yourself for the next period of your life.

The advice was well-meant, and eminently sensible for anyone
who wished to climb the conventional academic ladder. But
the subject on which Geddes's attention was fixed was the
universe, and although he might spend short periods when his
focus narrowed down to the most humble forms of life, during
the same afternoon it would draw back and embrace economics,
philosophy, psychology or painting—his view thereof embodying
concepts gleaned from the natural sciences. He once quoted
with approval G. Stanley Hall's description of genius:
". . . the best definition of genius is intensified and prolonged
adolescence, to which excessive or premature systematisation
is fatal".

Throughout his life Geddes needed, and often lacked, a body
of men and women of sufficient calibre to support his ideas,
criticize them intelligently when necessary, and help him carry
them out. He sometimes recruited such people from his classes,
and he was never more fortunate than when a young man called
J. Arthur Thomson decided to desert theology for a while in
order to study natural science. He proved a brilliant student,
and Geddes hung on to him.

In March 1883, when he was twenty-two, Thomson declared

he would put off returning to his theological course for a year, adding:

> In my best mood I am more disposed to be a minister than anything else. When oppressed with a sense of unfitness, with intellectual difficulties, with a feeling of the responsibilities involved, I feel most inclined to escape all these by turning to science . . .

By December of the same year he was writing:

> . . . but I doubt I shall ever do any scientific work worth speaking of, I should not like to be a mere teacher and to do no constructive work. And I am so unhappy when I resolve to give up the idea of being a minister that I cannot bear it . . .

At the time he was spending a period at Jena University and attempting to translate an article of Geddes's into German. Nine months later while doing some holiday tutoring in Scotland, he still felt under-motivated:

> . . . days of deathful stagnancy—as pipe in mouth I lay by the hour—on the links—a lanky figure—ostensibly peering up into the infinite, but in reality almost squashed flat by the finite . . .

By 1885 he was still travelling and studying science. No doubt it was Geddes who particularly encouraged him to visit Paris. From there he wrote:

> Paris surpasses tenfold all my expectations. . . . Porridge and the shorter catechism don't just tend to rear an organism likely to sympathise right away with Frenchmen . . . but this paradise-city, and the glory of buildings . . . do help to enable one to understand them. The seamy side does rumple up at times and no Scotchman could help moralising . . .

A few months later he was in Berlin researching sponges, and "battling to find a firm standing ground, a thoughtful rationalism, a synthesis which will satisfy my sympathies and compel me to synergy . . .". The phraseology is pure Geddes; the struggle was nearly over.

On 4th January 1886 he was still in Berlin and wrote:

> If you wish the sex papers *instanter*—*must* have them—despatch a postcard please, but I have had to bummel about these holidays and have got hardly anything done to them. . . . They are fearfully difficult . . . I shall be delighted to be your collaborateur for two years or more, provided I can *live*, till another *better* collaborateur is evolved—and then exit JAT to teach zootomy, spelling and morals to the heathen Chinese . . .

The next day he did return the sex papers, saying: "If we are to do any work together it must be *together*. . . ." Given the choice of commitment to God or commitment to Geddes, Thomson had chosen Geddes. The "sex papers" were to form the basis of *The Evolution of Sex* (published 1889) on which they collaborated, and they continued to collaborate on biological works, however sporadically, until Geddes's death. Arthur Geddes, commenting on his father's failure to express all his ideas in book form, wrote:

> . . . only Thomson could screw real collaboration out of him. (As Thomson said, this bled *him* of the last ounce of moral and intellectual energy!)

Thomson provided the stability, clarity and continuity needed for the production of popular scientific works, and brought to their shared projects his own romantic brand of moral earnestness that fitted well with the mood of the period. When, in August 1886, he became engaged, he wrote to Geddes:

> Long, long ago I was regenerated at the hands of faith, and all things became really new, nor have I lost all my early enthusiasm brought me. I was really born again in faith. A time came, however, with the dawning of clearer light when . . . by your help, I was slowly led, not without pain, to a wider synthesis and a surer knowledge. I was born again of hope, and under my impenetrable hide a new enthusiasm

burns; all things became a second time new in the light of a scientific synthesis. For this I thank *you*.

A third time, however, I have been born again, I have listened to a third regenerating voice. All things are again new, though my new enthusiasm can coexist with the old. I have been born again of love.

After his failure to get a university chair, Geddes was in a rather precarious position, both professionally and financially. In July 1883 he again applied for recognition as an extra-mural lecturer in Zoology, but again this was denied "while you hold the University office of Assistant to a Professor," and he discontinued his lectures. The *Encyclopaedia Britannica* had progressed from I to M, and he contributed articles on Mimosa and Mulberry. He demurred slightly at Millet, but acquiesced after the editor had written:

I quite agree that there should be an article on Plant-movements, but I fancy it must be Plants, Movements of, which is a good way ahead. . . . As regards Millet, I am unwilling to go to a new contributor for an article which you can certainly do quite well. Every man has occasionally to do work beyond his particular last . . .

Advice that was rather superfluous in Geddes's case.

Denied a central point within the university from which to operate, he renewed his alliance with the Positivists, and considered starting a Positivist centre in Edinburgh. Richard Congreve appeared gratified when he officially joined the society, though Geddes himself felt more allegiance with another of its leaders, Edward Spencer Beesly, who wrote:

I am becoming more and more of the opinion that the way in which Positivism is presented by Dr Congreve and his friends—liturgy (now much developed), prayers, (etc.)—although it may attract a certain number . . . drives away many more . . .

He tried to enthuse his old, as well as his new, friends with his beliefs, and his one-time schoolfriend Harry Barker desperately attempted to keep abreast of all his new departures. Geddes was beginning to consider radical concepts for the education of children (some of which he was later to put into practice with his own family), and Barker wrote to him on the birth of his own first child: "Hope you will have *that school* ready for my daughter when she is old enough . . . !" But sadly the child died after sucking matches when she was eighteen months old, and Positivism provided hollow comfort. Barker wrote to Geddes:

> I also feel it acutely in a way I cannot describe—it is a peculiar experience in which the Positivist philosophy offers no consolation—Is it not odd that I welcome and am strangely comforted by all the sympathy and satisfying assurances of Christian religion?

Geddes was not unsympathetic to people's personal tragedies, but perhaps to avoid the feeling of helplessness and guilt that they inevitably tend to induce in an onlooker, he seldom spent much time over them when there seemed nothing immediately useful that he could do. It is not very surprising to find Barker writing, four months later:

> If I lived in Edinburgh I would be a faithful disciple and attend all your lectures and read the books you selected and really follow up tho' many leagues behind—Give me a fresh trial old friend—I believe in you as fully today as 15 years ago—and am (at the moment) enthusiastic still for myself in the idea of a possibility of usefulness in a small degree acceptable even to you—I am year by year more painfully reminded of your prophecy long ago that in the future you would claim me as a "specimen" just as much as any beetle or crab—and still it is unpleasant to feel oneself only a specimen and how little understanding of it I have—I never hardly write to you—I feel you have no time to waste on me and when I have seen you so busy with such piles of important correspondence such grand schemes of philanthropy, research, exploitation etc. etc. I have positively felt it unkind to trouble you with myself and my mind and drag you even for half an hour into my humble life and affairs.

The two men were as unalike as chalk and cheese, and their relationship was strained almost to breaking point more than once. Nevertheless, it survived until Geddes's death.

Apart from his brief remark in the letter of 1881 to Jessie that he had "time enough" for matrimonial concerns, virtually nothing is known of Geddes's pre-marital emotional life. A fragmentary diary kept in the summer of 1883, when he went on an eleven-day tricycling tour with a friend, H. Baildon, does, however, give a rare glimpse of him in a relaxed mood. One entry starts by describing their lodgings somewhere between Darlington and Boroughbridge:

> Pleasant family. Goodman. Goodwife also supper: pretty Dulcinea—granny 82 mended my bag. Bakehouse—Cakes. Wet morning. Went to see church. Dulcinea—dinner. Dulcinea—tea. Dulcinea—market parting. O O O! Ride on at 3.30 to Boroughbridge. Tea at gardener's wife's with bonnie bairns. Then on to Knaresboro through clay—like flies in treacle. Temperance Hotel in Market Place. Whiskey fetched by goodman to celebrate B's birthday. Jollification till 2! Disturbed sleep.

Even without this slight evidence of his reassuringly normal susceptibility to a pretty girl, one would be able to gather from Geddes's writings on sex (which are discussed elsewhere) that he was very sensitively aware of the delights and problems of youthful passion. The tour took him and Baildon right down to Brentford in Middlesex, where they separated, and Geddes then set out to sail to Holland on his way to Jena to visit Arthur Thomson and talk with Ernst Haeckel, the evolutionist and inventor of the word "ecology".

Although there is no record of any early romance in Geddes's life, he obviously enjoyed the company of women at the varied social gatherings and intellectual groups which he attended, and particularly the more serious of them found him attractive. George Murray once referred to a girl called Alice Gray who "seemed to have a great opinion of you", going on to make a jokey connection between her hair which looked as if it had been "brushed by machinery", and Geddes's own "erect" head of hair by mentioning "capillary attraction". And Murray's own sister, Anne, a nurse, was clearly nonplussed by one of

Geddes's swift changes from one enterprise to another, after falling under the spell of his enthusiasm:

> You promised me a thing most wonderful by which I am to win my way to all men's hearts—a "Sesame to Kings' Treasuries", and I am not even to have· the trouble of learning the Greek alphabet. The grandest possibilities open up to my view. Equipped with this wonderful amulet I am to face fearlessly the stoniest-hearted doctor and professor.
>
> I wait patiently week after week, month after month, building the grandest castles in the meantime, then you come and in the coolest way possible pull the whole construction about my ears and bury me in the ruins. Was it not cruel of you to tell me after all the hopes you had raised "Oh, I have buried all that".

Many of the discussions and meetings, including those with Positivist links, in which Geddes was involved at this period, took place at the home of James Oliphant. Oliphant ran a private school in Edinburgh, and had wide literary and philosophical interests. His wife, formerly Edith Morton, often invited her elder sister, Anna, to visit them. Anna liked to exchange the somewhat restricted atmosphere of her parents' home in Liverpool for the liberal toings-and-froings of the Oliphant household. She was a serious, musical girl who claimed she would have liked to work with Octavia Hill, the London housing reformer. From the start, she was impressed by Patrick Geddes. In March 1883, when she was about to return home to Liverpool, she wrote to him:

> I am *very* sorry to find that we shall not be able to go and see you tomorrow afternoon.
>
> I wanted to thank you very much for all the pleasure you have given me during my visit, but I must content myself, I suppose, with writing my goodbye and thanks.

Whether prompted at all by conversations with Anna Morton we do not know, but Geddes's ideas began to focus towards the practicalities of housing conditions and social reform. Edinburgh itself was laid out like a social parable: the dignified and elegant streets of the New Town facing across

Princes Street Gardens to the piled up, dirty, and often semi-derelict, tenements of the Old. Geddes's own rooms in Princes Street faced directly on to the gardens, so that he could stand in the window and watch the old buildings, high on the hill ridge, darkening in silhouette against the evening skies, and terminated by the dour profile of the castle fortress. The beauty of the gardens was now broken by the railway, which had been thrust, against much opposition, into the heart of Edinburgh, so that intermittently bursts of steam and smoke would erupt noisily between the trees and grassy banks.*

The conditions of most people living in the Old Town were abysmal. The tenements were bleak, dank and insanitary, and yet there was something about their structure, their arrangement in a tough, urban landscape that fitted well with the dark rocks and skies of Scotland, that made them not unfitting. If one believes in such a thing as organic architecture, they certainly sat more naturally in their setting, under the brooding Salisbury Crags and Arthur's Seat, than did the geometric squares and crescents of the Georgian New Town. They still do. Geddes realized that they need not be beyond the pale; improvement and renewal were possible. By November of 1884, James Oliphant was writing to his sister-in-law Anna:

> . . . the Environment Society which is now being set on its legs . . . a preliminary meeting was held . . . only a few select friends of Mr Geddes's to hear his statement of its scope and aims. . . . It is a scheme for the organisation of all benevolent enterprise! But its special aims are to provide or rather improve existing material surroundings, by decorating halls and schools, planting open spaces, providing musical and other entertainments for the people, etc. etc.
>
> He and a Mr Deas . . . have been working it up. I have been made Treasurer and Mr Geddes is secretary. You will hear more of it when you come. Mr Geddes has been here dining today and discussing the matter. He came last night to do so but Mr Black was here. He is more comical than ever but very nice.

* Not all technological change is for the worse. The diesel trains which now go into Edinburgh are relatively clean and quiet, and do not disturb the office workers sunbathing in the gardens during summer lunch hours.

It did not remain the Environment Society, but became the Edinburgh Social Union; nineteenth-century terminology superseding a word that was not to be bandied around very much until eighty years later—and for precisely the same reasons as those outlined in Oliphant's letter. In 1884, Geddes had realized what Theo Crosby expressed succinctly in 1965:

A city must be able to regenerate itself, to heal its own tissue, to retain its values so that it remains economic gradually to rebuild and renew its buildings. This is partly a problem of economics, partly of sociology, partly of architecture.[1]

The membership card of the Social Union was unique. It had four columns for recording members' subscriptions, headed by four symbols. A purse indicated the money column, a city plan denoted gifts of houses or land, a bale of goods signified contributions in kind, and an hourglass symbolized "time generously applied". It was an ambitious venture, and if it was to succeed it was important that Geddes should be financially secure and operating from a position that would carry some weight with municipal authorities. Some of his students already called him "the Professor"—with his lengthening beard, volatile speechmaking and slightly eccentric manner it seemed inevitable—but he needed a legitimate claim to the title.

Towards the end of 1884, the newly-endowed University College of Dundee was inviting applications for its Chair of Biology. Geddes began to marshal together his testimonials once again, with much encouragement from scientist friends in Dundee—particularly Frank Young, a botanist whom he had known since schooldays. He was reluctant to visit Dundee in order to do some discreet lobbying in person, although W. Peterson, the College's principal, urged that "no one will suspect you for canvassing if you merely call to let the electors see what manner of man you are!" Geddes's supporters considered that this would be a wise course of action, since they felt the electors would be impressed by him, and that the more fanciful stories concerning his unconventional academic reputation would be seen to be unfounded.

However on 30th November, Frank Young was forced to write:

Sundry rumours have been afloat last week regarding your religious tendencies. You seek to eliminate "the spiritual element from the natural world". You consider special creation inconceivable, etc. etc. all of which we have hunted down to one divine who boasts of being a broad free-churchman but who has in this matter much to the surprise of all his friends shown the priestly intolerance and fear of scientific truth of the very narrowest of his breed. . . . Now my dear Pat whatever you may hear in this affair you must not now *on any account* withdraw as I fear you might for on you is fixed the hopes of all our local working naturalists and the encouragement and growth of Biological truth in our minds to say nothing of the best interests of the College by having it plainly established that nothing theological shall be suffered to enter therein.

. . . Peterson is to be in Edinburgh tomorrow and may visit and enlighten thee.

A little delay in the election naturally follows but your friends are firm and sincere.

Another Dundee backer, James Cunningham, also wrote to Geddes at the same time, asking: "Would you be inclined to write me a short statement of your philosophical and theological standpoint, which I might use or not at discretion?"

Stung, Geddes immediately settled down to draft a reply:

. . . though I should prefer simply looking at the humorous aspects of the matter (notably the illustration of the beautiful uniformity of cause and effect offered by the association of Britannica articles with heresy-hunts), you must pardon me the liberty of distinctly pointing out, that by in any way raising the question of my real or supposed relation to the faith at all—I allude not so much to your letter as to the numerous private enquiries, which are no secret, even here— the Council or its Committee of Inquiry would be dis-regarding the first clause of the one "fundamental condition" of the Constitution of the College, announced in the preface to its Calendar. In short I am compelled, in the interests of all candidates alike, respectfully to deprecate the serious inconsistency of first giving the utmost publicity to the condition "that no Student, Professor, . . . etc. shall be required to make any declaration as to his or her religious opinions, or to submit to any test" thereof . . .

. . . My philosophic position may be outlined thus. Just as a painter has an eye for composition, or a musician an ear for harmony, so I have an instinct for fitting details together, for piling facts into larger and larger masses of knowledge, call it faculty of generalisation, power of synthesis, or what you please . . .

. . . My leisure just now is going in to the problem of the Organisation of Beneficence with a practical beginning to which everybody is invited—Liberal & Conservative, capitalist & socialist, artist & philistine, scientists & women have alike accepted—in which I have reason to hope the Free Church Clergy will be cordially supported by the Catholic and in which the Clergy of Giles Cathedral and the leaders of the Secularist and Socialist Societies expressed cordial concurrence.

A minister entered the fray on Geddes's behalf, and wrote to Peterson, who replied:

. . . you may depend on it now, that if Mr Geddes is unsuccessful, it will not be because his religious views may not square with those of some of the electors.

But by 7th December, Frank Young was writing frantically:

You should not have stated anything to Peterson about Mrs Besant . . . the *very mention* here would ruin your chances, but Peterson will say naught I believe.

Geddes had known Annie Besant since his student days, and only recently she had cordially acknowledged copies of some of his notes which had contributed towards a series of lectures on the "Evolution of Society" she was giving at that time. This was before her involvement with Madame Blavatsky, and at a time when her separation from her vicar husband, and loss of custody of her daughter, were considered by many to be scandals of the deepest iniquity. She had left her husband because she had lost her faith, which would not have seemed very scandalous to Geddes. It was not only Annie Besant whom Young was worried about. In the same letter he said:

From what I hear *very confidentially* Ray Lankaster has not done you much good. . . . I don't like him and have endeavoured to neutralise anything he may have said.

It appeared that Lankaster had decided to back another candidate, D'Arcy Wentworth Thompson, who was six years younger than Geddes and a Junior Demonstrator in the Physiology Department at Cambridge.

On 14th December, Peterson wrote to Alexander Dickson—who had already supplied a warm testimonial on Geddes's behalf. Peterson's letter asked for amplification of Dickson's opinion of Geddes along the following lines:

1 as a teacher. This is the most important aspect in which any candidature can now be viewed. We have ample evidence to the *scientific* qualifications of at least three candidates, Hoyle, Thompson and Geddes.
2 as a lecturer. In Dundee, as elsewhere, a Professor is occasionally called upon to address popular audiences, though, of course, not necessarily off-hand.
3 as a colleague. You must know a great deal of Mr Geddes in this capacity. We have heard of his "eccentricity" "egotism" and even "impracticability"; though many of his friends are ready with their testimony that these supposed qualities lie most on the surface. The impression made on those who would be his colleagues, in the event of his election, is, I may say, that *should he be found the best man in other respects*—the residium of truth which may underly such charges does not involve any risk which might not safely enough be run. We have heard also of his "discursiveness", for which, I imagine, there would be less opportunity should he give himself over to a complete and definite course of Biological teacher.

Dickson, who presumably was having to bear some of the brunt of his younger colleague's exasperation and anxiety while all this was going on, replied firmly

I am not fond of dissecting character, but I do not think that *egotism* is more marked in Geddes than in other people; and if he has a good opinion of himself he is well entitled thereto.

As to the charge of *discursiveness*, he may perhaps be a little open to that, but I look upon it as the natural outcome of an unusually active mind, and I do not doubt that attachment to a chair would concentrate his energy in the proposed subject. As to his being impracticable I can only say that I have never found him so; and if the person who made this suggestion has had disagreeable experience of him I should be disposed to infer that the impractibility was not all on one side.

The meeting to select the Professor of Biology was at last arranged for the afternoon of Monday, 22nd December. On 16th December, Frank Young wrote to Geddes:

Are you coming through on Saturday night in order to have a Sunday's rest before meeting the Council? You could also come to church with me, the last visits have done much in your favour. Heard the fear was and may be in the minds of one or two still that you are a belligerent Darwinian.

He followed this two days later with the exhortation: "Be sure and brush up your long hat and go in for a masher collar and tie." Geddes was apt to be careless of his appearance.

The appointment went to D'Arcy Thompson. By prearrangement the candidates had agreed that the successful one should treat the others to dinner afterwards at the Royal Hotel. Thompson recalled that "it was a sorry affair indeed", he being the only one in high spirits. One of Geddes's friends wrote to console him:

Some of us had set our hearts upon having you settled here as a means of increasing our intellectual and social pleasures. . . . Thompson may suit the College very well but he will not be to the naturalists of Dundee all that you could have been.

Characteristically, Geddes invited Thompson to stay with him in Edinburgh while he was transferring from Cambridge to Dundee.

One wonders what his feelings must have been as he talked to his younger visitor (Thompson was only twenty-four) about the latter's plans for his department at Dundee. He would not have felt any personal resentment towards Thompson, who later became a colleague and who was also closely concerned with social reform. But he must have felt both bewildered and outraged by the power held by strangers to prevent him from taking what many felt to be his merited place in the academic establishment.

He was thirty years old, unmarried, and underpaid. If the establishment would not recognize him, he had to find a way of operating outside it.

Chapter 5

ECONOMICS, EVOLUTION, SEX

THE CHRONOLOGICAL NARRATIVE of Geddes's life is broken in this chapter in order to give a brief summary of his thinking as expressed in his writings of the 1880's. He is not a man whose work can ever be separated from his life, but this may be a more convenient way of indicating the scientific and philosophical observations from which his actions sprang. However, his passionate belief that "it is only by thinking things out as one lives them, and living things out as one thinks them, that a man or a society can really be said to think or even live at all" must never be forgotten.

"The Classification of Statistics and its Results" (delivered to the Royal Society of Edinburgh 1880, printed 1881) reflected nineteenth-century interest in statistics as a force for social reform. Florence Nightingale was nicknamed the "Passionate Statistician" because of her enthusiasm for statistics as a means of testing the effectiveness of social legislation. At the start of the paper, Geddes examined the need for uniformity in the collection and classification of statistics in different countries. He was concerned to dispel "the popular belief that (statistics) is an inexpressibly dreary accumulation of numbers by which anything may be proved", preferring to regard it neither as a science nor a method but "simply a quantitative record of the observed facts or relations in any branch of science". The facts which statistics could record, and which related to every society, he claimed fell into four basic groups: (1) those relating to the limits of time and space occupied by a society; (2) those relating to the matter and energy utilized by the society from surrounding nature; (3) those relating to the organisms composing the society; and (4) those relating to the application of the utilized matter and energy by the given organism. These groups were then broken down into a complex system of tables, one of which related to (2) and covered the dissipation and disintegration of matter and energy. It is an excellent example of the umbrella method by which Geddes's mind operated:

Loss
{
1. Of raw materials
2. In exploitation
3. In manufacture   by
4. In transport
5. In exchange
6. Of ultimate products
7. In remedial effort
}

{
1. Physical agencies, e.g.,
    avalanche
    earthquake
    volcano
    flood
    storm, etc.
2. Biological agencies e.g.,
    insects
    fungi, etc.
3. Social agencies, e.g.,
    crime
    war
    folly, etc.
}

His audience was no doubt relieved when he admitted that his system would initiate "a task even more than that of any of the preliminary sciences—needing innumerable lifetimes broad and long". But whereas such a remark might enable some to feel they were let off the hook, there were a few who leapt eagerly towards the huge concept of collecting enough knowledge and information to enable the world's ledger of resources to achieve a near balance.

When he came to discuss the section of tables covering political economy, he was at his most lucid:

. . . although political economy is said to deal largely with material things, and largely with organised beings, there is probably no department of modern literature, not even poetry or romance, so little leavened by the recent advances of our knowledge of the laws of matter and of life.

He concluded that as far as the scientific development of economics was concerned (and every action is an economic one in that it involves some disintegration and dissipation of energy) the highest order of consideration must be the ethical one:

When the counsel of economics and of morals coincide the action may be regarded as ratified and its ground as verified, while a discord between the two must similarly be regarded as indicating that the proposed course of action whether ethical or economic must be in error.

Among others, his mentors for this section of the paper were Ruskin and Kant.

Four years later, in 1884, Geddes came to the Royal Society with another three-tier paper, this time entitled "An Analysis of the Principles of Economics", which was very much a development out of the statistics paper. Again there were four categories into which he divided economic considerations: the physical, the biological, the psychological and the sociological.

Physical economics was a way of visualizing production and consumption as one vast mechanical process, which could be measured in units of matter and energy, as partially previewed in the Statistics paper. The energy units represented manpower, or man-days, and this was the first sociological application of the modern concept of energy. Geddes believed that the production machine should not be geared to more and more ephemeral consumables, but should aim for more goods with a lasting aesthetic element. There was a balanced optimum of needs for a civilized existence, and it was just as harmful to exceed this balance as it was to fall short. This optimum applied internationally, and to all societies.

Biological economics viewed the effect of economic processes on man as a part of nature. Geddes severely criticized economists for their ignorance of the effect of occupation on man, and for not drawing parallels between man and the two causes of degeneration in the organic world: deprivation and over-abundance. Deprived of food, light and air, living forms decline; and given an over-abundance of nourishment and too little activity they become parasites. In society, Geddes suggested, these two conditions were labelled "poverty" and "complete material wellbeing". In a later paper[1] he was to say:

For were man bathed in an ocean of nectar and ambrosia, he would not only come to multiply as fast as the tapeworm, but degenerate as far.

Psychological economics grew from a correct biological approach, and reflected Geddes's belief that co-operation is a fundamental human characteristic. The "iron law of competition" could not, he claimed, ever form a true basis for an economic system, since it denies the altruistic side to man's nature. Later he was to write in *Evolution of Sex*:

> . . . it is not for the sake of production or distribution, of self-interest or mechanism, or any other idol of the economists, that the male organism organises the climax of his life's struggle and labour, but for his mate . . . also for their little ones . . . *the species is its own highest, its sole essential product.* (my italics)

His concept of sociological economics was not included in the paper, and indeed was not expounded until many years later. His intention since his student days had been to write a comprehensive study of economics, but as his ideas proliferated, so it became more difficult to pin them down. He was all the time aware of such a complex input of information, and could not leave any area of inquiry unlit, so that it became impossible, in the limited periods of time he left free for such work, to reduce his scenarios of related systems into a manageable book. However, his thought as expressed in these two early papers on statistics and economics is fundamental to much that followed.

One of his best papers concerned with social conditions* was delivered at a conference in London organized by James Oliphant in January 1885 to discuss: "Is the present system whereby the products of industry are distributed between the various persons and classes of the community satisfactory? or, if not, are there any means by which that system could be improved?" Other speakers included William Morris and Alfred Wallace, and the lectures were extended and given again in Scotland during the summer of 1886. Here Geddes gave a rousing demonstration of his growing involvement with regional development and urban environment:

> Don't, for instance, invest in more foreign loans, nor even in more corn or cattle raising in America. We have plenty

* "On the Conditions of Progress of the Capitalist & of the Labourer."

of all these; but invest it in your own town, among the people who made it for you, and in permanent realities. Not in more smoke and nuisance, more percussion and corrosion, not in more factories, and more back streets full of workers in them—we have plenty of these, too—but in nobler dwellings, in giving the higher industries their long-delayed turn, and so producing a larger individual return for labour than is to be got by our too exclusive tending of machines.

He decried industry's veneration of production for production's sake, and claimed that while this system prevailed it was not enough for workers to worry simply about higher wages:

More wages for the ship's crew is all very well: I sincerely desire it. But if her course be wrong, and we are sailing towards where there will be by-and-by no wages for anybody, but simply ship and cargo, master and mariners alike on the rocks, it is needful to interrupt your golden visions with dry scientific questions of sextant, chart, and compass, and to be crying "'bout ship" first, "more wages" afterwards.

He totally disagreed with the system of *laissez-faire* (and used to refer to its supporters as "lazy fairies") and its links with the Darwinian principle that the best strains of species would emerge if they were uninterfered with and left to struggle. Society had to establish its aims, and control its means of trying to achieve them:

North, south, east, and west are only ideals of direction: you will never absolutely get there; yet you can never get anywhere, save indeed straight down into a hole, without them.

And for those who were frightened of the oppressive aspects of moulding society, he added:

There is no fear of being carried away by anybody's ideas, if you only read broadly enough.

One of the results of "reading broadly enough" was that Geddes never allied himself to any political party. It simply was not in him to find any merit in group competition and party in-fighting. Intellectually he was closest to anarchists such as Peter Kropotkin and Paul and Elisée Reclus (all of whom he knew well), though he had no wish to take part in political as opposed to general social reform activities and had no truck with the kind of activity he described as "mere fits of despairing hysterics and threats of dynamite".[2] He once made the rather charming suggestion that since a large number of prospective Liberal candidates who had been unsuccessful in a general election would presumably have a great deal of untapped energy and sense of responsibility at their disposal, they should combine to undertake a specific project of social reform.

In an article entitled "Co-operation versus Socialism" written for the Co-operative Wholesale Societies *Annual*, he argued in favour of co-operative enterprises. These, however, had got to progress far beyond the aims of cheap food and large dividends to a much fuller version of a co-operative society. While they had been dependent at first on the initiative of enlightened capitalists, he recommended that in an evolving society they would be organized by the artists and craftsmen: "who among even the capitalists have such power of resource and practical organization as the really effective architect?" His objections to socialism were that it too often meant dreaming dreams, but getting nothing actually done: "until everything and everybody is ready for the millennium nothing can be got ready at all". Whereas co-operation

> does the daily duties which lie nearest, refuses no bird in the hand to-day for the sake of two in the bush to-morrow, and thus not only lives and grows, but daily strengthens towards larger tasks; since, in fact, getting a bird into the hand to-day is the best practice for getting two out of the bush to-morrow.

He attacked the socialists' preoccupation with distribution, and the assumption that

> modify this, and all will forthwith be well. Here, of course, we have the central dogma and panacea. If you indicate a doubt of either the final completeness or the initial practicality of these, you might as well be a bourgeois at once,

and a speedy alternative between the sword or "Das Kapital" is the best that can be promised for your soul's health; while, if you express a timid belief that a little time of study and reflection might show that the resources of human thought have not been finally exhausted, even by the production of that important work, you are crushed with substantially the same rebuke as were the Alexandrian bookworms by the victorious Omar. For the Koran is complete.

But the moral warmth, the glow of social feeling, surely these cannot be amiss, even if the science be scanty? Granted; yet the Salvation Army has these, every wave of fanaticism the world has ever seen has had these, and it is surely time to recognise before rushing into new disasters that the theoretic and practical deficiencies of a system are not atoned for—nay, in history have usually been aggravated— by the religious fervour of its exponents.

Geddes's view of evolution, which formed the basis of all his social and economic theories, was expressed during this period in his scientific lectures and papers, *Chambers's Encyclopaedia* and the *Encyclopaedia Britannica*, and most specifically in the book which he wrote with Arthur Thomson, the *Evolution of Sex* (published 1889). This was commissioned by Havelock Ellis as the first volume in his Contemporary Science Series, and he wrote in his autobiography:[3] "To place such a subject at the forefront of the scheme seemed daring to many people, but . . . the book was well received and soon acquired high reputation and many readers." On the whole, Thomson contributed the more detailed scientific data, while Geddes tackled the wider issues.

The book contained an account of the contemporary theories of sexual selection (around which controversy was still raging), and it propounded Geddes's own view that progress and survival were essentially due to the subordination of individual struggle and development to species-maintaining ends. He viewed nature as a symphony of forces which, despite its complexity, was fundamentally an orderly and limited affair, and not the haphazard workings of an unlimited succession of natural selection. Evidence for natural co-operation could be found among the simplest forms of life:

... the greatest step in organic nature, that between the single-celled and many-celled animals, bridged as it is by loose colonies some of which are at a very low morphological level, is not due to the selection of the more individuated and highly adapted forms, but to the union of relatively unindividuated cells into an aggregate, in which each becomes diminishingly competitive and increasingly subordinated to the social whole. The colonial or multicellular forms, originating pathologically in all probability, may of course have rapidly justified their existence in the struggle for existence, just as unions of many kinds do in human society, but the Protozoa cannot be accused of any prevision of future advantage in remaining clubbed together in co-operation, nor indeed credited with much primitive altruism in so doing. None the less it is clear, that this greatest of morphological steps was directly due, not to any struggle, but rather to an organic sociality, or at any rate to a process which is not interpretable in terms of individual advantage.

The bulk of the book is concerned with a scientific analysis of sexual determination and reproduction among all forms of life, but a central theme concerns the characteristics of male and female, and has bearing on the chapters on sexual ethics which are of interest to the lay reader. Male characteristics were primarily "katabolic": active, disruptive, consuming energy; whereas female characteristics were primarily "anabolic": passive, constructive, hoarding energy. The sex of an organism was therefore determined by the relation between constructive and disruptive processes, sex being an expression of physiological activity. While fully accepting the widely differing proportions of male and female characteristics in each individual, Geddes always felt that although the sexes were assuredly "equal", they were just as assuredly "different", and no amount of activity on the part of women's movements could alter the fact:

We have seen that a deep difference in constitution expresses itself in the distinctions between male and female, whether these be physical or mental. The differences may be exaggerated or lessened, but to obliterate them it would be necessary to have all the evolution over again on a new basis.

What was decided among the prehistoric Protozoa cannot be annulled by Act of Parliament.

On the question of population and birth control, Geddes and Thomson took an impeccably virtuous stance, but were nevertheless strongly criticized for including the subject at all. *Nature* (10th April 1890) declared: "It is very much to be regretted that the authors have included discussion of certain social and ethical problems absolutely unconnected with the title of their book." The following quotations indicate the said authors' viewpoint:

The vague feeling that control of fertilisation is "interfering with nature", in some utterly unwarrantable fashion, cannot be consistently stated by those who live in the midst of our highly artificial civilisation. The strongest prejudice seems to be based in a moral cowardice, which gauges a scheme by its "respectability", while even more culpable is that consciously or unconsciously derived from the profitableness to the capitalist classes of unlimited competition of cheap unskilled labour. For never did the proletariat more literally deserve its name than since the advent of the factory period, their rapid and degenerative increase, indeed, primarily representing "the progress of investments".

... the survival of a species or family depends not primarily upon quantity, but upon quality. The future is not to the most numerous populations, but to the most individuated. And as we increasingly see that natural history must be treated primarily from the standpoint of the species-regarding sacrifice rather than from that of individual struggle, we see the importance of the general neo-Malthusian position, despite the risks which the particular modes of its practice may involve.

It seems to us, however, essential to recognise that the ideal to be sought after is not merely a controlled rate of increase, but regulated married lives. Neo-Malthusianism might secure the former by its more or less mechanical methods, and there is no doubt that a limitation of the family would often increase the happiness of the home; but there is danger lest, in removing its result, sexual intemperance become increasingly organic. We would urge, in fact, the necessity of an ethical rather than of a mechanical "prudence after marriage", of a temperance recognised to be as binding on husband and wife as chastity on the unmarried. When we consider the inevitable consequences of intemperance, even if the dangers of too large families be avoided, and the possibility of exaggerated sexuality becoming cumulative by inheritance, we cannot help recognising that the intemperate pair are falling towards the ethical level of the harlots and profligates of our streets.

Hardly stuff to herald in a permissive society eighty years in advance.

The two surviving private reactions to the book, both from women, are interesting in their outspokenness. The first is from a friend, Jane H. Clapperton:

My special complaint in regard to your weighty biological book is its treatment of artificial checks to conception. Experience goes against your inference that moderation in sexual indulgence secures infrequency of pregnancy and you base your theory of population reduction on that fatal assumption. Why not have frankly espoused neo-Malthusianism? For the ignorant, the gross, the degraded there is no other means—moderation forsooth in perhaps the only pleasure besides drinking that the base nature can enjoy! Cut off the breeding of that type and where is the social bad result? Drinking is infinitely worse to my mind.

The second came from a stranger, a Mrs J. Butt, of Eastbourne:

I owe so large a debt of gratitude to your book on "The Evolution of Sex" that I venture to beg you to increase that indebtedness by permitting me to ask a question which I much hoped I might find discussed there, and concerning which, in spite of much patient endeavour, I have been hitherto unable to find an authoritative reply.

In the earnest effort to do all that lay in a mother's power for the wellbeing of my children during the periods of gestation, it has been branded upon my mind, that much of the exaggerating sensuality that so often embitters existence might be spared mankind, if the natural aversion which (according to my own not very limited acquaintance of my sex) is so general during pregnancy, were more respected.

Circumstances having much brought under my own observation the appalling tendency among the young—and even infants—to habits pernicious to moral and physical well-being, I am greatly concerned to learn whether much of this unhealthy tendency may not be a forced predevelopment, due to the frequent violation of the natural desire for exemption from the most intimate duty of a wife, during the period of pregnancy; and whether even if inclination did not demand this exemption, she should not be taught, that abstinence at such time is the first responsibility of responsible motherhood, not only to her own children but to the race, that the *tendency* of their inheritance at least might be towards self-control.

If this proposition be true—and if as I have often read, although again I have never been able to verify that statement—an analogous instinct is almost universal outside Humanity, surely sirs it is high time that both parents should be taught that their responsibility is to the child as well as to each other, instead of being left in ignorance of the possible results of the endeavour to *stimulate* sexual desire, and create artificial response on the part of the mother, from her mistaken sense of conjugal duty.

How such self-control strengthens and cements the tie between father and mother, and the increased possibilities of the very functions themselves, by reason of intelligent unwasteful control, is perhaps only conceivable to the husband and wife of a true marriage.

But while it is easy enough for all the world to learn of detestable mechanical appliances for limiting offspring, while allowing animal passion full play, unchecked by any sense of responsibility, it is beyond measure difficult for ordinary unlearned and busy folk, to learn what is right and natural and beneficent—not to *one* only—but to the triple being that makes the whole of humanity. It may further illustrate how difficult, when I add, that a copy of your book which my husband offered to our new public library here was courteously rejected under the plea that it was quite impossible to have such books in a library where unmarried or young people might find them!

Unfortunately, there is no record of any reply to this letter. Sexual ethics, however, remained a preoccupation with Geddes, and he wrote an interesting chapter on the subject in another joint book with Thomson, *Sex*, published in 1914. This will be touched on in the next chapter for, although it is using it completely out of chronological context, it is the only direct information we have of Geddes's views on certain personal aspects of sex, and it does not at all jar with the known facts of his forthcoming courtship and marriage with Anna Morton.

Chapter 6

"LATE MARRIAGES GIVE TIME FOR INDIVIDUATION"

THE ACTIVITIES OF the Edinburgh Social Union, under Geddes's direction, slowly gathered momentum during 1885, but he was not satisfied with his life, and showed symptoms of unrest both in his bodily health and mental state. He suffered acutely from stomach disorders and severe headaches, and frequently castigated himself for not working hard enough. In fact, as well as his usual lecturing and writing, he was rushing around on behalf of the Social Union organizing projects to clean up slum dwellings, and generally endeavouring to fulfil the society's aim "to bring together all those who feel that misery of the poor arises in a large measure from the want of sympathy and fellowship between different classes". Whenever Anna Morton was visiting her sister he poured out his ideas and dreams to her and, according to Anna's mother, Anna had displayed her "*open* admiration" for Patrick Geddes right from "first acquaintance". However, Mrs Morton on hearing "you lived for your profession and the benefit of others less fortunate than yourself" had "often wished to know you but certainly did not contemplate a relationship . . .".

As Anna's admiration grew to love, she tried to conceal her emotions.

I was always so afraid of letting you see too much of what I felt, when I thought you were only kind to me as you were kind to so many others; and I went sometimes to the opposite extreme . . .

When this happened, Geddes simply threw himself harder into his work, but the emotional uncertainty contributed to his ill-health. He had not admitted he was in love with Anna, but there was a perceptible gap when she was not there to listen to his ideas. And as well as a companion, he must have felt the need for a lover.

In the chapter called "Ethics of Sex" from *Sex* which he and Thomson were to write later, he declared: "a man will be happier all his life if he can come to his wife a passionate lover, with a clean record". Whether he was describing himself, or expressing a regret, we do not know; but everything points to the former. He goes on to extol the virtues of "self-controlled men", while fully admitting the power of sex:

> We must face then the elemental fact of sex and love, making much not little of it, entering into it as into a great possession by which our own life and that of others may be enriched. And if there be a strong love, much may be forgiven—even when it sweeps men and women off their feet. . . . When the lover and his lass lose their heads before they marry, their loss of self-control will certainly not make their married life happier; but it may have a virtue which the "marriage for money", with all its respectability, never approaches.

The language he uses here seems generalized. Another paragraph has a more personal touch, despite its fairly clinical approach:

> It is often stated (by careful students of sex, as well as by the careless) that the normal Man's sexual appetites are, on an average, far keener and more insistent than those of the normal Woman. It is impossible for men without much (and obviously very difficult) consultation with good women to pronounce on such a matter, and perhaps there is a tendency to exaggerate the difference. . . . Our view of the matter is that sexual desire is quietened in most women because they are more moralised than men; because they are in the direction of sexuality more controlled, because they do not relinquish their first line of defence so readily as a man does, and so on. . . . It is not so much, however, that the sexual desire is not insistent in women, but that she is so constituted that from wooing to consummation it takes longer for the brain to become eroticised, and for this to relax the control of the centres which normally inhibit response to sexual appeal.

This last sentence is a particularly sensitive appraisal, and would appear to have parallels with Anna's letter, written two weeks before they were married:

> I can feel your arm round my waist, or my neck, turning my face towards you to be kissed, and I can feel your kisses on my brow and eyes and mouth. You know you used to kiss me that way sometimes. And once you said (didn't you?) that I sat quite passive and unmoved while you kissed me. I'm not sure whether you meant I was cold—you are my perfect, passionate lover whatever you said—but at any rate the impression the kisses made was a lasting one . . .

Exactly when their courtship became open and passionate is not ascertainable, but evidence seems to suggest that it all happened quite quickly. In March 1885 Geddes sent Anna a copy of his economics paper, and she replied in a straightforward, friendly way:

> I have waited to try and get an idea of the contents before acknowledging it. My brother and Mr Gibson after looking through the first few pages together, suggested that I had better write and thank you for it before I opened it, and so avoid the painful necessity of confessing my inability to understand it! I find it extremely interesting however, notwithstanding my ignorance, and I hope I shall at some future time read the larger work of which this is the sketch. Economics, as treated by you, is not at all a "dismal" science.

By July, Frank Deas was ticking Geddes off about the ambitiousness of his latest schemes, and they do not sound like the prelude to marriage:

> Here is what you want to do as I understand it . . . You want to rent 3 or 4 flats pretty high up in the houses on the east of the Free Church College. You want to live there yourself and expect to get some other people . . . to do the same "and bring their friends". . . . In a little while you hope to have working people—families—and generally any one who will come, and so to occupy the whole quadrangle and

be a regular community. Now all of it is quite a natural
outcome of your enthusiasm and kindness of heart. An
organized community! The "organization" appeals to your
head and your force, the "community" to your instincts of
brotherhood. . . . You will be the victim of depredations on
your time which are worse than pocket pickings—whose
room will be full of men when he does not want them?—
yours. Whose brain will be stimulated on all likely and
unlikely subjects till quiet work is impossible? Yours. Whose
biology and sociology will all go to the Devil? Yours.

Geddes's involvement in such schemes was worrying all his
friends. Arthur Thomson complained: "I am afraid you are
making a martyr of yourself for the sake of the Social Union.
You are too intense", and Anne Murray, whom he had invited
to be his nominal "sister" (perhaps as a way of easing over the
fact he would soon be publicly committed to Anna Morton),
wrote on 17th January 1886:

I know that I feel very anxious about your state of health.
. . . If you will allow me to advise you—*do* take that offer and
don't make the writing of that article a test. All the same I
hope the writing of it will not cost you so much as the last.
It must be dreadful for you—for you in particular to have
that incessant feeling of weariness and stupidity. . . . Do go
and see Athens, Constantinople . . . no one can think of
work when they are in such a state as to be threatened with
milk diet . . .

The offer that she mentioned came from James Martin White,
heir to a large estate near Dundee, who had invited Geddes to
accompany him on an extensive tour. It is uncertain exactly
when they had first met, but White was interested in the
development of imaginative scientific teaching and wished to
help Geddes regain his health. He assured Geddes, who was
three years his senior, that he must feel no embarrassment over
the cost.

If I can put a good scientific man in "real good shape"
consciousness of accomplished duty is my reward, for I
advance science. And you must in this instance remember

the pleasure I have in scientific company and yours especially. You are to be cashier and we are to travel unrestrained and joyously. I think you understand me.

Geddes accepted the offer, but Anna was in Edinburgh at the time. He sent her an invitation to meet him at the botanical gardens one Sunday morning in the middle of January. The gardens were closed to the public, and seem to have been chosen as the most appropriate setting for his declaration; even though they would be fairly bare in January they are always beautiful and peaceful—Edinburgh's nearest approximation to the Garden of Eden.

He asked her to marry him, and during their subsequent conversation explained that he thought she would be "a help not a hindrance" to his work. More romantically, he took an opal he had brought back from Mexico out of his pocket, and split it with a geologist's hammer. He gave half to Anna, and kept the other himself, as the outward symbol of their betrothal.

It seems that he needed to be certain of Anna if he was to reap any benefit from his tour. They planned to marry as soon as he returned, and he wrote to his friends claiming he had found a "she" who "is—oh well—everything".

However, he did not seem anxious to break the news to Jessie, his sister. She was rather possessive towards her youngest brother, and he may have feared she would view any prospective sister-in-law far too critically. She herself was now forty-five and middle-age had not relaxed her temper. To make it more awkward, she was staying in Edinburgh at the time of the engagement, and had already met Anna. Anna sent a note round to his rooms:

I am feeling very strongly that it is surely a mistake (is it not?) to put off telling your sister. Of course you ought to know best about her, but there will not be much opportunity, you see, before she leaves for us to get to know her better, and I don't see how you can keep it from her that you have postponed it if you wait much longer, and that would hurt her more than anything would it not? And again I scarcely like the idea of asking her to go to the club with me knowing that she may think afterwards I ought not to have concealed it.

And would it not be easier for her to bear if she were with you for a few days after you told her? You said she was to leave sometime next week. Could not you tell her tomorrow evening after you have seen me in the afternoon? She would still like to go to the club with me, I hope, and I should be able to get to know her more quickly—if she will have anything to say to me—you said she liked me a little already. You could go on with your work and she and I could go out for walks! I think this will be a rather long day without you . . .

There is no evidence that Jessie made difficulties, and Anna obviously went out of her way to ensure that she would have no reason to do so. She was already slipping into her life-role of protecting Patrick from unnecessary worries that might intrude into the time essential for his work. A visit was arranged to Mount Tabor, and there she was quickly absorbed as a member of the family—she and Alexander particularly developing an affection for one another.

However, it was only a week before Geddes and White were due to embark on their journey. Contributing keenly to Geddes's state of anxiety in the recent months had been financial worries, and at the same time as he agreed to go on the trip with White, he sought a loan from him of £200. This was readily granted, on the proviso that he was charged a lowish rate of interest ("as a matter of principle"), and agreed to repay the loan within two years. White reasoned that a fairly short period for repayment would provide "some time stimulus to take you out of the, in some respects, unproductive speculative", and push Geddes into getting his ideas down into book form and so make some money out of them. Optimistically, White spoke of the "position of independence, which I believe you can easily attain, from which standpoint a man can always work most advantageously". Geddes always agreed with the latter comment but the attainment never proved easy, and White was to provide a financial back-stop for several decades.

The two men planned to visit Venice, Athens, Constantinople, Rome, Cannes. Seeking advice from George Murray on the political situation in the Balkans before they sailed, Geddes was firmly informed: "...if war breaks out it might be unpleasant— but the *Bulgarians* will be civil even then. . . ." It was early

February when they left, and they were not due back until
early April—the date of the wedding having been fixed for
17th April.

Anna returned to her parents' home in Egremont, a prosperous suburb of Liverpool, and her letters to Patrick show the mixture of happiness and confusion that she was experiencing. Of
his travels there is no record—apart from references by Anna
to his continuing dyspepsia. Her new status as a woman about
to be married, rather than a twenty-eight-year-old spinster,
gave her a kind of confidence that she had previously lacked.

> It is quite another matter now dressing myself, and there is
> some pleasure in preparing the things—not that I was
> *always* indifferent before, but I was very *often* careless—
> because there was no one very greatly interested in looking
> at me.

Her father, Frazer Morton, an Ulster Scot who had settled in
Liverpool, was both a strict presbyterian and a prosperous
merchant. There were six children in the family, three brothers
older than Anna (who was born on 19th November 1857),
and two younger sisters, Edith Oliphant and Bex—who still
lived at home and of whom Anna was very fond. Like Geddes,
she had found the combined ethic of money and nonconformist Christianity restrictive and stifling, and although
an intelligent woman and gifted musician, she had taken
awkwardly to some of the social activities expected of girls at
that time. Contemporaries praised her looks (Arthur Thomson
once described her as "looking like a young goddess, very
nimble and joyous"); from her photographs she seems
womanly, both purposeful and sensitive, rather than handsome
or pretty. She herself described her temperament thus:

> I have often felt that for anyone whose chief means of
> expression is in music there is a tendency to vagueness and
> indefiniteness of expression. . . . I think I am usually either
> very logical or very dreamy and seldom hit the medium.

She grew very close to her mother during the period that she
waited for Patrick to return, and Mrs Morton was much more
sympathetic to her daughter's humanitarian and a-religious

views than Mr Morton could ever be. She was also able to
unbend a little on the matter of propriety, now that her
daughter was almost married.

Mother and I got into a warm discussion about the amount
of liberty that should be allowed to girls and how much
attention should be paid to the proprieties; and your *prim,
conventional* friend gave utterance to some exceedingly
outrageous opinions on the subject. Please don't jump to
the conclusion that these opinions were the result of the
late *conversion*, I instanced my own behaviour in regard to
Mr Gibson last spring and also some of my escapades with
yourself in past times as examples of what would be termed
most improper conduct by mother if other girls had been
guilty of them, and maintained that I would encourage other
girls in the same courses if I thought they had sufficient
self-respect. Mother's horror of any *talk* about a girl is the
cause of her regard for what is considered *proper* of course.

It seems Mrs Morton was fairly captivated by her prospective
son-in-law, and thus able quite genuinely to share her daughter's
happiness.

I'll tell you what mother said about you this evening. I was
saying how it made my happiness perfect that she and Bex
(and everybody) liked you so much, and then she spoke very
lovingly about you, and said you were so very affectionate;
and she compared you with Jim Oliphant (who is a *great*
favourite) and said that of course she could not have got on
better with anyone than with Jim, but that you were more
demonstrative and expressed your affectionateness more—
and she liked that in you.

When Anna felt lonely, she would bring out the opal and
gaze at it:

I was going to tell you last night when something interrupted me, what I had been fancying about the different
colours of it, and I am half shy about putting it into writing,
but I suppose you will say I must. Well, the red represents
to me your love, because it is passionate, and the strongest

of the colours and the others seem to fade beside it . . . and because too it shines out every now and then where one does not expect it at all. And then the green—I think that is all your wonderful knowledge. . . . Then the blue—that is connected in my mind with the blue of heaven which spreads over everyone, and it symbolizes your loving tolerance . . .

Rather unfairly Geddes demanded even more passionate declarations from his future wife, apparently complaining a little of the coldness of her letters. She replied:

I have a feeling sometimes of a piece of ivy that has been trailing on the ground amongst the damp grass and out of the sun, but that at last has found the tree that it can twine itself round and grow into, and by which it gets into the sunshine. Pat, I *wish* I could please you as much by my letters as you do me by yours but you know that is impossible . . .

There were of course also the more mundane practical matters of the wedding to be attended to:

Do you know I'm quite maliciously glad to be able to tell you that it is one of *your* friends who has brought us the first electroplate for a wedding present. Mr Miller has sent a case of fish knives . . .

The wedding duly took place from Anna's home on 17th April, and by the evening they had travelled fifty miles north to Lancaster, where they spent three nights at the King's Arms Hotel. A bill shows that on the first and second nights they had a fire in their room, together with a bottle of hock on their wedding night, and, less extravagantly, threepence-worth of ale the night after. The whole bill came to £2 11s. 3d. By a strange coincidence, Jack Geddes got married in New Zealand on the same day as Anna and Patrick, although they did not learn of this until later.

On their return to Edinburgh, they spent the first six months of their married life in Geddes's apartment. Hearsay has it that there were difficulties of adjustment. Geddes was used to having only to please himself as far as his strenuous timetable was concerned. Now there was Anna to consider. She could not always be a willing lover and active helper if her own needs and feelings were overlooked. Before their marriage she had announced her eagerness to aid him in his schemes, saying "'Yea and amen' to them with all my heart", but it was never easy to organize Geddes into a realistic schedule. There were no doubt periods when she resented his long hours away from home, or the hours when their rooms were full of people engaged in earnest discussions, and she may have longed for periods when they could just simply enjoy their new domesticity together. The one thing that always restored her, music, she could not really share, since Geddes was singularly unmusical. But although any early difficulties may have been momentarily painful, they were not deep-seated. Anna Geddes had indeed "found the tree" which would lift her "into the sunshine", and Patrick always remained her lover and friend, as well as her husband.

On the margin of one of his manuscripts he wrote much later: "Late marriages give time for individuation." He and Anna were developed adults when they married, and unlikely to subjugate their personalities too much for the convenience of the other. Anna's slight coolness and holding-back might sometimes irritate the more excitable Patrick, but together they were representative of a much wider range of characteristics and talents than they were when separated, and they were mature enough to appreciate rather than resent their differences.

Chapter 7

THE ROYAL MILE

AFTER SIX MONTHS of marriage, Geddes began to carry out
the plan he had once outlined to Frank Deas. He left the rooms
in Princes Street, and took Anna to live in a rented flat on
the second floor of a tenement block in the Old Town. The
elderly housekeeper, who had looked after him since his
bachelor days, went with them. The block was in James Court,
one of the closes off the section of the Royal Mile called the
Lawnmarket, not far from the castle. Alterations were made to
the property—a bathroom added, and a balcony, but the close
itself was dank and dirty. In the flats beneath them lived a
cobbler, a plumber and a street sweeper—all of whom "kept
clean homes"; but the tinker families on the upper floors were
infested with vermin and had violent rows. In the eighteenth
century James Court had housed "persons of consequence in
society" (including David Hume and James Boswell), but, as
the plaque at one of its entrances succinctly states, it "declined
c. 1790 with rise of New Town". The Royal Mile, which
stretches from the Palace of Holyrood to Edinburgh Castle,
had once been reckoned the fairest street in Europe, but by
1887 it had become a decaying historical façade concealing
crowded slums in every hidden close and courtyard.

By moving to such an apparently uncongenial area, the
Geddeses intended to show, by practical example rather than
mere rhetoric, that pleasant homes could be created in un-
promising surroundings. Their own flat was furnished with old
furniture that had been bought cheaply from second-hand
shops and lovingly restored—this at a time when antique
furniture was not at all fashionable. (Harry Barker wrote
self-deprecatingly of his own more conventional home: "I am
afraid you would scold at some of our *mahogany* . . .") The bare,
uneven floors were stained and polished—though Anna's
mother did send some drugget, saying: "It will do until you

get better and we don't want it." A somewhat earnest friend
of Anna's, Kate Crooke, wrote encouragingly:

> I am much interested in your removal and wish you may
> have fine weather for it. The gas fires would be delightful
> and viewed from the respective sides of cleanliness, health
> and convenience are certainly superior to coal. With careful
> use the price ought not to exceed coal, I should think.

Alex Michael, a young printer who idolized Geddes and was
anxious to better himself through self-education, was shocked
when he first realized his mentor had moved to such shabby
surroundings:

> . . . when I walked down the eastmost close and gazed up
> astonished at the grimy, towering houses, I could hardly
> realize that you lived up there but the row of flower-boxed
> windows suggested to me your whereabouts.

Having made their own home, Anna and Patrick proceeded
to persuade their neighbours to share in communal improvements. Light pastel colour washes made an enormous difference
to the confined spaces hedged around by high buildings and,
donning an old nightshirt as an overall, Geddes proceeded
to paint some of the external walls in James Court. He
wrote:

> . . . the improving external surroundings soon begin to
> reach upon the homes: to let in more delight, to bring in
> flowers is to show up dirt, and to show it the way out also.
> Windows are cleaned; size colour is found to be just as good
> inside as out, and so on. It is in such ways that a better
> standard of living arises; and that the poorest hovel feels
> it may again become the beginnings of a new and better
> home instead of merely the wreck and ruin of an old one.
>   . . . in many ways the collective improvement brings with
> it a new atmosphere, that of a more collective and social life:
> the court is no longer a mere huddle of sooty hovels, pile
> upon pile; but a pleasantly varied and harmonious whole:
> something like a village again, perhaps by and by a village
> pulled together.

As well as painting the walls, he organized proper dustbins and a urinal for the court, while Anna tried to help some of the women to achieve a higher standard of home-making. On Saturday mornings she held a sewing club for young girls in her flat, at which the girls used to sing as they worked. However, with so much effort being made, Anna felt she was still missing out on some of the quieter rewards of early married life. She visited her family in March 1887, and wrote to Patrick:

> I have been thinking that though I would not for anything in the world give up working together, still we miss something of what husbands and wives here have—I mean the freshness of coming together in the evening; and that I am not enough *home* to you, (tho' you call me so) and that that is one of the duties I must give more attention to when I go back, especially if we are to take more leisure in our evening. Bex and I have been talking over the two women characters which she has been studying lately, and trying to see if we could get some light from them on the general question of women; one was a type of moral enthusiasm and lofty ideality; the other of womanly good sense . . .

But however hard Anna strove, there was never to be any solution to the fact that Geddes was always involved in more practical and educative schemes than there was time to carry them out, and that these involvements meant an endless trail of visitors—however worthy and pleasant they may have been —to their home. Pressure was added when Geddes rented three flats in a nearby tenement, and turned them into a self-governing student hostel—the first of its kind in Great Britain. There were seven study-bedrooms, a sitting-room, a refectory and a kitchen, and the students were responsible for the entire running of the place. The hostel was called University Hall, and inevitably it was Anna who had to undertake much of the cleaning, refurbishing, and acquiring of cheap furniture. Since she was in the early stages of pregnancy, she must have been exhausted by the time it opened in May. But there were great compensations. The young people from the university, and those, such as Alex Michael, normally excluded by the circumstances of their birth and upbringing from the charmed circles of higher education, found stimulation and delight in the Geddes's involvement in their work and problems, and showed it in their spontaneous gratitude and friendship.

Meanwhile, in the summer holidays, Geddes organized what was to be the first of a long series of summer schools. Later these developed into elaborate affairs, visited by radical scholars from all over the world, but the first was limited to two short courses in "seaside Zoology and garden Botany". The motto of these summer meetings was *Vivendo Discimus* (By Living We Learn), and it is reflected in the way the zoology and botany were based on imaginative fieldwork in and around Edinburgh. Geddes's initial idea of holding a summer school was based on one he had heard of in Chautauqua, New York, and those recently established at Oxford and Cambridge. He was also very involved in an endeavour to launch the University Extension Movement in Scotland, and the official report from St Andrews University in support of the scheme said:

. . . special mention must be made of Mr Patrick Geddes, to whose zeal and energy the formation of a large committee of university professors and others is entirely due.

It was not only practical and academic learning that Geddes was anxious to make accessible to a wider public, but appreciation of the arts as well. In 1887 and 1888 respectively, large art exhibitions were held in Manchester and Glasgow, and as a commentary to each exhibition he published two pamphlets entitled *Every Man His Own Art Critic*. These are marvellously optimistic pieces of writing, encouraging people to enjoy the very varied schools of painting available to them. Alma Tadema was praised for teaching the uninitiated more about classical Rome through his paintings ("magic windows") than a "whole race of academic pedants". People are warned against criticizing impressionist paintings as inaccurate, and accused of wanting "an opera glass, a telescope for distance, and a microscope at hand", when all the time the impressionistic images "may be truthful as a camera obscura". The pre-Raphaelites must be forgiven for "their timid shrinking from a sordid, unintelligible every-day world" and offered gratitude for their "saintly vision of . . . spiritual ideals". And Turner's landscapes are extolled as "piled-up magnificence of all things terrestrial and celestial". Some of the writing is rather long-drawn-out and occasionally almost perversely uncritical, but there are insights and shrewd observations, such as this one:

. . . by the most rapid of tests you can tell how small a proportion of the visitors in a gallery have learned to see the pictures other than as a kind of illustrated newspaper, by noticing how they begin, in almost every case, by looking up their catalogue to "see what it is called". They never dream of beginning with the picture first, and looking at it quietly, till they are ready to mark on their catalogue what it *is*. This has been the making of the literary painter. Only connect a title with a pun in it, or turn up a happy quotation from Longfellow; give us half a page of Scott, a good pathetic sermonising, or a dog that plays funny tricks, and an engraving of your picture shall adorn the British drawing-room, you are safe to become an R.A., you stand a fair chance of being knighted.

Anna had her baby in October 1887, a girl whom they named Norah—the Irish abbreviation of Honora. With this added family responsibility, it became more urgent for Geddes to find a better job. After his marriage he had taken up a lectureship in botany at Heriot-Watt College, as well as continuing his work in practical botany under Alexander Dickson at the university. Then, in the Christmas vacation, Dickson died very suddenly. "He was curling, skip of his rink, keen as the ice itself, when he stumbled and fell into the arms of his fellow-skip, dead."[1] Geddes applied for the Chair, and he must have felt that this time he would be appointed. Although his social activities were multifarious, he had restricted his official teaching activities in recent years to the one subject, botany— as so many of his friends had advised, and the list of his scientific publications (see Appendix II) which accompanied his application was impressive. His printed testimonials included five by successful former students, one of whom, Harvey Gibson, was himself already a professor. Also he must have felt that his initiative in starting University Hall should count in his favour. The plight of poor and lonely students had recently been underlined when one boy was found dead in his lodgings—an event which the local press treated as something of a scandal, criticizing the general lack of concern for student welfare.

But the appointment went to Isaac Bayley Balfour. Balfour's father had held the Chair before Dickson, and he was a member of a prominent local family. He vacated a post in Oxford to return to Edinburgh—a post for which Geddes immediately considered applying. Schäfer advised against it, adding sadly: "It is thrown in our teeth by your opponents that you have worked at everything but Botany . . ." Geddes's activities outside the confined circles of natural science were almost obsessively mistrusted by many of those working solely inside. It is a pattern familiar to us today: jealous specialists regarding any tendency towards polymathy as mere intellectual adulteration. For them there could be no useful link between botanical research and whitewashing a courtyard. For Geddes, nothing was separate; everything was part of an interlocking synthesis. Unfortunately E. M. Forster's evocative command "Only connect . . ." had yet to be invented.

It was a particularly bitter rejection. Geddes had settled himself at the heart of Edinburgh, renewing, restoring, re-vivifying, re-educating, and the university, symbol of enlightenment, had once again ignored his altruistic ambition. He had made Edinburgh the centre for his social operations, but without a decent salary he could not reasonably continue. And although one can imagine the reservations the university curators had about Geddes, and must not condemn them for behaving in exactly the same way as most established bodies would have behaved, one cannot but wholly regret their decision. It upset the balance of Geddes's social-improvement operations by driving him partially away from the city of his choice. It may be that an Edinburgh chair would not have prevented the dissipation of his energies. But it might have done.

As it was, when Geddes wrote congratulating Balfour on his appointment, he also handed in his resignation to the university. It should perhaps be emphasized that Geddes did not aspire to a professorial chair simply because it was impossible to conduct his operations without the salary and status such an appointment would bring. He also needed one because the role of teacher was absolutely integral to his nature, and only as a professor would he have the autonomy to organize his teaching in the manner he wished. He was never more creative nor more eager than when given the opportunity to guide, instruct and enthuse a group of willing young people. And, as Arthur Thomson underlined, "you forced your students to think"—an invaluable ability. What was always difficult for him to accept was that so many students simply were not capable, or would not allow themselves to be, of taking on his synoptic approach.

His friends were concerned about his academic frustration, and Martin White came up with a compromise solution. He was prepared to endow a Chair of Botany in memory of his father at Dundee University, provided that Patrick Geddes was allowed to inhabit it. Furthermore, it was to be a part-time appointment, requiring Geddes to reside in Dundee for the three months of the summer term only, so that he could continue with his activities in Edinburgh and elsewhere. The yearly salary was to be £200 (out of which Geddes spent £100 on an assistant to carry on when he was not there, and from which he had to provide some of the initial equipment), plus two-thirds of the fees collected from the students. It was by no means a princely appointment, but it provided a sheet anchor for thirty years.

The university authorities were not entirely happy about the conditions of the appointment, and Geddes had some difficulty in persuading them to allot him a small portion of the grounds, plus the services of a gardener, so that he could create a botanic garden. He loved building gardens, and a good deal of his teaching took place in this one. His students were mainly from the medical faculty, and initially somewhat impatient at the statutory botanical course contained in their first-year studies. However, many of them were won over by Geddes's method of first introducing them to the wonder of plants ("the highest modern botany . . . finds its rise and climax in watching the blossoms open and the bees come and go") and then leading them into systems of classification, herbalist remedies, and the significance of evolutionary theories. They were also, of course, given a great deal of sociological information and speculation, which in the long run would have a bearing on their work. Dundee was all too suitable for field-study, containing as it did some of the worst industrial slums in Britain, with a subsequent high rate of disease.

His academic life settled, Geddes had an unexpected family

sorrow. In May 1888 his sister Jessie died at the age of forty-six,
leaving Alexander Geddes, at the age of eighty, to care for his
blind wife. Local help had to be arranged, and their far-flung
relations informed of Jessie's death.

The following year, Geddes once again involved himself in
prolific activities among the decaying properties of the Royal
Mile. To do this he needed yet more financial support from as
many as were willing to back his schemes, and he achieved
considerable success. At his instigation, Lord Rosebery and
Dr Barbour undertook responsibility for the restoration of
Abbey Cottages and the renovation of Whitehorse Close
respectively. While in October 1889 Geddes himself applied
for permission to make alterations to Riddle's Court, a sixteenth-
century mansion which he had recently acquired with the help
of backers. This became an extension to University Hall, and
he was able to offer accommodation to thirty-three more
students.[2]

In order to keep some equilibrium and efficiency in his many-
stranded life, Geddes continued to rely heavily on his close
friends for moral and practical support. Arthur Thomson in
particular, who was an integral member of the Old Town
community, and also in the no doubt difficult throes of
collaboration on their *Evolution of Sex*, came close to breaking
point in September 1888. He wrote to Geddes saying that he
felt he must seek an independent, better-paid post (he was at
the time lecturing on Natural History in the Edinburgh School
of Medicine):

... your ideal is high and wide, I wish to do something *soon*;
you have done many things and have the thews and sinews
of confidence, I have done nothing and wish to win my spurs;
your genius makes it indifferent whether you remain
specially efficient or not; my want of genius makes it
necessary to strive after efficiency in my chosen subject. I
have been forced to listen to all sorts of criticisms of your
Botanical course, which made me despairing of the attempt
to fight too overtly against the conditions of modern education. Must one compromise here as elsewhere? ... I have
been betrothed more than two years, and I know no reason
why I should be ashamed of saying—what till lately I would
not have said—that I wish to get married.

Geddes evidently replied at some length, justifying his modes of operation, and three days later Thomson recanted:

> . . . feeling rather ashamed of myself than otherwise. I suppose most people go insane now and again. I do not require any vindication of your position—it was only because it seems unattainable to me that I think of returning to the house of bondage. . . . But enough of this. Our bargain is made, and we shall see what comes of it. Only don't let me become an incubus . . .

He was able to get married the following year.

Geddes always found it difficult to compromise with his colleagues by gracefully accepting less effort from them than ideally he would have liked. Sometimes their apparent lack of will and enthusiasm made him angry or despairing. Then those who rallied to his support tended to display perhaps too fervid a brand of enthusiasm. At the time when work on Riddle's Court was beginning, and he was trying to find more sponsors, a close friend, Mrs Jean Craigie Cunningham, wrote to him:

> Do you know that Mavor* speaks of you as a "modern Christ". There are some folks who appreciate your work now and love and honour you and feel themselves grow strong . . . and full of life-giving power in thinking of your work.

The "modern Christ" kind of support had its dangers. There was something prophetic about Geddes, and it was all too easy for his detractors to ignore the fact that his forecasts and theories were founded in scientific and humanistic common-sense. But it was never enough for him to stay with the practical. In his persuasive rhetoric, the cleansed courtyard or hygienic kitchen invariably became a symbol for more complex universal regeneration. And scoffers then conveniently forgot that actual courtyards had been cleared, and real kitchens equipped and decorated.

There is always a strong element of unfairness in claiming to gain knowledge of people through reading fictionalized versions of their characters—yet so often those versions do contain an original element of truth. A version of Patrick Geddes was

---

* James Mavor, editor of *The Art Review*.

presented as Professor Grosvenor in an occult-tinged narrative called *The Cruciform Mark* published in 1896. Its author, Riccardo Stephens, had come from southern England to study in Edinburgh, mainly because he had heard of Geddes's reputation and wanted to live in University Hall. For him the experience had been disappointing. Perhaps some of the elements that contributed to his disappointment are presented accurately in Grosvenor—whom, interestingly, he made a professor of psychology.

. . . he was a most astute diplomatist, interested, as he smilingly said, in many things more than in psychology, surprisingly frank at one time, but at other times working for his object in an unscrupulous and round-about way that made one imagine he must enjoy underhand methods for their own sake. He would mine and countermine, diplomatise and intrigue for nothing at all, and then chuckle openly over his cleverness to some intended victim, being not only surprised but grieved when the said victim showed the slightest disposition to profit by experience. He was sanguine to silliness, yet far-sighted and intuitive to an astonishing degree. He would promise heaven and earth to anyone at any time, if he thought it necessary for his schemes, which were many, and on failure had always a little bit of heaven left, to tempt one to further idiocy. I have known him turn aside quite unnecessarily to do a stranger kindness. I have never known him spare a friend who seemed to stand between him and success. One was taken up and dropped frankly, according to one's momentary usefulness or uselessness. When the appropriate moment returned one must be ready to reappear, or the Professor was hurt beyond measure at what he was pleased to term disloyalty. He never spared others, and, to do him justice, was equally hard on himself . . .

For another, undisillusioned, University Hall student, F. A. E. Crew,* the experience of meeting Geddes was very different:

At the end of such an evening it really seemed that it was possible to alter the course of history and moreover that to
* Later Professor of Public Health and Social Medicine at Edinburgh University.

this end one had become dedicated. This sense of exaltation dwindled, of course, but there remained permanently the notion, firmly grasped, that life would be a dull affair if one did not at all times attempt to the best of one's ability and according to one's conscience to remove from the social organisation the many faults and flaws that disfigure it.

One young man who stood up to Geddes more strongly than most when they found themselves in disagreement, was Cosmo Burton. He was the son of the late Historiographer Royal of Scotland, and his mother, Mrs Hill Burton, and painter sister, Mary, were close friends of Patrick and Anna. In 1889 he acted as Geddes's assistant at Dundee, and was also developing a relationship with Anna's youngest sister, Bex. The following year Geddes invited him to come to Dundee again, and when Burton demurred because of what he considered were defects in the professor's teaching methods and organization, Geddes invited him to list these defects. One concerned his lecturing methods:

> You say that you cannot write notes for your lectures, which I don't believe, you could if you tried. To read from beginning to end would be better than getting along as you too often do. I know what you feel about the freshness of a spoken lecture . . . and I believe in this too, so long as you will tie your own imagination to that of your class and go no farther ahead than they can follow you. . . . That your lectures are always special pleading I have told you very often, only I don't think you quite believe it.

Then he added a remark which shows how far ahead of his time Geddes's concept of teaching was:

> I understand that you want teaching, not linear, as usual in books, nor plane, as usual in lectures, but *solid* or three-dimensional.

While this correspondence went on, Bex consulted Geddes privately about Cosmo Burton's prospects and achievements. He was at an uncertain point in his career, not sure which talent or subject to develop, and Bex obviously trusted Geddes's judgement and advice above any other, and felt no disloyalty in consulting him. At one point Burton agreed to go to Dundee again, warning Geddes:

> I hope you will be reasonable about what you expect and that you will remember that you are *very* difficult to work with . . .

But then he suddenly applied for, and was offered, a job in Shanghai. He married Bex, and they left their families and friends to start an independent life. At the end of the year they both caught fever. Cosmo died, and Bex returned home. This sadness brought the Geddes and Burton families even closer than before. Patrick wrote to Mrs Hill Burton:

> I wish to say how glad and thankful I am to find you all as I did—bearing sorrow as sorrow should be borne—not shrinking from the rest of life;—still more do I want to say that all I wrote in my first letter to you—or said this morning—I literally and exactly mean and desire to fulfil— That is you are to consider me your son so far as you can; . . . and the more you assume this relationship fixed so long as I do not cease to deserve it, the better I shall be pleased. That amid my multifarious interests and cares I give too little time and presence to my own parents and indeed even to my own household—and so may well seem at times forgetful of you and yours—is indeed true—but you are not to hesitate to recall me . . .

During the brief winter Cosmo and Bex had spent together in Shanghai, Anna and Patrick had travelled in Europe, accompanied by two young women and Norah. It was not altogether a happy tour. Anna wrote to Mary Burton:

> Oh dear Mary, earnest steadfast spirits are more and more needed especially amongst us women. As I have told you before I know it is always good for me to be with you. . . . At Strasbourg again we only stayed two nights. Pat found the University so cold and dead and dreary, and was so depressed at the signs everywhere of German oppression that even this one day was almost insupportable.

But eventually they arrived in Montpellier, where one of Geddes's friends from his student days in Paris, Charles Flahault, was professor of botany at the university. There the red anemones were blooming under the gnarled grey olive trees, and an atmosphere of scholarship and friendship welcomed travellers. Geddes always loved Montpellier, and Anna's only complaint was of scorpions under the floor matting.

As well as renewing academic friendships, and hearing of new research and ideas, Geddes made these fairly frequent visits to university towns because he was anxious to instigate reforms in Scottish universities. He felt the latter had much to learn from their European counterparts and had said so forcefully in a long closing address at the end of the 1890 summer term at Dundee. He was also trying to revive the Scots College in Paris (built by the Bishop of Moray in 1325) as a co-operative Franco-Scottish enterprise. This would not be a teaching or residential college, but would aid the British student in Paris "in the arrangement of his studies, and in finding friends among his teachers and fellow-students [and] . . . a suitable lodging with all due economies". Any student, he felt, "needs a better greeting than the railway porter's when he arrives at his destination", and the University Hall in Edinburgh had been partly inspired by the better facilities for students that he had experienced on the Continent.

Invigorated by his stay in Montpellier, he started negotiations on his return to Edinburgh for what was to be in some respects his most important purchase along the Royal Mile— Ramsay Lodge and the adjoining land in Ramsay Garden. Ramsay Garden stands on the edge of the castle esplanade, overlooking Princes Gardens, and away across north Edinburgh to Leith Harbour and the Firth of Forth. Ramsay Lodge was a Georgian block of garden homes built by Allan Ramsay, the poet-barber, and his son, the painter. Over the following three years, Geddes was to have this Georgian core heavily re-modelled, and a new block of six large flats built on at right-angles, making sixteen homes altogether for students and teachers. The remodelling and new building, undertaken by the architect S. Herbert Capper, followed the old Scottish domestic architectural tradition of rough-cast cement with red freestone dressings, plus a plethora of projecting eaves, windows, balconies, and towers. Some may regret the masking of

Ramsay's original steady Georgian design. However in the circumstances it is fascinating to see what building Geddes perpetrated when given a free hand on this, the most public and noble site available for private building in the whole of Edinburgh.

The fragmentary diary he had kept during his cycling tour with Baildon eight years previously, also has a few entries for his following visit to Europe to see Arthur Thomson. One of these describes the train journey from Jena to Cassel:

Delightful run—every village perfect picture (and sociological life). Timbered houses: $\frac{1}{2}$way between wattle and daub and Palace Beautiful.

There are strong links between the immediate image made by Ramsay Garden, and the phrase "$\frac{1}{2}$way between wattle and daub and Palace Beautiful". The block has its foundations, so to speak, in domesticity, community, family, cosiness, but its roofs and towers are magical and ornamental, and its decorations denote historical links and private fantasy. It stands in complete contrast to the dark, stark, sensible buildings silhouetted along the Old Town ridge—the only other immediately apparent extravagance being that elaborate but solid guardian of Mammon, the Bank of Scotland. Ramsay Garden could be read as a statement of defiance against the sombreness of Edinburgh, a permanent expression of Geddes's belief in the necessity for a rich and delightful living-background, be one student or professor. It was also designed to include a home for his family, and in later life he said: "It was a seven-towered castle I built for my beloved. Did you ever count them?—There are seven."[3] It should be added that Anna had every material right to her "castle", as £2,000 which had been left to her by her father, significantly helped to finance it.

Its erection entailed, however, some periods of separation for the Geddeses. Their second child, Alasdair, was born in June 1891, during their summer stay at Dundee, and given a grand christening in the hall of Martin White's palatial home, Balruddery. Norah later remembered: "On a Chinese stand was a great bowl or ornamental basin generally filled with flowers. This served as a font and the ceremony was performed by a clergyman." But when the Dundee session was over, Geddes was in urgent need of earning more money, and undertook to do various courses of lectures in London during the 1891/2 winter season. It was therefore decided to rent a flat in Hyde Park Mansions and base the family (accompanied by Bex and two other female friends) in London. However, in between the lecture courses Geddes fled back to Edinburgh to supervise the design of Ramsay Garden, raise money, and undertake various other activities. Frequently, it seemed, he broke promises in regards to the date of his return to his family in London, and the following extracts from Anna's daily letters give a clear picture of the tensions in their domestic life:

7th December: I must confess to feeling a good deal of the heart sickness of hope deferred, dear love, at this last disappointment, but your coming cannot be delayed much longer. Only do let us try to have one day if possible without a heavy burden of business before the freshness of your homecoming has worn off.

21st December: I'll only be too glad to stay at home on Sunday [25th] if you're just arriving; but I fancy you're only putting off the evil day of telling me you *won't* be here by Xmas—eh? Perhaps you'll be able to go home to Perth?

22nd December: No word from you again this morning . . . is there any chance I wonder of your being home for Xmas? . . . If you are not coming you might send Norah a Xmas card to let her see you remember her. . . . I feel so in the dark about you.

27th December: This is very sad news, but there's no use mourning about it; and further I much prefer knowing when I am to expect you than being put off from day to day.

27th December (written at night-time): I scarcely told you in this evening's letter how I long for your return, and perhaps you will be disappointed that I don't *seem* to want you more. But you need not be afraid. It all seems to a certain extent like *wasted* time that is spent without you, though I endeavour as much as possible to do the things for which I have not so much time when you are here—and

also the things you would like me to do while you are away.
I know quite well that you will come back to us at the first
moment possible. I am so glad to think your lectures do not
begin till Jan. 16, and that you may perhaps be able to take
a day or two of complete holiday when you come back. I
would rather you would stay a day or two longer and really
finish up as far as possible than have things to finish up when
you come here, and spoil the first pleasures of your return.
So work away, sweetheart until you can feel yourself—if
possible—without that crushing burden of work that *must* be
overtaken whether you feel fit for it or not. You say you work
better in Edinburgh than here, and I suppose you have
better assistance, and I don't want you to feel that I am
murmuring at this prolonged absence. I understand and
sympathise too much with the quantity and the importance
of your work to be in that mood.

2nd January (written after Anna had attended Dr Congreve's
service): Poor Miss C. trudged off in the cold yesterday
though I offered to send Kate with a note (I couldn't go
myself because of visitors), to Kew to tell about changing
the next meeting with the students, and was evidently a
little aggrieved when she found your telegram had arranged
everything, and that her 3 hours in the cold, which is more
trying to her than the rest of us, was for nothing. I don't
want to reproach you, dear in the least, nor would she
probably wish me to mention it; but if you could remember
just to *say you're sorry*!

4th January (written from Ryde, where Anna was staying
with Robert and Maggie): Yesterday I missed writing to
you for the first time, because it was too late by the time we
reached here to send out letters for north mails. . . . R. said
he knew "you didn't want to come"—which I denied—
partly of course telling a little fib, but partly there is
foundation of truth in my denial isn't there? Robert is so
kindly and affectionate when one comes, that one repents of
not having wanted much to be with him, and of course he
doesn't want to argue with me so much as with you. . . . Of
course I'll be back on Sat. to receive you, whenever you
come, in the infernal hole you are good enough to call home!
I appreciate the compliment.

5th January: Norah's very pleased with your beautifully printed little letter.

12th January: I do appreciate your morning letter. Thanks for writing so regularly. But you don't say when you are coming home?

There were some compensations for Anna. With three companions to help her look after the children, she had time for visiting the British Museum to read books on music—though sometimes these visits were curtailed because of fog, which meant it was too dark for the museum attendants to find the books in the store. She also made calls, which included the Sidney Webbs, and generally enjoyed some privacy and freedom away from the home. She kept in touch with Mount Tabor, where Captain and Mrs Geddes were also experiencing the inconvenience of the uncertainty of Patrick's visits. Alexander wrote to Anna:

We are glad to hear that we are to have a visit from Pat in a week or two but Mother says that he is not to come unless he has to come to Edinburgh or Dundee on business, nor is he to come if the weather is severe, as at present. But should he come, she desires that he shall be *punctual in giving her a day's notice* that she may be with him instead of airing sheets, etc. etc.

As Geddes's family endeavoured to underpin his energetic enterprises with a domestic pattern of regularity and affection, he was covering pages and pages with notes, scribbles and diagrams, all relating to his latest purchase in the Royal Mile: a somewhat odd-looking building, situated just below Ramsay Garden on Castlehill, and called Short's Observatory. This had belonged to an optician, who had added a turret to the original burgh house, in which he had installed a camera obscura. With the aid of this instrument one could stand in a darkened turret room and scan the panorama of Edinburgh and its environs in a continuous series of concentrated images. This phenomenon had caught Geddes's imagination, and he was planning to fill the whole building with concentrated images of one sort or another, and reveal to the citizens of Edinburgh an "index-museum to the universe", all cascading

from the turret-view of their own locality. The building was to
be renamed the Outlook Tower. As a symbol of what Geddes
stood for, its significance still persists. In 1899, Charles
Zueblin described it as "the first sociological laboratory in the
world".[4]

Chapter 8

THE OUTLOOK TOWER

THE DEVELOPMENT OF the Outlook Tower was in many ways inseparable from parallel activities that stemmed from Geddes during the 1890's in Edinburgh. Having created dwellings for over 200 teachers and students along the Royal Mile, he was endeavouring to initiate an extra-mural cultural programme that would draw together both academics and townsmen into a forceful, thoughtful community. The hostels just about kept head-above-water financially, and this encouraged him to seek backers to support him on these wider schemes. As well as the Outlook Tower, there were the Summer Meetings, the Old Edinburgh School of Art, a publishing company, a country-house club—all of which will be examined later. But as, to quote Cosmo Burton, "the *solid* or three-dimensional" expression of Geddes's thought, the one which contained his real pioneer work, the Outlook Tower is the most significant. He was aided in its establishment by many people, and it only remained at the peak of its effectiveness for a limited time, but at this peak it provided an extraordinarily imaginative perspective of the earth and its inhabitants. Besides being a sociological museum, carefully planned so as to have a cumulative effect on the visitor, it also provided a centre for its active members where new creative and educational practices, particularly in the fields of geography, nature study and art, could be catalogued and performed.

Geddes preferred visitors to start their journey through the Tower from the top. This could be reached by a winding back staircase, which bypassed all the rooms, and he liked to lead people up it at breakneck speed. When they emerged onto the narrow balcony around the turret they would be gasping for breath, and he claimed that they experienced the sudden panoramic views more intensely when the blood was circulating rapidly through their bodies. Soon they would be led into the

darkened turret room, where the images from the camera
obscura were projected onto a white table. The instrument
worked by means of a mirror, housed in the cupola above,
which could be rotated at will by a lever, and which reflected
its images through a camera lens. The effect of the device was
to concentrate the images of the surrounding environs, both
near and far, in a manner which Geddes likened to modern
painting—both the perspective and colour being compressed
into a form easily assimilable to the eye. To go immediately
after this experience onto the flat roof below the turret, with the
wide Edinburgh landscape stretching all around and the sharp
light making it difficult immediately to focus the gaze at all,
was for Geddes a symbol of the change from the artist's view—
the aesthetic and emotional view—to the limitless panorama,
impossible to absorb in one go, of the geographical or scientific
view.

This flat turret roof, equipped with a field telescope, was
called the Prospect, and standing on it Geddes would lecture
visitors on the evidences of meteorology, history, geography or
geology which lay before their eyes if only they knew how to
look. There was also a small herbarium in one corner, and geological diagrams were inscribed in one wall. Other exhibits,
including meteorological instruments, would be added from
time to time. Whereas the camera obscura view had been the
child's view—naturally integrating everything into a harmoni-
ous whole, the Prospect view was that of the questioning adolescent or adult, anxious to know what elements made up the
pieces that fitted together into such a complex city.

But before such a quest could become too parochial, the
visitor was reminded of Edinburgh's position within the vast
scale of the universe. In an octagonal room adjoining the Prospect were astronomical charts, a huge hollow celestial globe
that one could enter in order to see the whole sphere of stars
from within, and a model of the earth as though it were trans-
parent and seen in perspective by someone standing in Edinburgh, so that continents and oceans on the other side of the
world were seen inside out, and Scandinavia appeared huge
when compared to distant Australia.

After this the visitor went into a small, cell-like room,
equipped with just one chair. Following the "outlook" experience of the camera obscura, Prospect roof, and models of the

universe, this bare room was supposed to provide a brief opportunity for meditation so that the visitor could digest what he had
seen, and prepare himself for the "inlook" experiences that were
to follow. It was also a symbol of the idea that it is only through
understanding himself, his own psychology, that man can hope
to understand his environment. The gains of science, its "body
of verifiable and workable truths", are worth nothing if they
entail the suppression of "other (and it may be more important)
truths".[1] This welding of outer and inner knowledge was essential to Geddes's thought and teaching.

After the quiet pause came the storey known as the Edinburgh Room. This housed relief-model maps, paintings, drawings, photographs, documents relating to mineral, industrial,
educational and social resources, and displays concerning the
growth of Edinburgh over the centuries. It was from his experiences in relation to this room that Geddes's later well-known
city exhibitions evolved. A small room adjoining the main
Edinburgh display was called the Civic Business-room, from
which was organized the practical work of the Tower and its
various endeavours towards city improvement. The next storey
was devoted to Scotland as a whole, and outside the door stood
a large botanical globe, which among other things vividly illustrated the way geographical conditions have influenced history.
After Scotland came Great Britain, which was extended to
include all the English-speaking countries—Geddes considered
that the language bond with the United States was a far
stronger one than the merely territorial claims imposed on the
non-English speaking parts of the Empire.

The next storey concerned Europe, and three of its walls were
covered with a vast coloured chart illustrating European (or
Occidental) history from the fourth to the nineteenth centuries.
This was an example of the kind of graphic display Geddes
liked to initiate, and included widening and narrowing bands
of colour to represent the growing and receding influence of
various powers: purple for the Roman Empire, yellow for the
Goths, green for the Moslems, etc. Also on this floor were displays made by the Current Events Club that was housed in the
Tower, whose members endeavoured by means of press cuttings
to illustrate the complex developments taking place in Europe
and elsewhere. Then on the ground floor came the displays
devoted to Oriental civilization, and general anthropology.

Clearly, all this was not arranged in a day, and the whole process of establishing the Outlook Tower proved fairly uphill work. Having spawned the idea, Geddes was not always on hand to help with its implementation. Much of the day-to-day responsibility fell on the shoulders of a Christian-spirited young man called Thomas Marr, who in October 1894 was engaged as Geddes's winter assistant at Dundee. Twelve months later he was invited to continue the running of the Tower. The following selection from his correspondence with Geddes, starting with the latter's rather-difficult-to-grasp dream of the Tower as a college/workshop (or civic laboratory as he sometimes called it), illustrates the frustrations inherent in trying to span the gap between ideals and reality, particularly as the reality was supposed to include keeping the Tower on an even financial keel by attracting substantial membership subscriptions and daily attendance figures. 24th October 1895. Geddes to Marr:

> Herewith oldest jottings of notes for this Tower of about four years ago, which I had entirely forgotten. I shall be glad if you will keep this and the big bundle that has been accumulating through the summer. . . . The reason for this is of course that it tends to furnish a kind of teaching series for the essential thing I have got to teach. The gradual re-crystallisation of development of small beginnings, the gradual building of Castles in the Air into Castles of Stone, of floating fancies into schemes of culture.
>
> Everybody has these floating ideas, every conversation lets some drop; no bright gathering of young men or women but scatters plenty of them. But the whole tendency of modern life and what is officially called education is of course to filter off the crystal nuclei which at first make the mind solution cloudy, to stamp down the germinating points by the hurrying feet of the busy world. . . . The one thing that is never done by the elder folk is to respect these and let them grow, the one thing that is never done by the younger folk is to respect these themselves enough to let them grow—the patient culture necessary to *make* them grow.
>
> So out of these once boyish sentiments and fancies and Castles in the Air I build you and your comrades this small towerlet of that great Northern citadel of Culture I have so often dreamt of but must leave others to build.

Some of you may think it finished. That has been the way with most colleges. Some of you, (with whom I should personally have more sympathy), will think it a very small affair after all. If so, go on and do better. It should be easy to do better now that you have some little starting point. The real difficulty (on which my personal life has been mostly wasted) has been in getting any foothold at all.

In this connection pray look up my own notes marked "Collaboration, Elaboration, Independence" and let us try to organise a real students' workshop in which a man could steadily progress (as you yourself have been doing) from one to the other. My point is that if we could really organise a definite series of crystallising pans we should have for the first time a genuinely productive College. Men would of course crystallise out at all levels of intellectual size and clearness— would grow at different rates . . . that everybody should be growing after his measure is the main point.

28th June 1896. Summary of Marr to Geddes:

It seems impossible ever to see you now, and personally one naturally regrets the old times when one could profit a little by the time you now give to great schemes instead of to small people. [He goes on to say how it would have been nice to take a walk together and discuss the plans for the Tower.] Probably you have everything quite cut and dry—only I cannot get the details, and I should like to have them. . . . The tactics I would recommend are to emphasize 1st geography and 2nd history. Perhaps it may be partly because of my present interests [he was planning a book on climatology] but it is not altogether so. By making geographical matters prominent we may gain the support of the R.S.G.S.,* and it would be a very great pity if there could not be co-operation with them. [Goes on to say that some of the Society's members are anxious to help, but have been scared by reports about it being a Social Museum] and there would be no hope of getting the R.S.G.S. to support such a scheme. . . . You have evidently spoken over the heads of practical men, who failed to have any concrete conception of what you wanted to do. [Suggests it might be a good idea either] to

* Royal Scottish Geographical Society.

call it a Geographical Museum until people were educated
enough to appreciate the Social Museum into which it might
slowly evolve [or to keep the main part geographical] and
keep social matters in an inner room for those willing and
fit to enter . . .

3rd May 1897. Summary of Geddes to Marr:

[Tells him to buck his ideas up over the organization of the
Tower, and suggests that they are alike in preferring the
initial conceptual, and later teaching, aspects of museum
work to the acquisitive.] Unfortuntately the speculation is
largely past and the teaching largely future; and the actual
work of the Tower is of the third order, viz. the daily ac-
quisition and putting in order of things, in which you have
(1) no congenital or natural aptitude, so far as I am aware,
(2) practically no training . . . and (3) (am I unjust?) do not
appear to have made any *sufficient or adequately sustained daily
effort* since you undertook occupation a year ago. (If on the
other hand I am unjust, and you *have* been working steadily at
the Tower, then the result is too disappointing. You see I put
the dilemma as it appears to me, quite uncompromisingly.)

Poor Marr said once again that he would like to meet and talk
at length with Geddes, and on 12th May received the following
brief message, sent from Dundee:

I fear I am too busy to see you this week, as every day I am
occupied and with Edinburgh visitors to boot. What about
next Tuesday?

. . . you speak of the thing of more active organisation, and
you point out in this and former letters that ideas have not
come to you. I had intended to go on working at the Tower,
but pending definite understanding from you it was really too
unsatisfactory, and so I have just gone on thinking, towards
complexity and simplicity as the case may be. I never write
of these subjects: Life is too short . . .

Despite Marr's doubts and Geddes's criticisms, most of the
best display material for the Tower was in fact being created

during this period. The major globes and relief models were designed by Elisée Reclus, and his brother Elie's son, Paul. Elisée and Elie Reclus, eminent geographer and anthropologist respectively, were prominent figures in the international anarchist movement, and, together with Peter Kropotkin, were well-known to Geddes; Elisée in particular often lectured at the Summer Meetings. While Geddes never believed that in certain political situations violence might be justified, he was very closely attuned to much of their social and scientific thinking which he termed "constructive anarchism"; the sort espoused by Elisée Reclus when he rejected the idea of isolated free communities, saying: "We must not shut ourselves up at any price; we must remain in the vast world to receive all its instruction."[2] Paul Reclus had fled to Britain after the assassination of President Sadi Carnot in Lyons, when thirty anarchists were accused of having formed a criminal association, and he worked in Edinburgh under the assumed name of Georges Guyou. Geddes's attitude to anarchism is perhaps most clearly expressed in a letter he wrote to a friend in February 1896:

> Now Socialism. "We are all Socialists now" the politician says; yesterday we municipalised tramways, today it is telephones, tomorrow old age pensions—till even professors of economics believe and tremble. So far you are with me, but now *Anarchism*. And here with most people you stop . . . I thoroughly agree that it is a most ill-chosen and unlucky word; and that its constant misunderstanding is almost inevitable. But . . . it simply means what it says, *an archy, without government* i.e. social order maintained without *governmental compulsion*, the social love and the individual conscience having to keep each other true.
>
> It is an ideal, a Utopia—granted at once; they don't know how to realise it;—granted too. . . . Yet give men the ideal of getting *northward* to the very pole; and they realise it more and more approximately.

The presence of anarchists at the Tower's activities did not go unnoticed. It was one of the factors that contributed to the Edinburgh establishment's unease over Geddes, and for several years the reporters working for *The Scotsman* were instructed not

to cover events at the Outlook Tower. In circumstances such as
these, Geddes appears never even to have considered trimming
his sails to comply with the prevailing wind of opinion. He
would have scoffed at the conventional image of an anarchist:
black hat, smoking bomb and furtive expression. His anarchist
friends were men to be proud of, tempered by the fervour of the
1871 Commune whose influence had still been strongly felt in
the Paris of his student days. (In his autobiography, Havelock
Ellis rather disarmingly described Elie Reclus as "a delightful
personality, simple and genuine, an Anarchist of the finest
quality".)

Three stained-glass windows were designed for the stair land-
ings in the Tower, and these contained symbols of many of the
ideas Geddes valued. The anarchist black flag was included in
one called *Arbor Saeculorum—Tree of Life*—as well as the red
socialist flag and the cap of liberty. The main part of the
design of this window showed two sphinxes guarding a
tree whose roots are in the fires of life, and whose branches
represent the successive ages of man. Smoke from the fire
curls up through the branches to indicate how each generation has been blinded to the thought and work of their ancestors. Emerging from the smoke wreaths at the top is the
phoenix of man's ever-renewed body and the butterfly or
Psyche of humanity's immortal soul. A second window was
called *Lapis Philosophorum—Philosopher's Stone*—and symbolized
the reintegration of the arts and sciences in a graphic representation drawn from Geddes's thinking-machines: an early
appreciation of the dangers inherent in a split between the two
cultures.

The third window was a straightforward illustration of what
he called "A typical Region: Mountain to Sea with fundamental occupations"—a representation which he frequently used in
various forms in his teaching, and which he called "the valley
section." He regarded the valley section as the characteristic
geographic unit of western Europe and parts of America,
a convenient image to summarize the geographical components of a region and its fundamental occupations. (He
probably evolved this generalized concept from Elisée Reclus' more particularized course of geography, *Histoire d'un
Ruisseau*, published in 1869, and his own early memories of
the Kinnoull Hill, River Tay, Perth, valley section.) On .it,

also, could be depicted the workings-out of Le Play's three sociological elements—Place, Work and Folk. It could be shown that historically the hunter was joined by the woodman and then the miner to influence the environment of the mountains and woodlands; the shepherd and the peasant used and cultivated the plains according to the climate and soil; the fisherman set up his habitation on suitable parts of the estuary and coast. Occupation and environment then tended to lead to the development of a dominant psychological type within each community. Later urban developments were influenced by the balance of natural resources, and the valley section could then be used in more complex form to demonstrate the origins of the fundamental city professions. Thus quarrying, goldmining, forestry, hunting, sheep farming, arable farming, cattle farming, market gardening, vineyards, hopfields, and fishing village in turn created the urban iron and steel foundries, goldsmiths, timber and paper merchants, furriers, woollen mills, bakers, butchers, greengrocers, jam factories, breweries and ports. By understanding the origin of city professions in the natural occupations of their rural ancestors, Geddes claimed that planners were better placed to undertake the re-creation of the city region.

Like so much of Geddes's iconography, the valley section now appears old-fashioned and picturesque, particularly when related to the electric modern city rather than the Victorian industrial one, but it had a psychological significance beyond its environmental implications. Geddes wrote:

By descending from source to sea we follow the development of civilisation from its simple origins to its complex resultants; nor can any element of this be omitted. Were we to begin with the peasant hamlet as our initial unit, and forget the hinterlands of pasture, forest, and chase (an error to which the writer on cities is naturally prone), the anthropologist would soon remind us that in forgetting the hunter, we had omitted the essential germ of active militarism, and hence very largely of aristocratic rule. Similarly, in ignoring the pastoral life, we should be losing sight of a main fount of spiritual power, and this is not only as regards the historic religions, but all later culture elements also, from the poetic to the educational. In short, then, it takes the whole region to make the city.

In fact the method of intermixing personal and general symbols in the stained-glass windows does not perhaps look so old-fashioned in the 1970's as it did during the heyday of the modern movement, when cool functionalism and anonymity were characteristic not only of architecture and design, but also of much of the thought and expression of society as well. In these present times of sticker badges, Blakean imagery, and a certain (admittedly often shallow) familiarity with the scope and strangeness of, say, Stonehenge, 2001, black holes in space and alchemy, the Geddesian attempts to make pictorial syntheses have a certain familiarity. And one of the more ambitious visual effects which he once suggested for the Tower has definite links with photographic and film techniques which have been widely used in exhibitions during recent years. He wanted to have prepared several series of slides, each devoted to a particular area of Edinburgh, which could be projected so that one "melted into the other as a dissolving view" thus showing the historical development of each area. Jotting down possibilities in a memorandum, he wrote:

Can we show the ancient University building giving place to the new one, and then grow the dome upon it? Can we similarly project the Medical School upon the empty meadows or the McEwan Hall and Union upon Park Place?

After considering many similar suggestions, he concluded:

This is enough to show the general scope of the whole scheme, that of presenting cities as dissolving views—Emerson's "foam bells"—as expressing the conception of art as not simply something concerning marks on paper, or even colour on canvas, or even the shaping of marble or bronze, much less talking about them, but as a cosmic and a human process, the construction of cities for the one, the perfection or creation of landscapes for the other.

The purpose of the Outlook Tower was not merely to provide a shot-in-the-arm to schoolchildren bored with Victorian classroom teaching, or citizens unaware of their surroundings. The term "laboratory" was applied to it with serious intent, for it was here that Geddes grew fully to realize the importance of the process of comprehensive survey as an integral part of planning for the future. "Survey", in the widest sense of the word, was what the Tower was about, and was the content of its laboratorial work. As has been mentioned, from the Edinburgh Room grew the later important city exhibitions which Geddes organized, and from them and the arrangement of the Tower as a whole grew much of the content of the writings and talks by which he later influenced a new generation of town planners. In 1889 Charles Booth had started publishing his social surveys, *Life and Labour of the People*, and the range of subjects covered by the Outlook Tower perhaps represented the other side of the survey coin. Booth's work was meticulously detailed and rigorous, limited to definite contemporary circumstances, while the Tower's work embraced the sweep of geographic, social and economic history that had contributed to such circumstances. Only when all the factors were understood, Geddes felt, could a really concerted intelligent and humane attempt be made to improve society. In the Outlook Tower, he strove to make such knowledge visible, graspable and, above all, relevant.

But even though sandwich-board men were employed to patrol the main Edinburgh streets to attract visitors to the Tower, attendances were never really high enough to make it a financially viable institution. Men like Marr, Paul Reclus, A. J. Herbertson (who later became an eminent geographer) and Edward McGegan (who subsequently took over the running of the Tower from Marr) tried, between their other professional activities, to improve the displays and generate interest; but the gap between the ideal and the necessities of reality remained. Geddes was by no means unaware of the gap, but he simply had not the time available to fill it by the one means that seemed to work—his own presence. When he took visitors around the Tower, his vigour and powerful intellect forced them to stretch their imaginations, and such a conducted tour might well inspire sufficient motivation and curiosity to bring them back for more leisurely visits on their own. Geddes came to acknowledge that the Tower was equipped to appeal to "visuels" such as himself ("those who learn by eye-gate rather than ear") and that it might therefore lose the interest of the "auditifs". What he perhaps did not fully comprehend was that he alone could bridge the gap for the "auditifs" by his flow of speech in a way which others found impossible to imitate. And to reduce his rhetoric to an encapsulated, printed documentary to augment the illustrative displays would have defeated most people.

In 1886 Martin White had urged Geddes to move "out of the, in some respects, unproductive speculative" and to get his sociological ideas down in book form. The Outlook Tower was concrete rather than speculative, but it did need a parallel, authoritative, written work by its founder, crystallizing the scope of its contents, if its significance was to be fully understood. Geddes's friends knew the danger of the dictum he had impatiently expressed to Marr, that "life is too short" for the written expression of ideas. For if all his verbal expression was to be left to the vagaries of seminars and conversations, and the dilution of broadcast by disciples, it would inevitably suffer. One such friend, William Macdonald, wrote to Anna:

Again I say to the Professor that the best thing as it is also the easiest and honestest (to himself) way of solving his difficulties of publication is to *dictate*—dictate copiously, systematically: make it take the place, in the routine of his life, which that infinite personal explanation, casual exposition and ceaseless unprofitable hole-and-corner unrelated piecemeal propagandism—mere pumping of the water of life into any vessel that comes to hand!—has hitherto occupied. One third as much time thus differently directed would give, within any equal period (say of three or five years) thirty times the increase.

One of the contributing factors to Geddes's failure to produce such a book at this stage, was that the Outlook Tower represented one huge, personal experiment and he was forever seeing ways of modifying, extending or changing its many-faceted components. Like a sculptor, he could mould, elide, enlarge and attenuate, but he could not bring himself to the stage of completion when the work was deemed final and sent for petrifaction at the foundry. Also these periods of modification were interspersed by travels abroad, teaching in Dundee, lecture programmes in London and elsewhere, so that each time he returned to the Tower after any considerable absence, he had a whole range of new experience to influence his reactions to the current stage of progress.

But despite the lack of final completion, either in words or images, which might have made the Outlook Tower more immediately accessible, the work accomplished there established it as the pioneer centre for regional survey and the forerunner of the concept of environmental education. Through it Geddes was able to demonstrate the necessity of engendering in people a sense of civic understanding in order to equip them to contribute usefully to the improvement of their own surroundings, and he thus created the new discipline which he called "geotechnics": the applied science of making the earth more habitable.

Chapter 9

THE TOWN & GOWN
ASSOCIATION LIMITED

My bedroom door was opposite the dining-room door, and
lying in bed at night the noise of conversation over the dinner
table more or less kept me awake, especially when foreigners
were being entertained. At the age of eight or nine I used to
get out of bed and raid the cupboard in the hall for lumps
of sugar . . .

THESE ARE NORAH's early memories of the flat at 14 Ramsay
Garden, to which the Geddes family had moved in 1894. Compared to James Court it was positively luxurious, having twelve
rooms, including a double drawing-room divided by a wide
archway, with bay and turret windows at either end. The
wakeful nights that Norah recalled probably occurred most
frequently from mid-July to mid-August when visitors to the
Summer Meetings were being entertained.

During the 1890's these Meetings were at their height. Attended by about 100 people, mainly teachers—including ones
from America, France and Germany—there were over 200
lectures, excursions and opportunities for practical work from
which they could select their courses. Among the foreign lecturers were the Reclus brothers and Edmond Demolins, whose
talk on Le Play had had such an influence on Geddes when he
was a student; and distinguished visitors to the Meetings included Ernst Haeckel and William James. Geddes himself
headed the general course with twenty lectures on "Contemporary Social Evolution", while Arthur Thomson ran the
biology and practical zoology. About thirty other lecturers and
demonstrators covered subjects from comparative psychology
to sloyd (a system of instruction in practical woodwork which
had been developed in Sweden), and in the evenings Anna
gave music recitals with her friend Marjory Kennedy Fraser—

well-known for her collection and performance of Hebridean folksongs. Riccardo Stephens was twice in charge of the general arrangements for the social functions at the Meetings, and one year they included "a series of *Tableaux Vivants* illustrating the history of the sciences" performed by the students for "one of the evening conversaziones of the British Association". It is impossible not to believe that these ironical paragraphs from *The Cruciform Mark* derived from his experiences:

Grosvenor, with his usual taste for paradox, held to the theory that holidays were the time when everyone was best able and most anxious to work. This demand must be supplied, which justified the importuning of lecturers, eminent and otherwise, to take their holidays in Edinburgh, and spend them in lecturing, with or without pecuniary profit to themselves. For this was the summer holiday-time, and in holidays one does not work; therefore to lecture in the summer holiday-time was not to work. Besides, were there not scores of folk, nay hundreds, thirsting for knowledge, and could one be so hard-hearted as to deny them ever so little of one's own abundant stores?

So sundry easy-tempered souls promised to lecture, and then it became necessary to find an audience. The lectures, as a rule, were caviare to the multitude, and come they would not, in spite of advertisement. Here and there a hyper-conscientious soul came along, but the average young man and woman turned up their noses at these attempts to sell them what they didn't want, and tramping off to hillside and seaside, unconsciously did the best thing possible towards accumulating health for the next twelve months. Then an audience became problematical, and free tickets being issued to certain sections of the community, it was interesting to discover how few people preferred lectures to fresh air. However, a hundred or so turned up of misguided souls who lost their holiday, and of people who, making life one long holiday, found a pretence at study amusing, and the whole scheme must have been thought a success, since a great educationist, who also looked very much overworked, was prevailed upon to come and congratulate everybody in a polite and well-delivered speech.

Even though Stephens may have considered the Summer Meetings too much like Geddesian bandwagons preaching mainly to the converted rather than successful attempts to reach the people, there were travellers in those bandwagons who derived much benefit from their experience. And the purpose of the teaching methods of the Summer Meetings was echoed in numerous academic practices and recommendations by the teachers who attended them. Geddes expressed their purpose thus:

Starting from the familiar idea of working from the concrete to the abstract, from the senses towards the intellect, it is attempted in each subject of study (1) to freshen the student's mind by a wealth of impressions; (2) to introduce him to the advancing literature of the subject; (3) to supply him with the means of summarising, arranging, and more clearly thinking out these accumulations of observation and reading. Hence (1) the insistence upon demonstrations, experiment, and field excursions; (2) the introduction in several subjects of the Seminar, which, with its guidance to the world of books and activity in using them, is so marked a strength of the German University; (3) the extended use of graphic methods.

   The student, though first of all freshened as an observer, is regarded not as a receptacle for information, but as a possible producer of independent thought. Hence the examination method, everywhere falling into such merited disrepute, is here definitely abandoned; a keener stimulus, even a more satisfactory test of progress, being found in accustoming the student to take part in his own education by attention first to the increase and systematisation of his materials, next to the occasional contribution of his best results, to the common stock of class notes and summaries, and thence to fuller collaboration with his teacher. . . . Thought, then, does not exist by and for itself, nor has it merely application to life, as is enforced by the dominant school of Technical Educationists. It arises from life, and widens in proportion to its range, not only of observation, but of action, and even of social intercourse. Hence the advantage of associated residence.

The "associated residence" was provided by the University Hall accommodation, vacated by students for the summer, and the lectures and seminars were mainly held at the Outlook Tower and Ramsay Garden. For four weeks Geddes had a sizeable flock under his wing, and the means by which to house and educate them. His own course of lectures started the morning at nine o'clock; in the afternoon he headed sociological field visits "so as to familiarize the student with the problems (hygienic, architectural, financial, etc.) of actual improvements in progress in the neighbourhood"; and in the evenings his home was filled with those attending the music or literary recitals, and foreign visitors invited to a late supper. On some evenings he also lectured on the methods and aims of regional survey, and on Saturdays there were day-long excursions to places like Stirling, Melrose or Abbotsford. One fine night he even went round the neighbourhood rousing as many as possible of the Meeting's members and inviting them to join an expedition up Arthur's Seat, the highest peak in Holyrood Park. At the summit of this extinct volcano, gazing round the moonlit landscape, he talked of the early Celts and his hopes of reviving aspects of their culture. It was for him, no doubt, the perfect end to a virtually perfect day. With his shock of hair and lengthening beard, his crumpled suits and long cloak for inclement weather, his rapid walk and non-stop speech, he had become a very well-known figure in the Old Town, and never was he more frequently visible than during that summer month when he showed Edinburgh to his visitors. It used to be said that in a city of professors any reference to "the Professor" was always taken to apply to Geddes, the epitome of the professorial image.

Much of the art content of the Summer Meetings was organized by W. G. Burn-Murdoch, Charles H. Mackie (whose work was influenced by his friendship with Gauguin), and John Duncan. Geddes admired their work and tried to act as patron by providing the premises for a small art school and opportunities for commissions. Known first as the University Hall School of Art and later as the Old Edinburgh School of Art, it was founded by Geddes and Duncan in the hope that its work would provide an aesthetic vision to set beside the more practical content of most of the Outlook Tower. Geddes wanted its products to be decorative and symbolic, suitable for inclusion into quite simple homes, and developed along the lines of Celtic art, frequently using metallic materials, "for if there is literal gilding within a building, it will free its occupants from the lust for further gold". He deemed the most appropriate subject for such decorations to be a kind of personal almanac, incorporating anything from signs of the zodiac and illustrations of the passage of the seasons, to particular events in the family's history.

> Here then is a task for the artist. Given but the sordid sand of daily life, soiled by the wreck and jetsam of a stormy past, driven hither and thither hopelessly by every wave of circumstance, to weave these into magic coils, to fasten them is our task.

What he wished to avoid was the creation of beautiful but expensive objects that were outside the means of ordinary people, and he condemned William Morris for failing to change a situation where "art has always been the treasure of the ruler, not the daily environment of the people", despite his socialistic intentions. Burn-Murdoch and Duncan were commissioned to do external decorations and friezes around the Royal Mile properties, and the Witch Well by Duncan can still be seen on the Castle Esplanade near Ramsay Garden.* The Art School was involved in paintings and decorations for the Outlook Tower—including the stained glass windows and a frieze by James Cadenhead in the Edinburgh Room. Duncan painted a frieze illustrating the history of bagpipes (said by some to be the one musical instrument Geddes really appreciated) in the drawing-room of Ramsay Garden, and there were numerous panels and murals depicting Celtic legends in the public rooms of Ramsay Lodge and other University Hall premises. However, the money to sustain these activities and their creators was not abundant.

Duncan to Geddes, 6th November 1895:

> Miss Baxter tells me that she is approaching the completion of her work in the Common Room, and we must decide what she is to turn her attention to next.

* Unfortunately the water supply has been discontinued and the public tend to use it as a litter basket (see illustration no. 18).

You surprised me very much by saying that your understanding was that she was just engaged for the present job, and that after that was done she could go about her own business. On engaging her that was not expressed, the words you used being that she was to be offered the same terms as Miss Hay.

But apart from this I must have been under some misapprehension all along.

You gave me to understand that you were eager to form a School of Art. That this School was not to consist primarily of a great band of students, but of a body of artists and their assistants working together with common ideals.

The work of this school was not to be the making of mere studies, but to be directed towards the execution of actual work for public and other purposes.

You assured me that there was abundance of work to be done, and exhorted me to make converts, telling me at the same time not to bother my head about financial matters as that was your business.

I need not remind you of the various efforts we as a body made to carry out these ideas. In one thing at least, amongst all my failures, I was successful, and that was in getting together four ladies able and willing to work sympathetically into my hands. I spared no effort in teaching those young ladies all I knew about ornament, and their decorations show that they are now thoroughly competent designers.

Then at the moment when I expected you to incorporate them into your School of Art and get them to work—you tell me you have no work for them to do!! Miss Mackie's offer of assistance is repulsed, Miss Mason, after getting one or two small jobs to do, is dismissed, and Miss Baxter is threatened with the same treatment.

What am I to think?

The other day when we talked over these matters you spoke of want of money, but told me in the same breath that the School of Art had been voted another supply by the Town Council. So I can't see why there should be any talk of a reduction of a staff which I understood your first object was to increase as rapidly as possible.

Geddes to Duncan, 7th November 1895:

... I said to you before, and I say again, that I thoroughly appreciate the work you have done and are doing, and thoroughly value the assistance of the ladies you have trained. Do you see that if at this stage I were, as you fear, willing to let the school drop—it would be a greater failure to my life as an educationist than to any of yours as artists! The Hall, the School of Art, the Summer Meeting, are not these the very things for which I work?—my books, my pictures as it were?

Which was probably not very helpful to Duncan's predicament. Once again, there was a gap between ideals and reality. Where was the public that would want a combination of Celtic and personal imagery, with art nouveau associations, painted on their walls, and where would the money come from to pay for it? Geddes tried to work out a paper entitled "Art for the Public", but in a note to Marr dated 28th January 1896, admitted:

The artist reading my papers is not satisfied; to Mr Duncan or the like, such treatment is quite unsatisfactory. Agreed. I am perfectly aware of it. It was not written for him; it was written for the half blind kittens whom we call the public ...

"Half blind kittens" was in fact an alteration; his original term had been "blind idiots". If Geddes's attempt to inspire a popular art seems rather fanciful, his reaction to the now famous design by Charles Rennie Mackintosh for the Glasgow School of Art, which won a competition in 1896, was very positive:

The real artist is he who, like Mackintosh in the Art College of Glasgow (one of the most important buildings in Europe) gets his effects within the sternest acceptances of modern conditions. For here never was concrete more concrete, steel more steely, and so on.

However, as he reached forward to the new architectural aesthetic, so he continued to widen his interest in the Celtic revival.

A visitor to the Summer Meetings, William Sharp—who had written biographies of Rossetti and Shelley, as well as poems and romances—began in 1893 to publish mystical Celtic stories under the pseudonym Fiona Macleod, and they were extremely successful. Geddes decided to set up a publishing company, based in the Outlook Tower and partially specializing in Celtic literature, and invited Sharp to become its manager. The company, called Patrick Geddes & Colleagues, lasted effectively for about four years. The Fiona Macleod works which it published (notably *The Washer of the Ford* and *The Sin-Eater*) were successful, but the organization itself was far too lackadaisical. Sharp lived most of the time in London, and his yearly managerial fee of 100 guineas was barely earned by his infrequent visits to Edinburgh and editorial correspondence; and besides this, he was in poor health. While the Macleod books were successful, others were not, and by 1896 the royalties due to Sharp were delayed from one month to the next because the company had insufficient money to pay them. Two men who had probably put up much of the money for the firm, and who were certainly included in the "Colleagues" for the services they gave, were John Ross and Victor Branford. They were accountants in partnership, with offices in Edinburgh and London, and Branford in particular became very close to Geddes. He was a rather Elizabethan-looking man, with a long narrow head, pointed beard and thin nervous lips, and Lewis Mumford wrote much later that "in his character were mingled a worldly shrewdness, an ability to appraise all the mischief and madness of his fellows, with a wild devotion to losing causes and remote ideals".[1] The "wild devotion" meant that, unlike others, he never seemed to grow impatient with Geddes's ideas, while the "worldly shrewdness" enabled him to run a successful business life.

In 1814 it was decided to combine the talents of the Celtic artists and writers with the scientific-sociological idealists of the Old Town community, and produce an occasional "Northern Seasonal" journal called *The Evergreen* (after a publication of the same name which Allan Ramsay published in 1724 to stimulate a return to Scottish tradition and the natural world). Geddes, Branford and Sharp loosely shared editorial responsibility for the written contributions, while Duncan, Burn-Murdoch, Mackie and others provided the illustrations and decorations. At one stage John Ross, who tried to keep a weather eye on the publishing activities, warned Geddes that the Art Committee was becoming too dictatorial and might well ruin the magazine. In all, four editions were published during 1895 and 1896, each linked to one of the seasons. It was a handsome publication, if somewhat uneven in standard overall, with limp leather covers embossed with a design by Mackie, and it was acclaimed by the *Sunday Times* as

> the first serious attempt we have seen on the part of genius and enthusiasm hand-in-hand to combat avowedly and persistently the decadent spirit which we have felt to be over-aggressive of late. . . . We have in this first number some score of articles, sketches, and tales written round Spring and its synonyms, whether in human or animal life, in nations, in history or in literature. And the result is a very wonderful whole . . .

Another reviewer was not so enchanted, however. In the issue of *Nature* dated 29th August 1895, H. G. Wells attacked the *Evergreen*'s artwork for its "ugly and unmeaning distortions", and said that it could not be regarded

> as anything more than the first effort of amateurs in art and literature—and it makes that claim—it is bad from cover to cover; and even the covers are bad. No mitigated condemnation will meet the circumstances of the case. Imagine the New English Art Club propounding a Scientific Renascence in its leisure moments! . . . Mr Thomson, for instance, tells his readers that "the conception of the Struggle for Existence as Nature's sole method of progress," "was to be sure a libel projected upon nature, but it had enough truth in it to be mischievous for a while." So zoologists honour their greatest! "Science," he says, has perceived "how false to natural fact the theory was." "It has shown how primordial, how organically imperative the social virtues are; how love, not egoism, is the motive which the final history of every species justifies." And so on to some beautiful socialistic sentiment and anticipations of "the dominance of a common civic ideal, which to naturalists is known as Symbiosis". . . . Now there is absolutely no

justification for these sweeping assertions, this frantic hope-
fulness, this attempt to belittle the giants of the Natural
Selection period of biological history. There is nothing in
Symbiosis or in any other group of phenomena to warrant
the statement that the representation of all life as a Struggle
for Existence is a libel on Nature.

This review is particularly interesting, because it fore-
shadows how Geddes's and Thomson's co-operative idealism
was to fall into comparative obscurity as the modern era of
world war devastation gradually drew near. This devastation,
which Wells anticipated, was also foreseen, if less specifically,
by Geddes, who all his life had hated what he called
"Prussianism" and "jingoism" and was scathing about the
nationalistic overtones of so much political activity. But his
reaction was to prescribe a cure: civic renewal. He claimed
that if people were living in a prosperous and efficient society,
and allowed to participate in its affairs as fully responsible
citizens, they would be less likely to be persuaded into war.
He later wrote in *Cities in Evolution:* "People volunteer for war;
and it is a strange and a dark superstition that they will not
volunteer for peace." But over half the twentieth century had
to elapse before this creed became widely accepted. In 1895,
the year Oscar Wilde was imprisoned, Geddes's and Thomson's
moral idealism probably seemed little different from Victorian
religious restriction to Wells, who was struggling to support a
mistress and a wife and suffering from painful, and at that time
apparently fatal, consumption. It was the year in which he
published his first books, including *The Time Machine*, whose
final pessimistic message was to be characteristic of a whole
era, blotting out the programmes for regional, self-help
co-operation outlined by writers such as Geddes and
Kropotkin. At the end of the novel, the narrator remembers
the Professor, who had again disappeared on his time machine:

> He, I know . . . thought but cheerlessly of the Advancement
> of Mankind, and saw in the growing pile of civilization only
> a foolish heaping that must inevitably fall back upon and
> destroy its makers in the end.

Wells no doubt found Geddes's vision of the future complacent.

But its brief for community action now finds favour in a world which has not quite sunk beneath the darker Wellsian prophecies.

In August 1896 Arthur Thomson undertook to edit a science series for the publishing company, but he was soon complaining to Geddes that "unless my editorship is to be the merest fiasco, will you give me, in writing, authority to draw up . . . draft agreements"; while a month later John Ross stated adamantly that he could not co-operate in any future publishing, or other ventures, as long as arrangements were made and entered upon without his being informed. In April 1897, Louis G. Irvine, author of *Nerves and Brain*, wrote to Thomson:

"P.G. and Colleagues" are like the East-India Company. You can't get at anybody in particular to come down upon, the Company perpetually eludes all attempts to fix responsibility . . .

and by November of that year Geddes was trying, unsuccessfully, to offload the whole venture on to John Murray. The operations gradually tapered off, though one successful publication did emanate directly from the Outlook Tower. This was a pamphlet on the Dreyfus Case, written in 1898 by Paul Reclus (under the name Georges Guyou), which ran into three editions and grew out of the activities of the Current Events Club.

By 1895 the financial structure of Geddes's proliferating enterprises was becoming untenable—particularly for Anna. Her £2,000 had enabled them to buy 14 Ramsay Garden (Geddes had based the whole building enterprise on persuading people to pay for apartments in advance), and she always reassured herself that should anything happen to her husband she would, like her friend Marjory Kennedy Fraser, be able to support herself and the children by teaching music. But in 1895 she was again pregnant, and Geddes's financial commitments to friends and civic worthies who had loaned money for his enterprises, were of alarming proportions. The Town Council had given grants towards the Summer Meetings and the Art

School, but these only covered partial costs and were not automatically renewable. As early as 1891 a legal friend had written to Geddes about University Hall:

> . . . I think we ought to call a meeting of university men and philanthropic persons, with a view to relieve you of all further responsibility (but not of the honour of having founded the institution). If Workman's Cafés and temperance clubs attract thousands of pounds, for which the shareholders are content to get 3 or 4 per cent of interest only, I should think *a fortiori* we ought to get the money for so excellent a purpose. My position, like that of so many others is this—that I should be delighted to take (say) £50 or £100 worth of shares; but I should hope that men who are ten times better off than I am would take a larger interest . . .

When his third child, Arthur, was born in October 1895, Geddes was deeply involved in plans to follow, somewhat belatedly, this advice. Aided particularly by Thomas Whitson, who had lived in University Hall and helped at the Summer Meetings, and was now partner in a firm of accountants, he proceeded to form a company called The Town & Gown Association Limited, which was to take over the financial management of nearly all the property standing in his name. This included private dwellings and warehouses as well as the University Hall buildings.

During the early months of 1896 he bought and rented further cheap tenement properties that could be renewed and added to the value of the whole concern, so that when prospectuses were first sent out to would-be investors, the total estimated value of all the property involved was over £60,000. The trustees of the company included an ex-Lord Provost of Edinburgh, and its directors were Bailie James Pollard, a city magistrate; Henry Beveridge, a Dunfermline philanthropist; Professor Alex Crum Brown of Edinburgh University; Francis Caird of the School of Medicine; Arthur Thomson, and Geddes himself. When the company was floated there was already a £25,000 loan-investment debt to inherit, and during the first year they were able to sell a further £21,000 worth of shares. The pattern of loans that had enabled Geddes to acquire so many properties included £700 from his father, £500 from

Harry Barker, £200 from Martin White, and £100 from Herbert Capper. There were larger sums from business acquaintances and trusts. When Barker had enquired in 1892 whether his investment was likely to yield any dividend in the foreseeable future, Geddes had replied briskly from London:

> I am sorry to have been so busy of late that I have not had time to write to you respecting your investments. . . . It is in fact impossible to give you full particulars in writing and you should run up and see for yourself . . .

Early in 1895 a Clerk of Works had been appointed to take overall responsibility for the physical care of the buildings. The urgent need for such a man was outlined in a note Geddes sent to Whitson:

> It is obviously very unsatisfactory for me to come to you at one time, Ross at another, Marr at a third, or Herbertson at a fourth, or Slater [a builder] direct at a fifth, with some structural improvement which none of us have time to attend to, special skill to design, knowledge to supervise, and most of all technical experience to estimate correctly.

Throughout these years Geddes was still, of course, spending the summer term in Dundee—accompanied by Anna and the children, and living in a rented house outside the town. He felt that everyone should have the opportunity to spend a portion of the year in the country, and one of the final purchases he made before the Town & Gown Association was formed was a large house called Craufurd, which still stands on the perimeter of Lasswade, about four miles south of Edinburgh. Lasswade is a sleepy village, grouped along the wooded banks of the Esk river, and Craufurd was to be a country house club, providing peaceful breaks amid natural surroundings for members of the Old Town community. The amount collected in rents from those who agreed to spend holidays there, did not ever balance satisfactorily with the cost of renewals, repairs, housekeepers, garden upkeep, etc., and Craufurd gradually became something of a white elephant. However, before that happened, Anna and Patrick had spent what they were to look back upon as some of their happiest family holidays in the rather plain-featured, tree-surrounded house.

Two months after Arthur was born, when Anna was still not very well, Geddes heard that Harry Barker's wife had died, leaving him with one child, Mabel—who was Geddes's god-daughter. He offered to go and stay with his old friend, an offer which was declined, but Harry turned to him as the one person he could pour out all his sorrows to by letter. Geddes was forty-one, and made particularly aware of the advance of time by his friend's bereavement, the weakening of his own parents—now eighty and eighty-six, and the fact that Norah and Alasdair were beginning to take their part in his schemes for developing new ways of teaching children. It was an age at which many other men dug their roots firmly downwards, accepting their professional and patriarchal positions, becoming permanent figures in a landscape. But via the Town & Gown Association Geddes was shedding some of his cares, and many worthy people were available who should be able to keep up other Old Town activities. As always, he had to lecture where and when he could in order to earn extra money (at that period the Tyneside Sunday Lecture Society could assure him that "We command an intelligent and attentive audience of 2,500"), but it was almost as though, having reached the watershed of forty, he was preparing himself for wider challenges that would remove any chance of ossification through so-called consolidation. During the rest of his life, Edinburgh was gradually going to become less and less the centre of his operations. Whether matters would have been different if the city had given him opportunities rather than forcing him to create his own it is impossible to say. It seems likely that he would have remained there much longer for a proportion of his time, but wholly unlikely that he would not have embarked on at least some of his ambitious travels. Already plans for participating in the forthcoming international exhibition to be held in Paris in 1900 were on his mind. Then, while the 1896 Summer Meeting was taking place, the Turks massacred some 7,000 Armenians, and thousands more fled as refugees into surrounding countries. Before outlining why it was that such a distant happening could divert Geddes's attention away from all he had created in Edinburgh and take him to Cyprus for three months, it is

perhaps worth recording a short, unsolicited testimonial that
he had received in 1895:

Dear Sir,
I take the liberty of sending for your acceptance, an old
Engraving of the Lawnmarket, a district for which you have
done so much deserves the gratitude of an old citizen.

Bryce Anderson

Chapter 10

"STIRLING AND DAMASCUS, STRANGELY MIXED"

ON 30TH OCTOBER, 1896, Geddes wrote to Robert Smith, a young botanist and one of his brightest pupils, who was working in Montpellier:

> I am going to look into the question of organising agriculture, possibly in Cyprus, for the relief of the Armenians, and so should like to utilise the peculiar resources of Montpellier for this purpose. Will you explain this to Mons. Flahault and ask him to let you be preparing any information you can for me in the meantime? Find out what you can about the vegetation and the possible agriculture of these parts, including besides the staples such as wheat, vine, silk, tobacco, cotton, etc., the accessory cultures, such as poppy and medicinal herbs, etc.
>
> Would there be any possibility of finding one or two capable fellows at the School of Agriculture for whom such work might afford places in Spring if all goes well?

A week later he drafted a letter—possibly intended for the relief committee set up in London on behalf of the Armenian refugees—of which the following is an extract:

> I am at present attempting to draft a scheme (of which I shall send you particulars by-and-by) of *non-political action* in the East, such as is open to private persons outside politics.
> This scheme is of actual industries, rustic and urban, agricultural and manufacturing, which might apply some European capital to the difficult task of, in the first place, relieving some of the more acute distress among Armenians (and for that matter, among Turks also!). This may further have the advantage of experimentally working out on a small

scale some of the ways in which the reasonable co-operation of these different Eastern races can be renewed.

I am personally thinking of leading a small group of our best organising people here to some suitable point in the East (Cyprus, Egypt, Smyrna, Philippopolis or Athens, as may be determined) for the purpose of starting there a Labour Colony for Armenians.

By the middle of December, Cyprus had been chosen as the centre of operations, and Patrick and Anna set out on the mission together, visiting Smyrna and Constantinople *en route*. They arrived off the port of Larnaka in Cyprus on 13th January; there was a rough sea and they landed in an open boat amid heavy surf. Norah, Alasdair and one-year-old Arthur (who had just had measles) had been left in the charge of Jeannie Bothwell Curry, a retired school teacher. Miss Curry was a friend and companion of Mary and Mrs Hill Burton, and frequently cared for the Geddes children at the Burtons' home on the shores of Loch Ness. Many friends had expressed their dismay at Geddes's venture, though others had provided money towards helping to rehabilitate the refugees. Not least among those who were dismayed was Bailie Pollard, who acted as chairman of the Town & Gown Association. The following is part of a draft letter, written by Geddes in Cyprus on 30th January, in which he was working towards a justification and explanation of his mission:

Here as at home I can honestly say that the general development of the schemes of the Town & Gown Association remains central interest. Despite the wealth of new impressions and interests, they all centre as of old; perspectives change, and new sides of educational and economic development present themselves—that is all; there is no loss of interest in the older and existing ones, which are seldom far away from my mind, in fact I hope that I may be of more use to these when I return.

Let me recall that I insisted before leaving on the use to the whole organisation of *devolving* as far as possible my ordinary responsibilities; (1) to directors and staff, (2) to younger men etc. Thus besides Town & Gown, and internal affairs of University Hall, the organisation of Outlook

Tower, of Summer Meeting of Publishing etc., are all being attended to; and, I doubt not, on the whole better than would have been the case had I retained the reins. Personally, as I explained, I wanted change of occupation and scene, freshening and maturation of own thought, botanical and geographical on one side, social, political and ethical on the other.

I wished too to begin my political education, with some understanding of the Eastern Question (with its minor Armenian one) and to test the geographical and economic hypotheses I had formed. Let me mention again the central one: To understand the general Unity and Continuity (and Tragedy) of History we have to keep in mind (1) that Europe, Asia, and Africa are not three continents (as foolish schoolbooks taught us!), but that of the great main Asiatic mass Europe is but the peninsular West; (2) A main-spring of History, as all agree, is the recurrent torrent of pastoral immigrations—and these again are to be explained by that gradual upheaval and desiccation of Asia, the desert thus driving out its children. With this comes the history of the Mediterranean peoples, as largely a destruction of their region. Disforesting for pasturage and agriculture, for building or shipping, brings with it destruction of soil— hills bared, to flood plains and choke ports—thus the history and the present ruined state of Cyprus, the general decay of the Turks, the special Armenian atrocities, or even the special madness (mania of suspicion, authority etc.) of the Sultan, are all explained within the same general thesis.

Why all this so academic disquisition? Because it is a basis of *action* as well—for Eastern question and Turkish question, general Historic or special Armenian question, *a type area may be selected—and this in Cyprus!* Here is East in West, and West in East, since the earliest times (always too in occupation by the Sea-Kings, be they from Tyre or London!). Here we can see the geographical ruin in all its stages; here too the social ruin, for in this wonderful island of tombs the British Museum excavations are but mechanical and super- ficial; the main survivals of the past, all the historic stages are in the living village, the living language, (thus British words survive into the present British occupation from the Saxon soldiers of Richard Coeur de Lion!). This little town of Nicosia, (itself reminding you of Stirling and Damascus strangely mixed, as in a dream), lies on the middle of the central plain between two mountain ranges, and thus commands a view of the essentials of the whole island . . .

In other words Geddes had found an historic but neglected Valley Section which cried out for interpretation and remedy. There were two practical issues affecting the whole island that caused him particular concern: the roads were carelessly planned, acting as "tentacles of the towns, not the arteries of the village", and the means of irrigation had fallen into disrepair and disuse, thus impoverishing the agriculture. Some of the concepts expressed in the letter to Bailie Pollard might sound rather full of abstract grandeur, but the sojourn in Cyprus was in fact an occasion when the two sides of Geddes's nature, the scientific and the imaginative, found immediate and successful expression. Besides Anna, he was accompanied by one of the students from University Hall, a Mr Fox Pitt, and they were later joined by an Armenian from the Montpellier School of Agriculture, Mr Salmaslian. Between them, they accomplished a great deal.

After landing on 13th January, their first two days were spent in Larnaka visiting houses that had been allocated to Armenians, seeing local authorities and listing possible occupations suitable for the refugees (of whom there were about 500 on the island), and looking at farms and gardens that might be cultivated by them. 15th and 16th January were spent in Nicosia, staying with Mr and Mrs J. R. van Milligan, who became close friends. Mr van Milligan worked for the Ottoman Bank, and proved a mine of information about the possibility of acquiring land and property on behalf of the refugees so that they could develop their own occupations and industries, and participate in those that were well-established—such as silk-farming and fruit-growing.

17th–27th January was spent at Government House, where at first the authorities were "hospitable and courteous but very reserved on Armenian questions". The Geddeses spent a week riding around on mules, studying the agricultural possibilities, and it did not take long before Geddes drew near to fulfilling the Governor's "practical man's desire for a well-digested scheme to be laid before him and adhered to". 28th–30th

January was spent driving with van Milligan to Limassol—through fever-striken villages and "wretched farming of beautiful valley"—where they visited many people concerned with the refugee problem. Mr Salmaslian arrived from Alexandria, and was immediately taken around the Limassol neighbourhood where he made suggestions for cultivating various neglected gardens that were available. Two young Armenians had found a fruit and vegetable garden which they wished to work, but they had not the necessary capital for a horse to work the water-wheel, a cart to carry the produce, or extra labour. Geddes reported to the relief committee:

> Salmaslian went into this with them and advised an advance of £20 which I accordingly have given them, half paid now and half when they need it shortly—on the understanding (1) that they employ never less than two and if possible three Armenian families, feeding them as far as possible from the ground, lodging them on the farm, and thus paying them less money wages. (2) That they give first offer of produce at lowest wholesale market rate to compatriots—thus cheapening Armenian living and finding them market. (3) That they pay no interest but repay in instalments in course of three years.

Similar arrangements were made with a towel-maker, who needed looms and facilities for training weavers.

One of Geddes's complaints was that available money from charitable sources was often specifically designated for women and children, whereas he deemed the main need to be to help men get established in work so that they would be able to support their families.

By March, Salmaslian had set up a silk school in Nicosia, "to grow and distribute the wonderful cocoon of the island; one of the biggest, trickiest (and quite the strongest) in the world, but which has been almost killed out for lack of the ordinary Pasteurian precautions". A 1,500-acre farm was purchased nearby in Geddes's name, so that mulberry trees could be cultivated for feeding the silkworms, and he started negotiations for a second, larger farm, with the help of van Milligan. An Armenian monastery offered 100 acres of land rent free, to which about fifteen families were moved.

Small workshops for making agricultural implements and distilling flowers were also established. Geddes wrote to Mary and Mrs Hill Burton telling them of these successes, but also allowing them to see the darker side of colonial government in what is virtually a self-contained social parable:

> ... the woeful and piteous oppression of these poor people—of whose total agricultural yield of £500,000 or thereby, the government extorts (collects, the wise call it) nearly £200,000. ... Then the usurers (9% legal, 12% to 30% or even 60% really) get a lion's share of the rest; so the peasant goes hungry to the café; the strong, raw wine goes to his dulled head, his embittered heart; he quarrels, the knives flash out and a dying man is carried home. The police come but often not even the mourners will tell. So the Lord Chief Justice shakes his wise wig and writes a report (innocent of any glimpse of social facts or theories), saying (1) that there is widespread and increasing demoralisation in Cyprus and that an increase of the Police Force (doubled, nay far more since my occupation) is the one thing needful. So he gets it, and the best of the growing youths are taken off the fields to this army and new taxes are levied to pay for larger barracks and larger prisons. So these surviving peasants go to the usurer again to borrow once more—are then doubly poorer. New money = new crime = new report by Lord Chief Injustice = new police and so on, in downward spiral. This is what they call the progress resulting from British Rule.

As the time drew nearer for Geddes to leave Cyprus in order to prepare for the summer term at Dundee, he was beginning to hope that the nucleus might have been established in Nicosia for the formation of an international agricultural school, "to which I should like to bring by and by some of the young fellows who at present go to the Colonies without any preparation and too commonly come to loss and grief in consequence". Writing of this to a military acquaintance in London, who had shown interest in the Armenian projects, Geddes embarked into one of his more optimistic flights of fancy, as he tried to describe the kind of person needed to help organize such a school:

I want to ask your help in finding one of the men I still need—a (young?) soldier—preferably engineer—as my colleague—who is disposed to exchange sword for plough-share, yet bring his military training and virtues to the task. . . . Here I have a capital group of young colleagues already, but they need a soldier among them. Here for instance is no lack of agricultural science, fresh from Montpellier, or skill fresh from the soil. The business ability too is not lacking. I can temporarily energise (and I hope in some measure permanently awaken) such young fellows; but where I shall fail alone is that I cannot discipline them—I have not time—nor have I the discipline in myself! They need their habits formed—from early rising to regular breakfast hour and onward through the day's work and play —and here any steady sergeant would be worth academic senates. But I want more than this: an engineer accustomed to plan and survey—to irrigation work—yet who would not disdain our tiny dams and trifling tree-plantings, made with few labourers, and as far as may be with our own hands. All this an engineer sergeant could do and much more I doubt not; but I want more still, a student used to book and languages, or at least with some faculty for these, yet a student accustomed to think in the open air and not simply on paper in drawing-office and study, and who could not only learn to take meteorological observations but to reason on them, and not only to understand a geological section on paper or even in the field, but to be or become something of a hydro-geologist and so not only engineer surface water but see where (and how) to mine for deep water too. . . . Then, too, he must have that human element . . . he must care (as a good officer does) for his young fellows, he must care and teach them to care too for the villagers (Greek and Turk here are alike good fellows of whom anything might be made: it is only the Greek usurer, the Turk official who are bad, as I am sure you know). . . . What is he to get for this he may fairly ask? Well, pretty much what the army would give him at best: hard work and ample responsibility with as little pay as may be—but a livelihood and a life. Better than hanging about Pall Mall or the West End of Edinburgh.

Better indeed! (In fact the description was not hopelessly

unrealistic, for twenty years later it would exactly fit Geddes's own son, Alasdair.)

Amid their survey and organization work, Anna and Patrick managed to take a little time off for recreation. Mr and Mrs van Milligan's daughter Ruth, who was fourteen at the time of their visit, recalled such occasions in a letter written to Norah almost fifty years later:

I remember only such things as the picnics and PG being bolted with when he was riding one of our fiery ponies— and a series of tableaux, representing the historical procession which had passed through the island—Phoenicians, Greeks, Romans, Turks, etc. I still have that programme and photos taken of several of the tableaux—they were all inspired by your parents and worked up by my mother— though I can't remember PG being there for the actual performance. . . . I well remember the paraffin film as a protection against mosquitoes . . . and behind it all, as a delightful restful background, was your mother's playing of the piano.

For Geddes, this opportunity to apply his geological, botanical and social knowledge to a beautiful but neglected island, was a "freshening" of the highest order, and inevitably his thoughts ranged beyond the immediate needs of the refugees. He could read a landscape and its inhabitants like a mathematician can read a complex equation, but he could also add to his reading images from history, poetry and philosophy. To see an area, be it rural or urban, in an impoverished condition, provoked in him an urgent need to act; not in the role of owner or conqueror, but more as a practical healer, so that the place concerned could quickly be restored to its people in a state of health and utility. When he left Cyprus at the end of March, he had every reason to believe that his work on behalf of the refugees would continue to bear fruit, and some hope that his ideas and suggestions for the island as a whole would reverberate more widely.

In October, a company called The Eastern and Colonial Association was registered

to take over and farm and develop the two estates of Kouklia and Athalassa examined and purchased by Professor Geddes, in the winter of 1896–7, a half-share in the silk School and Establishment for producing silk worms in Nicosia, partly established by him, and to purchase, lease, develop and farm other estates and undertakings in Cyprus as the opportunity of acquiring the same on extremely favourable terms might present itself.

Its directors included Henry Beveridge, an engineer, and a spice merchant, with Geddes himself as chairman—a post he resigned six months later "because of other commitments". In January and February 1898 he delivered a course of three lectures on Cyprus at the Royal Institute in Albemarle Street. (The traffic problems of the day were alleviated by telling those invited to the lectures "that Coachmen may be ordered to set down with their Horses' heads towards Piccadilly, and to take up towards Grafton Street".)

Meanwhile in Cyprus itself, the one thing Geddes had not bargained for started to happen: the Armenians slowly began to leave the island, lured by the commercial opportunities elsewhere, particularly in America. There were still opportunities for continuing their agricultural developments for the benefit of the island, but according to John Ross, who was initially involved in the Company, Geddes had

> enlisted in the Company the support and assistance of men who only understood what he was after in their own limited and very so-called business fashion, and proceeded to get rid of him and all the rest of us who had any sympathy with him. In fact they said, "now that we have got rid of all these impractical ideas we shall begin to make things hum". Well he left them to it, but things never hummed and never have hummed and the thing slowly petered out.

All that remained of Geddes's initiative were some written comments on the agriculture, irrigation and reafforestation of the island—some of which did seep through to members of the Colonial Service.

Almost the last memento of Geddes's Cyprus adventure is a letter dated 30th April 1900, written to an official in Nicosia, negotiating the return of some antiquities which he had bought in 1897 and left behind in the silk school:

I would be very glad if you would instruct some capable person to pack up the collection in a safe way with layers of paper so as to stand the rough handling of the voyage. I suppose a lot of the pots and glasses would go best into some of the big vases, but I need not ask for all the big vases to be sent home. Would you care to accept them, or if any be of sufficient value for the Museum would you invite the authorities to accept them? Similarly for the big white marble lion. I could make good use of that here, and it might perhaps be packed separately. Still, if that is of any value to the Museum or yourself, I should not wish it to be sent home.

Then in a hurried postcript he recalls: "There should also be some riding boots, some underclothing, silk, etc.", adding "but if missing, never mind."

Chapter 11

FIN DE SIÈCLE

THE LAST YEARS of the century brought both sadness and new opportunities. Geddes was depressed by the rumbling prophecies of war; anxious to strengthen cultural ties with France and America, and to avoid the influence of "Prussianism" which he felt was infiltrating so many aspects of both German and English life. He wrote to a French friend; "Jingo seems just now as much the preponderant idol as ever Gladstone was; Rhodes is its prophet; Kitchener, Chamberlain, Rosebery, Balfour & Co. are his bodyguard or warriors and priests." The Cyprus expedition had strengthened his desire for international as well as regional co-operative action, and he was trying to envisage ways of participating in the 1900 Paris *Exposition Universelle*. Perhaps because he was pausing before seeking a wider sphere of influence, he was uncharacteristically dispirited when things went wrong in Edinburgh; he seemed for a while to lack the vigour or optimism to seize instant advantage from adversity as he once might have done.

One incident which upset him, and which illustrates the conviction of his moral earnestness as far as sexual matters were concerned, occurred in June 1897 at Ramsay Lodge. The housekeeper there reported that two servants were "living on improper relations" with a student resident. The maids were instantly dismissed, and the student agreed to leave, but not before he had revealed that other students had been involved. He was asked to produce them, but only one—who also left— owned up, the identity of the others remaining unknown. Geddes discussed the implications of the scandal with Thomas Whitson, and even went so far as to suggest it meant the failure of the whole University Hall scheme. He would not have felt like this if a student had been discovered having sexual relations with a girl because they were passionately in love; it was the deliberate involvement of several students with maidservants

for purely sexual ends which upset him. Whitson sent him a
comforting note:

> I can't get your wearied face out of my mind. . . . Of course
> the whole thing is beastly and I for one felt much inclined
> to throw over the whole show. It knocked the bottom out of
> me for three days. Your morals are no doubt very different
> and of a much higher grade than mine. Hence it is possible
> that you may feel it more . . . but I confess that I feel sur-
> prised that you let this be such a slap in the face to you.
> The idea of such a thing happening has all along been
> familiar to me and I thought to you also.

Two days later Geddes, on behalf of the Town & Gown Association, sent a long peroration to the residents at Ramsay
Lodge, concerning the responsibilities of self-government. He
concluded:

> Upholding as we do the principle of your liberty and self-
> government, we must all realise, must we not, that these are
> fraught with individual and collective dangers. Liberty must
> always have its dangers: that is why the old education went
> wrong and gave little of it! Hence it is that associations for
> purposes of material comfort alone, inevitably degenerate.
> For, just as our muscular tone speedily fails without active
> exercise, and our intellectual tone cannot exist without active
> mental culture, so our moral tone, without clearly formed
> moral purpose of one kind or another also sinks, and indeed
> most surely of all—most silently too, generally quite un-
> observed, until the necessarily resulting disaster.
>
> Happily, however, the converse is no less true: given any
> group or society with high corporate and individual feeling,
> and correspondingly defined aims, its members rapidly
> acquire and express these, and hence it is that the tradition
> of every college is founded not on its material comfort, good
> though that may be, but on things far more material to it:
> upon its pure and correspondingly strenuous physical life,
> its atmosphere of culture and intellectual ambitions, its
> individual spirit of duty, its collective soul of honour.
>
> You will not take this little discourse amiss; for believe us,
> we wish also to take it to ourselves.

The setting up of Town & Gown had not really eased
Geddes's personal financial position, and he still tended to dip
into his own pocket to solve minor financial crises. In November
1897, Marr asked for a grant of £400 from Town & Gown to
enable him to continue the development of the Outlook Tower,
but the directors could only vote him £50 to catch up on outstanding bills, and they set up a committee consisting of Crum
Brown, Herbertson, Geddes and Marr himself to manage any
further grant of capital. By May of 1898, Whitson was writing
to Geddes:

> I have your note and as requested have handed on to Dun-
> can a cheque for ten guineas. But when is all this to stop?
> Personally I quite understood that this the *last* panel for
> Ramsay Lodge had been paid for; it seems like the other day
> since we sent him £26 or something like that.
>
> Duncan must have got hundreds out of you. And you talk
> of giving him further commissions. For goodness sake don't.
> T & G can't afford it, still less can you and besides you can
> get something which pleases the average eye better . . . at
> less than half the cost.
>
> . . . Many things annoy me just now. We are being pressed
> for money for Outlook Tower and yet mark you there is not
> the remotest chance of *1d of rent* coming in. We must either
> get some wealthy person to guarantee the rent or as land-
> lords we must enter into possession and turn the place into a
> student residence or something.
>
> This sort of thing won't do. It can only have one ending
> and it has gone far enough already if not too far. There is
> no one in charge. You and Marr are both away. It is next
> to impossible to get a letter from the one and the other has
> too many irons in the fire already . . .

Whitson, who was later to become Sir Thomas Whitson, Lord
Provost of Edinburgh, probably did more than anyone else to
keep the feet of the Town & Gown Association on the ground,
but John Ross once remarked: "I have always felt that he had
little, if any, apprehension of, and certainly was not much
interested in, the theories which lay behind P.G.'s action." (In
later years Whitson's support for Geddes was spurred on by his
wife, who did sterling work at the Outlook Tower.) It may have

been to Whitson that Geddes first used a description of himself
that he was often to repeat when the inevitable accusation of
"too many irons in the fire" came up: he used to reply that he
was like the schoolboy who rang the bell and ran away. Certainly after Geddes's death, Whitson was to recall that in the
late 1880's the Edinburgh Social Union members had blamed
Geddes "for leaving them in the lurch after starting the organization and giving them the ideas", and to imply that similar
behaviour occurred throughout Geddes's life. John Ross, who
like Whitson was an accountant and an eminently practical
man, but more in tune with Geddes's ideas, just said: "Is the
Sower to be blamed because some of the seed fell on stony
ground?"

Another contretemps which occurred in 1898 particularly
aroused Geddes's anger. This concerned the authorities of New
College, the divinity school situated in Mound Place by part
of University Hall, where Geddes was organizing some street
improvements. In order to carry these out properly, he needed
to infringe on a portion of land belonging to the College, whose
legal advisers demanded £600 for it. Geddes retaliated by
offering them another piece of ground plus £300. The rather
complex interchange concerning these matters promoted some
genuine misunderstandings, but in the end Geddes became
furious at what he considered to be the Church's obstinacy and
niggardliness, and he wrote to the Reverend Dr James Stalker:

On the completion of a series of improvements which have
now extended over some fifteen years, permit me to offer you
the accompanying photograph and ground plan. These improvements have now touched or included some thirty-seven
of the Old Edinburgh courts and closes, and involved a turn-
over of upwards of £120,000, and while the undertaking has
been so far conducted on ordinary business principles without loss of principal or interest to any person concerned
other than myself, my accountants will certify that the whole
business while solvent has fully avoided the risk of any
criticism of excessive money making. I have for some time
been winding up this business, and removing it from Edinburgh to continue it in quarters where hygienic and architectural construction meets if not with less apathy at least
with less opposition. . . .

It is on my conviction of the prevalence of individual and civic high-feeling that I think it well frankly to inform you that the determining reason of this change primarily is sheer economy of life, and . . . I think it right that you should know and consider, for whatever you may think it worth, this very definite and discouraging impression: that, of all the harsh, i.e. not only ungenerous but to my mind unjust dealings of which I have been sufferer or spectator during twenty years of business your Body stands absolutely and unquestionably first. That so eminent and educative a Body, (of which the members not only individually but even corporately stood in my imagination, as in the public's eye, for collegiate ideals alike in architectural and non-material things, for a recognition of civic and hygienic improvement and not merely corporate gain, for the due infusion with the business spirit of some element of consideration for others, and of arbitration for force and law), should in practice conduct these affairs in so strictly legal a manner with a legal ability alike in general strategy and in detail management— from this I now retreat for good.

I need not recall in detail the innumerable large and small difficulties which we have had during a good many years, from the material vandalism which wantonly destroyed my gift of decorative paintings, to the material injustice of your many times renewed rejections of arbitration on each and every point on which I have protested against your exactions.

In making these criticisms I am of course prepared to justify them should your memory require. But my real object in writing thus strongly is not that of offering unasked criticisms, of grumbling over past disappointments or defeats, or otherwise of stirring bygones. I am clearly conscious too that I cannot always have been right, that I must have often laid myself open to misunderstanding, and to fair criticism; that my constant insistence on material improvements has made me a troublesome neighbour; but my real reason for saying these things is to ask you to consider whether your methods of confiding your affairs to the strictly legal, as distinguished from the business, mind is even for your material interest, for your good-neighbourhood, for your civic responsibilities, or your public example.

That in practical affairs caution and coolness are needed, my defects of temperament and training have brought me as many lessons as another, though in practical efficiency and moral result I submit that it is possible to carry this too far. Our Edinburgh legal idea of business which eliminates all considerations of feeling, individual or public, which attains the ideal and utmost coldness to all, coinciding with the lowest circle of the Inferno—that of Ice; for your own sake and that of others, why stay there?

The affair was smoothed over, but the letter was indicative of Geddes's increasing impatience with Edinburgh and it hints of his future involvement with a students' hostel scheme in London.

Early in the same year his mother had died, aged eighty-two. Janet Geddes had been bed-ridden for some time—not with any specific illness, but just a gradual weariness with life. Alexander Geddes, now ninety, knew that he would not live for very much longer, and as a token of his special affection for his youngest son, he sent him his watch. Patrick replied:

My dear Father,   16 April 1898
I was much touched by your kindness and thoughtfulness in sending me your watch, which I accept with great pleasure, handing my own one to Alasdair when he is a bit bigger. I cannot tell you how much pleasure it gives me almost every time I look at it, as it calls up so many old and happy memories of you and home, from the time when I used to creep into bed between you and mother, and tremble at the big B.O. and the fingers coming to gobble me, and then be amused and delighted with the golden face and tick-tick inside. So your watch not only tells me the present time, but calls up the old times also; the watch pocket also with its embroidery by mother's hands will always be a dear and sacred possession, and call up her kind face also.

Now that I have the responsibilities of a father in my turn, dear dad, it is a great thing for me to have your example to look back and fall upon. As I have told you before, I have been a pupil of many great naturalists, each of whom knew far more than you ever dreamt of, but I have to thank *you* for my love of nature and of gardens. Here I am making a beautiful old place, I trust, more beautiful: if all goes well and I'm spared, it will be one of the very nicest little gardens in the County, but the one thing I wish for it is your presence, to walk round it with me and let me show you what I have been doing with my little spade and barrow, since I used to trot round with the little "Express" after the big "Tally Ho".

I wish you could start your grandchildren as you started me; but I must try and do it for you, and as you used to do. Norah and Alasdair are good little gardeners, planting whole long borders of daisies and crocuses and sticking to their work very well, which is the best sign for their growing up.

Tomorrow being Sunday, we shall go round the garden together as you used to take us, and we shall think of mother and you and of dear Jessie too: and we shall call the new apple-trees after the children, and ourselves, so that each one shall have his or her tree as in the dear old garden at Mount Tabor. And the big, beautiful old pear tree (winter pears, like that on your wall just outside the window, but tall and grand like a forest tree almost) shall be "Grandfather's tree", and the old apple in the same way shall be "Grannie's"; and already it wears over its roots a great crown of white blossom —a wreath of memory, yet also of joy.

And last of all, dear father, the watch speaks of the future also. I am passing through middle age towards age itself; and believe me, I feel the responsibility; it helps me to look beyond this hour and day, into the years, and even to see things from the widest standpoint, of eternity.

Believe me always, Your loving son

Pat.

The garden to which he referred was the one at Craufurd, where the Geddes family were spending quite long periods, while letting their flat at Ramsay Garden. Other colleagues from the Old Town community would stay at the big house, and Norah, Alasdair and three-year-old Arthur learned to care for animals as well as plants. Norah, looking back somewhat tartly on her childhood, recalled: "In their capacity as earnest educators our parents saw to it that we had pets in order to foster kindness to creatures." There were a pair of ringed grey doves, miniature turtles, a pig, a collie, a donkey, and hens:

"I had not affection for hens . . . but to feed them was my daily chore."

The family were in fact never settled at Craufurd long enough for Geddes's whole plan of education to evolve there (and when they moved, Norah recalled that the animals all mysteriously disappeared). But the ideas he had in mind were outlined in a letter to a friend, Mrs Jane Whyte, who was anxious to send her son, Aird, out to Craufurd every Saturday morning to act as an apprentice gardener. Nothing inspired Geddes to write long, long letters more than enquiries for advice about education. His reply to Mrs Whyte ran to over two thousand words, and it explains how he wanted children to experience the occupations and possibilities of life as summarized in the Valley Section: thus, by the time they were adults, they would have experienced the types of existence symbolized by the Hunter, Shepherd, Peasant, Fisher, Forester and Miner:

. . . we have to choose clearly. (a) Have our boys educated by (1) a head master, (2) a don, and (3) finally by a game-keeper, as the prevailing manner is. Or (b) begin with the hunter, so as not to end there; educate them (1) with the fisher and naturalist-hunter (like J. A. Thomson at Lochalsh), then (2) with the botanist and forester (like Robert Smith with his map at Pitreavie), (3) with the shepherd. (Would I had one to name, but he should not be ill to find.) All this is still only primary education. Still, all that is good in the dominant culture may be thus reached, and much more. Then comes a higher stage, one of subtler pleasures and steadier disciplines than Law and Sport and War and Business together have to show. I mean the steady Chinese patience of the spade, brightened with the changing blossoms and fruit of the seasons. Thus your boy is raised to the level of a higher, deeper, and truer civilisation, the agricultural, which makes possible a true secondary and technical education. So this is what you good mothers and we thinking educationists have now to unite for—despite heads and dons, examiners and clubmen, gamekeepers, and the fashion generally—and from this elemental rustic plane of civilisation he may go on into many a paradise of culture.

His projects with his own children included many simplified

versions of the charts and tabulations which he always used for lectures. One such project, set for Norah, was aimed to discover "What became of yesterday's sunshine?" The growth of leaves (which later would change into other substances such as peat and coal), and the capturing of images of light by means of photography, were just two of the suggested answers. Another project concerned geology, and the action of volcanoes was to be suggested by the small explosions caused by throwing drops of water on the fire, while the erosion of stone by water could be demonstrated by the action of water tipped along the garden path.

An educational scheme of a more ambitious nature was absorbing him during 1898. This was to develop a company which would manufacture Elisée Reclus's designs for relief globes, 40 feet in diameter, and also publish a range of panoramas, maps and synoptic charts. These globes would hopefully be bought and displayed in museums and exhibition buildings, and pave the way for the really huge one (80 feet in diameter) which Reclus had prepared designs for, and which Geddes was hoping to find sponsors for in time to have it made for the 1900 Paris Exhibition. With this aim in view, he joined the annual meeting of the British Association for the Advancement of Science in September in Bristol, accompanied by Elisée Reclus, A. Picard (who was to be Director-General of the exhibition), Paul Reclus, and Tom Marr. He had been out of touch with the Association for several years, and enjoyed meeting up with old friends. As well as attending committee meetings and lectures, the party visited the Severn Tunnel, Chepstow Castle (returning "by Brunel's strange bridge"), Cheddar and Glastonbury, and Marr found time to make a brief survey of Bristol. They went bathing, Geddes writing to Anna: "old Reclus like a river god. Imagine his dripping beard and hair and mixture of grim and gentle aspects!"

Besides discussing plans for the globe, Geddes developed a plan to hold a summer school at the exhibition, designed to guide people around the many pavilions, and to relate their historical, cultural and sociological implications in a series of lectures. An international committee of patrons was to be set up in order to finance the school, and its teaching members were to be drawn from Britain, Europe and America. It was decided that Geddes should visit America to find patrons, and

John Stivenson

Alexander Geddes

Janet Geddes (*née* Stivenson)

Jessie Geddes

Patrick Geddes at fifteen

Mount Tabor Cottage in 1973

From the top of
Kinnoull Hill, 1973

Patrick Geddes, *c.* 1886

Patrick Geddes
at twenty-four

James Court, 1852,
thirty-five years before
Geddes's improvements

James Court, 1973,
sadly deteriorated,
eighty-five years after
Geddes's improvements

Anna Geddes with
Norah, Alasdair and
Arthur, *c.* 1899

Ramsay Garden, 1973—
the cupola and turret roof
of the Outlook Tower
can be seen in
the middle distance

Arbor Saeculorum, design for stained-glass window in the Outlook Tower

MINER   WOODMA

Illustrations from the Dunfermline report showing (*a*) actual
state of Monastery Street in 1903
and (*b*) suggestions for its improvement into Monastery Place

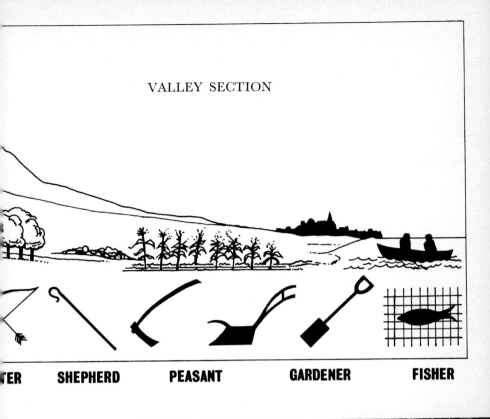

VALLEY SECTION

ER   SHEPHERD   PEASANT   GARDENER   FISHER

Pittencrieff Park, 1973

Patrick Geddes   Anna and Patrick Geddes, *c.* 1910

Patrick Geddes in India, *c.* 1915

also to endeavour to establish financial backing for the globe. However, as the estimate for making the latter stood at £200,000, hopes for its achievement were not very high.

Geddes intended to cover the costs of his American tour partly by lecturing, but he could not hope to cover all his expenses and once again he was in difficulties as far as his personal finances went. After a little gentle preliminary negotiation with John Ross as mediator, Martin White agreed to act as his guarantor for a £2,000 overdraft, but insisted on proper sureties. White wrote to Geddes:

> You have pulled through big things in the past and one has gained confidence, otherwise I should have listened to nothing. It would not in my judgement have been in your interest to do anything now if you had not been pretty successful. I must leave the matter in the hands of the lawyers to do what seems fair. Note I am not driving a bargain to squeeze anything out of you. I am getting absolutely nothing out of this and am only doing it to help a good old friend. You will get back all your securities on paying off the overdraft and relinquishing my letter to the Bank. You are therefore at no disadvantage.

Meanwhile, prior to leaving for America, Geddes was busy fermenting his globe publishing scheme, which he hoped to develop with the aid of John Ross and Victor Branford. He had a vision of forming an International Geographical Syndidate which would promote Globe Tower Companies (versions of the Outlook Tower) in different cities. However, as he commented in a letter to Ross and Branford:

> All this of course . . . is still unfamiliar to people. We need to bring it into the existing stream of ideas and that is where, as you know, I personally am weakest: I have not the aptitude for using or combining with existing organisations.

At the end of November 1898 Mrs Hill Burton died, and Geddes wrote to Mary:

> I, too (with my dear, dear father past 90—and my own mother also gone at the beginning of this year) feel the

solemnity and responsibility of standing in the elder ranks as
I thus practically do, and I think it is the feeling that there
is a younger world to whom we have to be something of what
our elders were to us that nerves me for life, more than even
the hope of still some personal work and career and achievement before the shadows close and the evening weariness
comes.

He went up to Loch Ness for the funeral, and wrote to Anna
from the Burtons' home:

Morning more beautiful than anything further south, in a
sombre glory of leaden blue and silver, of citrine and russet
autumn leaves, and birches wonderful in purple mists of
branchlets, yet here and there one in complete vesture of
gold, all unswept by the wind. Whin too, in blossom here
and there by the way, and gorgeous fungus patches and red-
berried holly; none of these more than bright incidents, yet
like jewels on the bright but gravely mixed tartans of the
autumn hills. Then the gloom of the shower and the sombre
brilliance of the farthest blue hills—all still waiting to be
fully painted. I felt the necessity of seeing as a main joy for
every life, and that, if one could but "teach"—i.e. perhaps
not even "awake" or "develop", but simply preserve from
destruction—the child's artistic sense, the whole of life would
be relieved at every moment, and its great moments rise to
ecstasies few have felt, and those rarely, which is why we
wonder at them and call them poets. And all this time I was
not forgetting the house of sorrow; but this solemn splendour
of winter pageantry was the right background for it all.

Then here, warmly welcomed, dried, warmed by the kind
greetings no less than by the material fire; then to the room
with the dear, dead face, like a bust in tinted marble, strong
and sweet as of old. In daylight, the whole house as it should
be and as she would have wished it. One thinks more than
one can set down; it is a great thing to have so much to
remember; friendships are so rare in the world, and this was
more; there was no exaggeration in our all feeling her as
"mother" and "granny"—but the simple fact.

Christmas was spent in traditional fashion at Craufurd, and

Geddes took the opportunity to write a 27-page letter to his nieces and nephews in New Zealand, describing in full the decorations, sweetmeats and present-giving, and opening out into a full-dress examination of their historical and philosophical implications.

He sailed for New York in the middle of February 1899, disliking the "stupid or clever but most horrid modern songs" enjoyed by his fellow passengers after dinner in the evenings, and taking pleasure from his children's parting gift—a bunch of snowdrops. After a rough and stormy crossing, there was ice on the sea near the Hudson river, "all golden sheen and violet". He found Manhattan at first sight to be "fearfully and wonderfully made—sublime and ridiculous in one". From the boat the skyscrapers were like

> a wharf piled with packing cases, standing on end, their hard skylines relieved into irregular ugliness by an occasional inverted piano-leg or paraffin lamp stand. Yet as the ship sweeps on, and you realise the appalling magnitude of these masses, which rise and rise into the sky above as you approach and change and drift with the ship's motion into the strangest skylines—you cannot but recall the piled up picturesqueness of Old Edinburgh, of Stamboul itself, and if one could but see this at dusk, it would have a quality by no means altogether inferior to either.

Leaving his baggage, he strolled up from the wharves into the city, where a blizzard had filled the streets with snow "covered with dirt, banana skins and ashes". But he found the air clean and smokeless, and the grid system "made it the easiest of towns to understand". He stayed at the University Settlement in Rivington Street, enjoying the simple accommodation after the "over-decorated showy ugliness" of the ship and was reminded of his time as a student in Paris. He was moved by the files of unemployed who lined the roadways every morning waiting to be organized for snow-clearing, momentarily regretting that he had no old breeches and boots to match his old jacket, so that he too might have taken a shovel and become acquainted with a few of the poor, just as he used to know some of the tramps in the Lawnmarket in Edinburgh. However, he was quickly involved in meeting university, museum, municipal

and newspaper men, and becoming acquainted with the central
part of New York. He found the "immensity and luxury" of
the new hotels to be "beyond description", but wrote to Anna
that "Ramsay Garden, Esplanade and Gardens are infinitely
better than Fifth Avenue and Central Park! If these are
millionaires, what billionaires we have been all the time,
without knowing it sufficiently perhaps". After a few days of
talks and visits to people's homes, he formed "the impression
of the Americans as a strange race, dwelling in elevators and
subsisting on ice-creams", their "nerve centres dulled by over
stimulation, your ice is mixed with four or five sorts for instance
—all coloured and flavoured differently, and they often eat
tranversely instead of successively, and that goes through all.
If need of reaction gives hope of it, the severest Emersonian
simplicity will soon again be having its turn."

He lectured in New York, Philadelphia and Chicago, finding a good deal of support for his ideas, and interest in the
possibilities of participation in the 1900 Summer School. However, it was not easy to solicit definite patronage without more
concrete financial support from the European side. By March
17th he was lecturing in Boston, from where he wrote a letter
to Anna and one to his children.

Darling winsome,
    . . . What shall I say? That absence does make fonder; that
it constantly makes me realise how great and rare our happiness is, how delightful and beautiful our home, how noble our
city and country—for oh, woe's me! this vast wealth and
energy as yet produces little save a pandemonium-city, its
very luxuries, of hot blasts and ice, of whirling electric cars,
of decoration and dress, of feasts and flare, making up an impression which is generally more painful than pleasant—and
which forces the impression that America is the martyr of her
own progress—from which we shall reap in time without the
whole turmoil of human life, the whole wreck of environment. Yet there are better things here from part beginnings
too of neotechnic future. And it is coming fast, a great ferment
of changes.
    This is not writing as I began—yet in a way it is: for home
and calm are the pendants to this restless phantasmagoria
here. And you, poor dear, must know it; there is work and

scope here for both of us—and though I would fain not have too much of it, some will be expedient and helpful and wise—strengthening and useful to ourselves and to others. And together we would be enjoying it more than I can alone.

People are moving fast in thought, and are more ready for what I have to say than at home; their own thought too is more congenial and complementary often than I find at home . . .

But, oh, dear lassie, how I long with it all for you, and to have you in my arms again—and all, and all—and *all*.

And the dear little ones too. I wish often I could see them at play and asleep and round the table.

I am glad to be coming home in time for my session, etc., though not I fear for much of Craufurd . . .

Dear Children Three,
Thank you for your letters; and be sure to write once more; Baba too can draw something. I am sorry to have so little time to see what the children are like here; but a great many of them seem very nice little people indeed. American teachers and mothers are trying very hard just now to understand children and make things very nice for them, so that when they grow up and have children in their turn, they may do better still, and thus every crop of children be a better one than that before. Isn't that a nice idea?

Your pets and your flowers are your children, are they not, so you are beginning with them already.

Now goodbye today. X X X from your loving Daddy.

Despite his hectic programme, Geddes had found that meeting new people and seeing new places had refreshed and stimulated him in a way that no amount of quiet work at home would have done, and perhaps the love letter he wrote to Anna during his journey home in April, reveals a little guilt at having enjoyed himself so much. But when he said "and together we would be enjoying it more than I can alone", he certainly meant it. Although he liked short periods of solitude, he always missed the day-to-day companionship of Anna, who alone was completely familiar with his needs and ways of doing things.

. . . But mainly(est) the reason of my letter is to say how

penitent I feel for not writing more fully and posting more carefully, though I really took more thought and care than you can have supposed (ship *very* wobbly). It was however a very *very* full and busy time.

But I'll be a better husband now that I come back, you'll see, and recover myself by every penitence and obedience and submission and devotion, and obeisance and penance and worship and adoration that the heart of man can offer and the heart of woman desire! Yes dear, our constant affection is only strengthened by parting for a season, and now it glows all the brighter as we approach reunion—need I say how I have counted the time, and now the days and nights and hours! . . .

I am very well . . . and shall be quite ready for the summer's work. (One result too will please you. I feel more ready to *write* now also.)

But this is a love letter dearest; and I feel as young as ever to write that, as I am sure you do to read it.

Once again, he did not care very much for the style of life on board ship: "Perhaps the presence of the millionaires may have a chilling effect, e.g., Astor of Cliveden with his children, vigorous barbarians all; Cornelius Vanderbilt, a paralytic and worn-out invalid, and others whose names and faces I know not, but who are I understand, of scarcely less magnitude."

He had been back in Scotland just a month, settling with the family in Dundee for the university summer session, when his father became ill. Now ninety-one, Alexander Geddes sorely missed his wife, and during the year since her death his own engagement with life had become gradually weaker. He was dying, and Patrick sat by his bedside. The drifting white blossom on the gean trees had fallen. In the garden, and up Kinnoull Hill, the plants were thickening and deepening in colour towards the massed, surging green of midsummer.

For the only time in Patrick's memory, his father was assailed by doubt. He had wanted to die because he wanted to see Janet. Suddenly he dreaded that the abyss might lead to nowhere. He sought consolation.

"Oh, will I see her, Pat?"

And Patrick many years afterwards told Arthur, still with emotion: "And I lied, lied to him for the first time."

He replied to his father, who had laid the stable foundation on which he could build his own co-operative vision of the universe without recourse to exclusive religious faith: "Yes, oh surely yes."

Shortly afterwards, Alexander Geddes died.

Chapter 12

1900: THE I.A.A.S.A.E. IN AMERICA
AND PARIS

THE INTERNATIONAL ASSOCIATION for the Advancement
of Science, Arts and Education was the not altogether wieldy
title given to the organization to promote the 1900 Summer
School. In 1899, the British Association and the French
Association had met simultaneously at Dover and Boulogne,
and Geddes had commuted between the two, enrolling sponsors
for the I.A.A.S.A.E. He had been particularly helped in this
task by James Mavor, who was now professor of economics at
McGill University, Montreal, and not long afterwards the
British section's membership had reached 500. Geddes acted
as the section's Secretary, and Sir Archibald Geikie and the
Rt Hon. James Bryce were joint presidents. (Archibald Geikie,
brother of James, was director-general of the British Geological
Survey; and James Bryce was at that time Member of
Parliament for South Aberdeen, and had recently chaired a
Royal Commission on secondary education; a man of
tremendous energy and breadth of knowledge, he once caused
Queen Victoria to comment: "I like Mr Bryce. He knows so
much and is so modest.")

The purpose of the Summer School was to be a centre of
information and interpretation for the *Exposition Universelle*,
reporting on the findings of its many conferences (in graphic
as well as verbal terms), and providing descriptive lectures and
guides to its wealth of pavilions. To Geddes, such an exhibition
was a kind of Outlook Tower or thinking-machine writ large:
the many strands of life important to the contributing nations
being woven and displayed in one great, inter-connected
spectacle.

He sought and captured distinguished sponsors (including
those who simply allowed their names to appear on the list),
like a single-minded lepidopterist. When visting Perth in

connection with some business over his father's will, he saw
Sir Robert Pullar, who had long been acquainted with the
Geddes family, and whose dyeing factory "Pullar's of Perth"
dominated the little town. Geddes told Pullar all about his
scheme for the Summer School and was rewarded by the offer
of £3,000 to be used at his own discretion to further his
plans.

This undoubtedly made his wish to go on another tour of
the United States, this time with Anna, much more practical.
As he wrote to Mary Burton in July 1899, he felt "greatly
comforted, encouraged and renewed" by his stay in America,
and he was looking forward to re-visiting the country where a
sizeable number of people were outgoing and enthusiastic about
his ideas, even if their life-style was not always to his taste.
Mary was in the throes of trying to sell her home, but she
promised that she and Jeannie Curry would care for the
Geddes children in their parents' absence, should this be
possible. In the end the children in fact stayed with other
friends, and Anna and Patrick sailed for America at the end
of December.

Their tour covered many towns in the eastern states, and
they also travelled north to Montreal to visit Mavor at McGill,
and east to Buffalo (seeing the Niagara Falls in heavy snow)
and Chicago. Executive offices for the American section of the
I.A.A.S.A.E. were set up in New York, Philadelphia, Boston
and Chicago; Robert E. Ely (later director of the League for
Political Education) was appointed co-secretary with Geddes;
and William T. Harris (United States Commissioner of
Education) and Robert S. Woodward (President of the
American Association) acted as joint presidents; and among
the 400 members recruited were Alexander Bell, Andrew
Carnegie, Woodrow Wilson, G. Stanley Hall, John Dewey,
Jane Addams, Mrs Julia Ward Howe and Louis Tiffany.

Geddes's programme for one day in Boston in January, gives
an idea of his activities. At eleven o'clock he gave the third of
a series of four lectures on sex (the first had been attended by
600 people, but the number dropped once people became
acquainted with the strenuous intellectual content and muffled
mode of delivery); he and Anna were then guests for luncheon
at the Twentieth Century Club, where he gave a talk on the
aims of the I.A.A.S.A.E.; afterwards he visited a college club,

then he dined with a Harvard professor, and finally he spoke at eight o'clock on "Nature and the Study of Society" at the Boston Normal School. To begin with reporters attempted to keep up with his lectures and précis them in their newspapers, but soon they gave up the struggle. For Geddes, however, the individual contacts he had made no doubt compensated for some lack of communication with the people at large. G. Stanley Hall, president of Clark University in Worcester, in particular became a friend. His philosophy had much in common with Geddes's, for he claimed to have been educated by practising on his father's New England farm as many as seventy occupations.

Chicago was the high spot of the tour. There Geddes met Jane Addams—whom he nicknamed "the Abbess of Chicago" —and he and Anna stayed for a while at Hull House, seeing at close quarters the work she was doing for deprived urban youth. He also met John Dewey and visited his experimental school. Dewey is said to have described one of Geddes's lectures as the greatest, and most idea-provoking he had ever heard, and wrote: "I found that we had a strong common interest because I was engaged in an educational undertaking which had the development of occupations as its central core." But whereas Dewey developed the practice of crafts within his school, Geddes thought that children should mainly learn them, apprentice fashion, in the real world.

He met up again with Charles Zueblin, who had written so favourably of the Outlook Tower, and he was particularly interested in the ideas of the economist Thorstein Veblen (who in 1899 had published *Theory of the Leisure Class*) at the University of Chicago. Mrs Emmons Blaine, patron of progressive education, was persuaded that John Duncan was just the man needed to run the arts department of the Chicago Institute, and the Geddeses had their first direct introduction to eastern thought through meeting Swami Vivekananda, teacher of the Vedanta. They were deeply impressed by the eastern tradition of combined discipline for body and mind, and learned some simple yoga exercises to teach to their own children. During their Chicago stay Anna was frequently unwell, and it became apparent that she was in the early stages of pregnancy. (Arthur was now four, and there had been a four-year gap between each of the children—which was probably planned rather than coincidental. Anna herself was forty-two.)

When Geddes learned that there was to be an international fair in St Louis in 1903, he visited the city for two days in order to ascertain the possibilities of holding a meeting of the I.A.A.S.A.E. at the fair. Then, in March, he and Anna returned for a final three weeks in New York. The one thing which they did not achieve during their stay was promise of financial backing for the Reclus globe. Staying with a wealthy grocer, Francis H. Leggett, in New York, Geddes is said to have broached the subject at the breakfast table, but Mr Leggett merely inquired what practical use the globe would have, and whether it would help anybody's business— and there the matter had to rest.

On his return to Scotland, Geddes applied for formal leave of absence from his summer term duties at Dundee, and nominated his assistant, Robert Smith, to deputize for him. Permission was duly granted, and he set about finding somewhere in Paris where the whole family could stay while Anna looked for a suitable flat. By the middle of April he had taken rooms at a *pension* in the Boulevard St Michel, and wrote to Anna: "Of course I am waiting anxiously for telegram saying how you are—for oh don't run any risk of travelling too soon." She and the children in fact joined him by the end of the month, and they later moved to a flat in the rue de Marignan. Bearing in mind that the *Exposition* was due to open in May, the combination of professional and domestic duties that Anna had to shoulder was almost overwhelming. The French governess who was helping to look after the children is reputed to have remarked: "The best thing Monsieur Geddes possesses, it is neither his ideas nor his kindness; it is his wife." Just before the exhibition opened, Geddes whipped off back to England and did a week's lightning tour of the universities of Liverpool, Manchester, Edinburgh, Glasgow, Cambridge, Oxford and London to generate interest in the I.A.A.S.A.E.

In bare statistical terms, the hundred people who participated as lecturers at the Summer School gave 300 formal lectures, 800 specialist talks, and conducted, or gave information to, "tens of thousands" of visitors during the five months that the exhibition was open. The School had lecture and assembly rooms in the Hotel Palais des Invalides and the Palais des

Congrès, and other rooms and information offices scattered around the *Exposition*. The extent of the latter was vast. It covered 279 acres (111 of which were roofed) as well as making use of the park of Vincennes; and there were 211 pavilions and special exhibits. One of the features of the exhibition was a *trottoir roulant*, consisting of two pathways moving at different speeds—one at four miles per hour, and the other at seven. Posts at intervals aided the less nimble to step on to the continuously moving platforms, and one fat friend of James Mavor was so paralysed with fright once he had stepped on, he was said not to have stepped off again until the machinery was stopped at midnight. Besides Mavor, among the people aiding Geddes as he mercurially visited and digested the impact of the exhibits being completed for the May opening day were Arthur Thomson, Edward McGegan, Tom Marr and John Duncan (soon to depart to his new job in Chicago). They were quickly joined by Jane Addams and Swami Vivekananda, who were among the more permanent lecturers in the School, and other friends from America. Peter Kropotkin and the Reclus brothers were in Paris, and many more members of the old Edinburgh Summer Meetings. Another man who visited the School, and who was to become a close colleague of Geddes, was Jagadis Bose, the bio-physicist,* of the University of Calcutta.

The exhibition's scientific and industrial exhibits were grouped together rather than being separated nationally, and they created an excellent opportunity for Geddes to expound his concept of the Paleotechnic and Neotechnic eras. Taking the Old Stone Age (Paleolithic) and the New Stone Age (Neolithic) as his symbols, with their development from rough stone implements for mainly warlike or hunting activities to skilfully chipped or polished ones for peaceful agricultural purposes, he tried to illustrate how modern science and industry should evolve. The Paleotects of the industrial revolution had been intent on extending their markets at the total expense of the working man and his environment. This in turn had created a social psychology where war was acceptable (war

* Bose's invention of an instrument capable of magnifying plant growth 10,000,000 times enabled him to undertake research which still forms the basis of current programmes to demonstrate the sensitivity of plants to external stimuli.

being "but a generalising of the current theory of competition as the essential factor of the progress of life"),[1] and the great industrial machine was easily adapted to the manufacture of the implements of war. Once, however, the Paleotechnic era was recognized as not only bad but also unnecessary, the Neotects could start to use science and industry for peaceful, hygienic and pleasurable ends: "The applied physical sciences are advancing beyond their clumsy and noisy first apprenticeship, with its wasteful and dirty beginnings, towards a finer skill, and more subtle and more economic mastery of natural energies."[2] (Unfortunately it turned out that this finer skill and more subtle mastery was also employed for weapons and environment-destroying factory plants. Geddes had initially imagined that one of the main goals of the Neotects would be good quality houses for all "and with them the substantial and assured, the wholesome and delightful, contribution to the sustenance of their inhabitants which gardens, properly understood and worked, imply".[3])

Shortly after the exhibition opened, and when the initial attendances at the Summer School were proving rather disappointing, a double tragedy occurred. Mary Burton died very suddenly of a brain haemorrhage while staying in Rome, and Anna had a miscarriage. The unhappiness this must have caused Anna and Patrick was increased by the bewildered, bitter letters they received from Jeannie Curry. She had been the first to know of Mary's death, and immediately informed the Geddeses. It appears that Patrick offered to go to Scotland to see her if she felt she could not manage Mary's affairs alone, and she was deeply hurt because in fact he did not go (though nor did she specifically say she could not cope). What is not clear is whether Anna was ill just before or just after the news of Mary's death—but probably the latter. And from the correspondence it would seem that Jeannie Curry was not immediately told of her miscarriage, so was not aware of the personal as well as the public commitments that held Geddes back. She accused him of being more concerned with his "play things" in Paris than his friend's death, and it was not until September that she wrote: "I shall bury [the affair] in my own heart and it shall never pass my lips."

Anna's friends at home were extremely worried about her health, and one, Dora McNeill, wrote to her:

I am very concerned about you, and hope that Norah is beside you, for I am sure no one else in that house you are in will have any time except for exhausting you! . . . You have had all the suffering and none of the joy. I do hope you will take time to get better and not get up and run about too soon. Leave the Exhibition business to be governed by you on the horizontal.

Jane Whyte, no doubt hearing that Geddes was thinking of remaining in Paris for a while after the exhibition closed, wrote offering Anna a gift of money if that would enable her to make her headquarters in Edinburgh for the winter, saying that she could have the three children working with her own in a class at her brother's house. These friends clearly recognized the seriousness of a late miscarriage at Anna's age, as well as the strain that looking after three children could be on someone in poor health.

Meanwhile attendances at the School were improving, and Victor Branford wrote to Geddes that he had heard that Robert Pullar, who had recently been to Paris and seen the School in action, was "immensely charmed with the results of his visit". When Anna was recovered, James Mavor arranged a special walk around central Paris for the Geddeses, Mrs Kropotkin, and the latter's daughter, Sasha. The walk was conducted by a very old man known as Le Français who had fought behind the barricades in the 1830 revolution (when he was a child), then again in 1848, and finally had joined the communist rising of 1871. He demonstrated how parts of the city had been readily convertible into miniature fortresses, and how, by throwing up barricades, those parts were easy to defend. Geddes also took time out during the summer to go on a brief walking tour of northern France with Mavor.

However, in August there were two more unpleasant occurrences that clouded the contained, busy world of the *Exposition*. On the first of the month, Anna received the following letter from Annie Cobden-Sanderson, who together with her husband had invested in the Town & Gown and Eastern & Colonial Associations:

I am sending you a copy of a letter which I have addressed to the Directors of the Town & Gown Association to be read aloud at the shareholders meeting on the 7th.

I have already expressed to you my views on the subject
of the neglect of all the aims which tempted some of us to
invest in the Town & Gown Association but there is no sign
of improvement, in fact things grow worse, and I must now
protest aloud, and shall continue to do so till things are
mended or ended!

I am very sorry to trouble you with this, but I prefer you
should hear it direct from me.

> Believe me dear Anna
> Your affectionate friend . . .

Anna's reply to the criticisms outlined in the enclosure was
cool, concerned and totally supportive of her husband. She
thanked Mrs Cobden-Sanderson for the frankness of her
criticism, but added that she felt it would have been fairer if
they could have seen a draft of the letter to the directors before
it was sent in order to clear up some misconceptions. She said
that it was simply not true to write that "Mr Geddes has
practically given up Edinburgh": apart from that particular
year, he always spent much longer there than the university
arts professors whose teaching year lasted only five months.
She utterly denied the accusation that "all the ideal side of his
work has fallen through, and he retains merely a brick and
mortar interest", pointing out that the previous October,
November and December had been mostly devoted to the
Outlook Tower "which is the most complete expression of my
husband's ideal and ideals" but "which you seem to leave out
of the question, because (is it not so?) you do not understand
it". She went on to say that she and Patrick could not be
responsible for the wave of imperialism which had recently
swept Edinburgh, but simply had to continue quietly with their
work at the Tower for "its ideas and aims appeal to the real
type of Scottish student, not to the imperialist athlete who since
our Halls began is the growingly predominant type in
Edinburgh". Then she referred to the many problems which
they had tackled and solved over the years: "I might tell you
many instances of our difficulties in Edinburgh as for instance
of the long and troublesome negotiations with the Free Church
lawyers, which cost more time, energy, and worry than would
have gone into the writing of three books. . . ."

On 28th August, Robert Smith in Dundee died very suddenly

of appendicitis, aged twenty-six. It must have seemed to the Geddeses that however bright and auspicious the festive meeting of nations to welcome the twentieth century might be, there was an obdurate streak of misfortune dogging their lives and those of their friends. Besides helping with the teaching at Dundee, Smith had, in 1899, successfully revised Geddes's very personal *Chapters in Modern Botany*. (This was a University Extension Manual, which had evolved from Geddes's lectures, and whose first edition had appeared in 1893.)

The *Exposition* closed in October, and until the end of the year Geddes was absorbed in a plan to save the best of the pavilions which had made up the *Rue des Nations* feature, and to house in them a selection of the most interesting exhibits. Once more a committee was formed, and strenuous lobbying of all interested parties undertaken. Germany offered her pavilion as a gift, and several other countries followed her example. However the legalities concerning who owned the land on which the pavilions stood proved intractable, and time ran out. The demolition companies had to move in if they were to honour their contracts, and the scheme came to nothing. If it had been successful, we might today still be able to visit a condensed version of the 1900 *Exposition Universelle*.

One of the people Geddes had tried to involve in the scheme was, not surprisingly, Sir Robert Pullar. But despite Pullar's reported favourable reaction to the exhibition, he was not so impressed by the amount of fees gathered in by the Summer School. Although visitors had made use of it in many ways, the hard core who signed up for full courses was not all that large. And at the end of November, Marr sent to Geddes some extracts from a letter he had received from Pullar:

I also have heard more than once from Professor Geddes who I see is interesting himself in this grand idea of utilizing the *Rue des Nations* for more permanent purposes.

I trust this may prove to be a more successful scheme than the International Assembly but the public appear to be difficult to move in any educational scheme where money is required, and without this very needful element it is impossible to go on for long with any plan or purpose as has been fully exemplified in the financial statements the treasurers have made up of the International.

It seems to me that the sooner the whole matter is wound up the better.

Although it may appear that Geddes was extravagant with funds for his educational schemes, on a domestic level his household was run on very careful lines. When, on 24th November, Anna received a letter from McGegan (who was taking partial care of their affairs in Edinburgh) on which there was a fine to pay because he had forgotten to stamp it, she would not accept it. Instead she sent a postcard to McGegan saying:

Have refused a letter from you tonight because there were 80 centimes of extra postage to pay. Hope there was nought pressing in it.

Her accustomed thrift had no doubt become exaggerated by worries about their situation as a whole. At the failure of the *Rue des Nations* plan, Geddes had switched his attention to the idea of organizing another International Association assembly at the Glasgow Exhibition due to be held in 1901. Tom Marr, on hearing of this plan, wrote firmly that it must be dropped unless a really considerable sum of money could be raised; he added:

I am broke, stony broke with debts in every direction and nothing to organise Glasgow on. But we have I think come to the point where advances from you must stop. Firstly, it is not fair to you; secondly, it is merely postponing the day of reckoning.

That was a day which Geddes continued to postpone.

Chapter 13

EDUCATION FOR PEACE

JEANNIE CURRY INVITED Anna and the children to stay
with her when they returned from Paris, confirming Kate
Crooke's impression that during the previous summer she had
been "definitely unhinged by the continuous pain and not
herself". Geddes himself went to Brussels for three weeks,
writing to Anna: "How sad I was the day you left—all the
day there went through my memory the sad refrain of Macduff
—'What—all my pretty chickens and their dam—at one fell
swoop'!" Miss Curry was living in a house called Viewforth
(shortly to be renamed Innesforth) which had been bought
after the sale of the Burtons' old home. Situated just outside
Dunfermline, it was quite near to Edinburgh, and became
the Geddeses main centre for a few years. (During the summer
term they moved to a house on the Firth of Tay, opposite
Dundee.) Mary Burton had left legacies to the three Geddes
children, and Patrick was able to persuade the solicitors that
Innesforth could represent part payment of these legacies, on
the understanding that Jeannie Curry remained as tenant. This
provided the Geddeses not only with somewhere to live,* but a
resident teacher as well, and they were able to set up a little
home school for their children and Miss Curry's niece. Victor
Branford later wrote this description[1] of the school's activities:

> [Their] first approach to Latin was not in the pages of a
> grammar or even through the spoken word, but by song.
> The children opened the school day by singing in chorus a
> chant of the Roman Breviary. It was a memorable experience
> for a visitor in the Geddes household to hear the sonorous
> Latin hymn rolling from the fresh, true voices of the youngsters
> as they stood round their mother at the piano. Morning
> school thus begun was followed by two or three hours of

*14 Ramsay Garden was let in order to bring in some income.

book-learning not widely different from the customary. The afternoon course consisted of work in the garden, alternating with music or dancing lessons, out-of-door sketching expeditions, play-acting, masquerading, and concert-giving by the children, with seniors, guests, and neighbours for audience. Each of the children according to age and capacity rendered some practical assistance in the tasks of the working gardener—who was Professor Geddes himself. The hour or two thus devoted served also as an introduction to handicraft through the repair and maintenance of tools and the making of some of the simpler apparatus of the gardener's art. Alasdair also did odd jobs of carpentering for the household, and amongst more ambitious things built a tiled and glazed shed with the joiner. These practical tasks performed, the rest of the afternoon was the children's own to do what they liked.

Geddes himself always laid emphasis on the importance of what the children called "beauty feasts"—the display of flowers, leaves, fruit and shells found on their walks. And they were never given either pocket-money or machine-made toys. He wanted an education "free from premature thoughts of personal economic interest, and from aims of conventional success, prosperity, or position"; it should apply "to the realities of the skilled labouring existence" and express the "elimination of customary middle-class standards".[2]

In fact the fairly puritan regime of the Innesforth household did represent one kind of middle-class standard, though certainly not a status-conscious one. When Mrs van Milligan was thinking of sending her daughter Olive there for a period, Anna gave her an outline of their customary repast:

For breakfast as a rule—porridge, bread & butter & jam, and plenty of milk. Dinner 1 o'clock the principal meal—sometimes vegetarian, but generally meat or fish. The children are ready for a hearty "tea" at 5. They again have plenty of milk with bread & butter & jam, cheese or eggs or pudding or some little extra. As they go to bed early they often eat little or nothing after this, but on the other hand if hungry they come down at our suppertime 7.30 and take what is going.

Once when Arthur had eaten a boiled egg *and* a banana at tea, his mother reproved him, saying: "That was rather greedy." He remembered sitting there wondering if she were right: "I'd been hungry, and felt the good effects; *was* it really greedy? I thought . . . I'm sure it *wasn't!*" He was a much more delicate and nervous child than Alasdair, whose steady, practical (though not at all insensitive) temperament, better suited him to his father's regime. Alasdair was, however, a fairly late developer intellectually, and Norah remembered overhearing her father at the Paris exhibition (when Alasdair was only nine) say of him: "What a pity that courageous people will be so stupid."

Norah herself was entering adolescence by this time, and she experienced a conflict between trying to live up to her father's expectations of her, and obeying the dictates of her own temperament and capacity. In family photographs she looks the strongest-featured, most determined of the three children, and there is no doubt that Patrick's relationship with her was more complex than with the even-tempered, self-contained Alasdair. She remembered an occasion in about 1902 when

> I had formulated some interesting thoughts, as it seemed to me, and I made the great effort of showing them to my father. It would have been quite easy to have shared them with my mother but I thought I'd take the hard way and show them to him instead. He read them over and then said: "You are quite right to put down these kinds of thought: without buds there would be no shoots and flowers." But I who thought they were already flowers, was disappointed by this dictum. I felt my mother was a little hurt at being bypassed.

A young explorer, Rusmore Brown, often used to stay with the family around this time, and once he cut his finger while romping with Norah. As a result she got a spot of blood on her dress, which made Anna say that the games must stop, they "were not seemly". Norah felt "shocked and ashamed". Brown, who was a little in love with Norah, was not altogether happy about the regime imposed by Miss Curry when the children's parents were away, and tried to express his doubts to Anna:

I must thank you for another happy holiday at Innesforth which I returned from yesterday. It was indeed very kind of you to so readily agree to my proposal to go there on Saturday to see the children and I only hope that my visit gave as much pleasure to them as it gave to me and that I did not prove a source of trouble to Miss Curry for I find it very difficult, if not impossible, to agree with her in many of her opinions where she evidently seeks for agreement. And if I do differ from her it is, believe me, in no argumentative or self-assertive spirit that I do so but due to the real love which I have for your children and the feeling that I do in some degree understand them.

He went on to say that Alasdair's arithmetic was improving, and that Norah's Latin had advanced a great deal.

But what struck me most about Norah was that she seemed very subdued and was, in fact, only her own happy self when we were at Tulliallan on Sunday morning. I do not mean that she was at all unwell—I have never seen her look better —that was obviously not the reason. Doubtlessly her seriousness was due in part to her sense of responsibility in your absence which I know she feels and partly no doubt to her increasing maturity—and these two reasons, no doubt, explain the great part of Norah's mood.

Anna replied rather tartly, among other observations, that he might have been a more effective man himself if he had had such an influence as Miss Curry. However, he was not deterred, and wrote: "Do not be blind to the fact that Miss Curry's influence over the children is different to yours and to your teaching in many ways." He then asked rather crossly what Anna meant by the phrase "more effective man".

Long after both his parents were dead, Arthur wrote to Philip Mairet that Anna, while admirable in so many ways, lacked any manifestation of "over-flowing mother-love", saying:

It may be that while her discipline nerved her for sacrifice, especially the ten years in James Court, and made her face the possibility of PG's death and her supporting the family by teaching music with quiet equanimity, that a certain over-strictness or lack of easy warmth hardened Norah . . .

What may also have been true, is that Anna's strenuous life with Patrick, supporting and protecting him, and facilitating his schemes, made it impossible for her to be anything other than wholly disciplined. Such a life quells spontaneity and expression of personal instincts, neither of which had been lacking in the letters she wrote just before her marriage. (In a letter written in October 1901, a friend paid her the compliment of saying: "I always thought you combined a miraculous amount of Mary with Martha!") Arthur also suggested that his mother's moral earnestness aimed to emphasize and promote the similar side of Geddes's nature, possibly at the expense of his warmer, human side. They certainly put a great deal of earnest thought into parenthood, even if it did not always result in an easy understanding of Norah's occasionally obstinate individualism or Arthur's imaginative and nervous temperament. Their aim was to organize an "education for peace", one which would prepare their children "to go anywhere and do anything; and to know where they were, and how to make the best of it".[3] During the early 1900's when William James visited the household, long talks on the problems of educating adolescents took place. Victor Branford speculated that these talks may have contributed significantly to James's demands for constructive outlets for young people in order to provide "moral equivalents for war".

Each of the three children undoubtedly felt the pressures of being raised in this special way, set apart from their contemporaries for so much of the time; and their parents did not seem to realize that this could partially counter the good effects of their programme. It worked best for Alasdair, who could be receptive without loss of personal identity, but the burden of being educated as a wise co-operative citizen, while the majority of the rest of society was facing in the opposite direction, must have been heavy. That, however, is not to negate the experiment, some of the principles of which are now widely accepted and practised. To Geddes it would have been quite pointless to advocate educational ideas on paper and not make any attempt to apply them to his own children. Also he probably thought that it was just the type of education he would have benefited from as a child, rather than having had to undergo the Perth Academy timetable, without fully realizing the quite different position he had been in. He had known only the one home, in which he had been totally secure and permanently cared for by his parents and sister, while his own children had moved about frequently, were cared for by friends in their parents' absences, and above all had a much more forceful, problematical father to cope with than Alexander Geddes had ever been. The result of Patrick's upbringing was that he felt quite safe in the world, and could turn his penetrating eye upon it in order to develop the new science of making it more habitable—geotechnics. Norah, Alasdair and Arthur were more ordinary mortals who could not so easily distance themselves from the conflicts of society in order to practise useful diagnosis, since they encountered those conflicts within themselves, and were thus involuntarily bound more closely (despite their education) to the everyday world around them.

Two other people who were having difficulty in denying the tiresome reality of this everyday world, as opposed to Geddes's reforming advance guard, were Tom Marr and John Ross. Marr was still trying to leave the Outlook Tower and get a job so that he could afford to live, and Geddes was trying to persuade him to undertake the administration of the International Association's assembly which he was determined to hold at the Glasgow exhibition in the summer of 1901. On 22nd January, Marr wrote resignedly that he would do the work if the assembly was properly set up and he himself was properly paid. He added: "Your suggestion that I should combine collaboration with you in literary or other work with the work of organisation I find on careful consideration quite impracticable." Throughout February and March Marr tried to find another post, explaining to Geddes and Whitson that he would have to close the Tower because it cost £400 p.a. to run and only achieved an income of £100 p.a. John Ross backed Marr's statements, and indicated that he himself could not go on indefinitely helping with various Town & Gown activities. In a rather rambling, rueful letter to them both, Geddes suggested somewhat desperately that McGegan might sort matters out: "He is developing his teeth and claws and sometimes gives me a quite wholesome experience of them! You know him reasonable and fairminded and if I have so far the advantage of you in his mind in some ways, and in our relations, that is not too much so as to blind him to my defects or make him in any way afraid of me." Marr replied that he and Ross were not seeking concessions, but simply needed to take a new path, and shortly afterwards he became warden at the Manchester Art Museum and University Settlement. (In Manchester he promulgated Geddes's ideas, becoming secretary of the Citizens' Committee for the Improvement of the Unwholesome Dwellings and Surroundings of the People. He also acted as Father Christmas at "the Cripples' gathering".) On 20th March, John Ross tried to summarize their impasse:

> . . . each new scheme instead of bringing you help and credit, tends to harass and discredit your energies—I feel doubtful whether you yourself appreciate the reasons for this—and what it is that we all (more or less badly . . .) try to express. You seem to me too often to escape from the criticism, under cover of its defective expression. Now that you feel as though there has been practically a rupture between yourself and Marr and me—in one sense there has been and is none, viz: in the one direction which you yourself most value—sympathy in ideas. You find it hard to dissociate this from practical expression of sympathy by co-operation? Briefly put it appears to me thus—that with you at all times the brain is too far ahead of the hands, that you thus require as colleagues men who can utilise (not neutralise)—can ballast— this tendency. Personally I am obliged to confess myself unable to do this sufficiently, and the result of the continued and unequal effort is more than health will stand—that is the personal reason, and of course besides there are all the material consequences of repeated and continued failure. Find the man whose personality and character is sufficiently strong to enable him to shape and execute what you plan, and you will have success. As things are, we—you and I— only stimulate each other to undertakings, which we have not the qualities for effectively completing in co-operation. . . . I am not strong enough to ballast you—but you are too strong for me. I see no prospect of redressing the balance of power . . .

Inevitably it was the still-willing Edward McGegan who was persuaded to undertake the administration of the Glasgow International Association's assembly.

This was a much smaller affair than the Paris Summer

School had been, though again Geddest tried to sell the idea
that the best exhibits in any exhibition should form the nucleus
of permanent collections. Within the assembly he ran a conference on regional museums, which explored the methods and
value of museums individual to their locality, and issued a
"Report on Museums and Institutions possible after the close
of the Glasgow Exhibition of 1901", which concluded:

> Funds for the creation of at least several of the collections
> suggested above may also more readily be available than
> was the case in Paris, since in addition, if need be, to the
> public spirit and ready generosity so characteristic of many
> members of the Glasgow and Scottish public, the Exhibition
> surplus has itself, by a wise forethought, been allocated to
> the advancement of Science, Art and Education.

Unfortunately the "ready generosity" of the Glasgow public
did not extend to Geddes personally, and after the exhibition
had closed he was involved in a long and bitter wrangle about
expenses due to the International Association from the exhibition's financial sub-committee. On 20th October 1902 he
was still appealing to the Lord Provost of Glasgow, saying:
"They further inexorably withhold even the large amount
which a twelve month ago they admitted as due, in the certainty of sooner or later compelling me by their stress of personal poverty to accept this as full payment, or abandon the
whole amount." In the end he was forced to make good the
deficit (about £200) himself.

Another setback was that Mr and Mrs Cobden-Sanderson
were continuing their allegations against the Town & Gown
Association in general, and Geddes in particular, which cul-
minated in a long letter which Mr Cobden-Sanderson wrote to
him on 2nd March 1901. In it, he accused Geddes of "char-
latanism which exploits enthusiasm and discredits ideas by
their association with unreality". He painstakingly listed all the
Town & Gown's schemes, comparing their initial claims with
the actual financial results. He concluded:

> In the face of all this rodomontade and charlatanism I
> ask you to come to a stand, to consider seriously—once—
> the situation; and to devise means—once—which shall be

adequate to the situation and bring all your schemes and "Associations" to an end. If you do not do this voluntarily I shall do my own best to oblige the Associations with which I am, unfortunately, involved, to reconsider for themselves their "situation" and as far as may still be possible to wind themselves up.

Between the 15th and 18th March, Geddes composed a reply, whose draft ran to twenty-two pages. It began:

> . . . I am not Stoic enough not to feel, nor Tolstoian enough not to feel resentment, yet I can but honestly recognise, and even admire the artistic unity, the colour, the chiaroscuro of the picture—at least the cartoon—you hold up to my eyes. . . . There is no likeness to approach a really good caricature, no libel approaches a forcible presentment of partial truth.

He then went on to counter Cobden-Sanderson's accusations, demonstrating that some of them were inaccurate on specific factual bases. Bearing in mind this all happened in the midst of his disagreements with Ross and Marr, and at a time when it seemed hardly anyone could share and utilize his vision of the importance to European peace of the continuance of activities like those of the International Association, Geddes must have felt very heavy-hearted during the three days that it took him to write the letter. He was, after all, having to justify fifteen years of his life. On 23rd March, Cobden-Sanderson replied, saying Geddes's letter did not make him alter his views, but advising him to take a rest:

> Suspend—if possible give up altogether—your attempts to realize your dreams. The world is not ripe for them nor are the means at your disposal adequate. Give up your attempts to realize them and concentrate all your efforts in seeing them clearly. Then crystallize them in literature and let them stand an inspiration for the world to come.

It was a familiar exhortation. On 4th April, Henry Beveridge was able to write to Geddes that he had seen Cobden-Sanderson, who still seemed to maintain his views about Geddes personally but had simmered down *vis-à-vis* the Town & Gown Association as a whole. Undeterred, Geddes continued trying to get support for the founding of a university hall in Chelsea—a scheme he had been thinking about for some time—and this brought a fresh burst from Cobden-Sanderson, who threatened to expose the whole scheme in the papers. Even Beveridge was forced to admit to Geddes: "I think you very much too sanguine in your forecasts and too much disposed to make a great display on the basis of a very little material."

While the Glasgow International Association's assembly was taking place, Geddes again cast his thoughts to the St Louis World Fair, due to take place in 1903. He wrote to the Commissioner for the Fair, mentioning ways in which he might be able to participate, and offering to come out at his own expense to talk the matter over. But the offer was not taken up, and the I.A.A.S.A.E. was forced to grind to a halt. However, its British presidents, Archibald Geikie and James Bryce, gave support to another scheme which Geddes prepared early in 1902—a plan for a British National Institute of Geography.[4] This was to be both a geographical museum and a sociological laboratory, and would, of course, house Elisée Reclus' still-to-be-built globe, and an equally large celestial one by the French astronomer and architect Galeron. The plan was submitted to the Royal Geographical Society, who politely proclaimed their interest and suggested warily that it would receive serious consideration "in a year or two".

During August, Geddes lectured at a summer school in Cambridge on the teaching of nature study, a subject which he and Thomson had done much to promote as an official part of the school curriculum both in Scotland and England. At an afternoon tea in Cambridge he met a group of Northumberland miners, and offered to make them a present of plants for a botanical garden. At the time they had no land, but after returning and talking persuasively to the chairman of the local Mechanics' Institute, one of them wrote to Geddes to say they would like to take up the offer. After Cambridge he went to London to lecture on the same subject, both occasions backed up by an exhibition of nature study projects borrowed from various schools. (As with most exhibitions, there was a frantic relaying of messages as the exhibits got lost, or arrived at the wrong place at the wrong time.) Geddes's theme at these meetings was the same as he employed when teaching his own children: close observation of living things in their own habitats must precede any dissection or reading of text books. The latter were only to be consulted for points of information as needed; they were not the "book of the play", but simply embodied a "list of *dramatis personae*". The play itself was enacted in the fields and woods, parks and gardens, and that was where good natural scientists (of whom Darwin was one of the finest examples) did their long, preliminary work. Only later should pupils move into the laboratory for more detailed study.

"Nature-starvation", which was caused by an environment in which children had no opportunity to observe growing plants or to help to care for animals, led to stunted adults. If education was to "civilise man to peace again", it must, Geddes felt, include direct contact with the natural world.

Chapter 14

"WHAT IS TO BE HOPED FOR THIS LITTLE DUNFERMLINE?"

In March 1903, Geddes made a final attempt to obtain an establishment post in Edinburgh—this time as Director of Education at the Museum of Science and Art. Charles Booth was one of his referees, and J. Arthur Thomson (now a Professor at Aberdeen) another. Ray Lankaster also supported him, but D'Arcy Thompson felt unable to do so on the grounds that he himself had been an unsuccessful candidate for the same post the previous time it had fallen vacant. Various friends tried to discourage him from applying, indicating that they felt sure the authorities would be seeking someone with previous official museum experience. And so it turned out to be.

Having failed in his application, Geddes set about trying to find means by which to consolidate his sociological theories. He wrote to Charles Booth and William James to see if they could suggest institutions in London and America respectively where he might "drive in" his "many-armed signpost to the radiating paths of knowledge" and offer a course of lectures on "Index Museum, Synthetic Laboratory, Classification and Nomenclature in Sociology, and so on". He was also discussing with Victor Branford and other friends the possibility of starting a sociological society with its own quarterly or monthly journal, and wrote to the Town & Gown directors about the idea of establishing the Outlook Tower as a sociological college. At the same time he revived the Edinburgh Summer Meeting for the last time (it had lapsed since 1899), taking "Edinburgh and its Region" as the theme, and organizing a course that thoroughly explored all that he meant by the term "regional survey". The attendance at the School was not large, but by re-orientating Geddes closely to the process of city survey in general and the survey of Edinburgh in particular, its work was to bear fruit.

He had shown his plans for an Index Museum to Henry Beveridge, who besides being a director of Town & Gown was one of the members of the Trust which Andrew Carnegie had just set up and endowed with half-a-million pounds to benefit his native town of Dunfermline. Beveridge showed Geddes's sketches to Dr John Ross—Carnegie's solicitor in Dunfermline and ultimately his philanthropic alter ego in Scotland (and not to be confused with Geddes's accountant friend John Ross). Dr Ross was quite impressed, and in turn promised to show the plans to Carnegie, though preferring to present them as Beveridge's idea and not mention Geddes. Commenting on this, Beveridge wrote to Geddes:

My criticism of yourself and your doings is that you seem unable to impress yourself on the ordinary man. You are too mercurial and do not dwell on your points long enough to make them clear. You are always running off on some collateral subject and confuse the mind. You are always trying to kill 2 or 3 birds with one stone.

However when Dr Ross did lay the plans in front of Carnegie, Beveridge reported that he

unfortunately began at the wrong end. He started at the Paleolithic period and Carnegie at once stopped him saying we had nothing to do with the old world—Greece and Rome had no bearing on modern life etc. His interests are only in the present and in the future.

Despite this inauspicious encounter, in the autumn of 1903 Geddes and the architect Thomas Mawson were separately commissioned by the trustees to prepare designs and proposals for the use of the Pittencrieff estate, which Carnegie had recently donated to them for the citizens of Dunfermline together with the endowment of $2,500,000 in 5% bonds. His aim in making this gift was to contribute to the "monotonous lives of the toiling masses of Dunfermline more of sweetness and light", and in his deed of trust he challenged the trustees to "remember you are pioneers, and do not be afraid of making mistakes. Not what other cities have is your standard; it is the something beyond this which they lack." The estate, consisting of about 70 acres, lies beside the ancient Palace and Abbey of Dunfermline, and contains the ruin of the tower built by Malcolm Canmore, who became king of Scotland in 1058. The ruin stands in an area called the Glen, a small natural ravine divided by a winding stream, and incorporating a compact series of romantic vistas. By contrast, the park itself presents a gentle, undulating landscape, and contains a mansion house and formal garden.

The combination of historical associations and natural beauty, plus the order to benefit the lives of working people, could not have suited Geddes better. He had just celebrated his forty-ninth birthday, and this was the only time he had ever actually been invited to submit proposals for a community project, as opposed to undertaking schemes entirely on his own initiative. He wrote to Harry Barker:

> For the first time in my life, instead of *always*, as hitherto, thrusting wholly undesired theory and practice upon a reluctant university or public, I find myself this year in demand. Fancy being asked for one's help and even paid a living wage for it! Remember that till now my fiftieth year, I have been refused *every* job I ever asked for, without any one exception at all.

The next seven months were spent in preparing what Edward McGegan was to describe as "the sublimest poem I have ever read". It is probably the only time a planning report has been likened to poetry, but McGegan's judgement was not distorted by his admiration for Geddes. The care, detail and vision embodied in what Geddes entitled in full *City Development, A Study of Parks, Gardens, and Culture-Institutes, A Report to the Carnegie Dunfermline Trust** amount to poetry in the broadest sense of the word, and even his prose style is intermittently less circumlocutory than usual. Into the report he poured all the practical and philosophical yield of his experience, and Ebenezer Howard justifiably commented: "A copy ought to be in every public library, and in the office of every architect to every local authority."

* This is the title of the edition circulated publicly later in 1904. The first copies, printed by the Edinburgh University Press, were called: *A Study in City Development, Parks, Gardens and Culture-Institutes*, etc.

Needless to say the preliminary survey work Geddes under-took before starting the report was pretty exhaustive. Besides making detailed plans, contour maps and a geological inspec-tion, he asked James Norval, a photographer who was also one of the Carnegie trustees, to photograph each section of the area "from every point of view—in late summer verdure and in autumn colouring, in winter nakedness and in early spring—and as far as possible all these both in sunshine and dull weather",[1] thus revealing many unexpected prospects of interest and beauty. He used a few of these photographs to illus-trate how some areas might appear after improvement, by showing the original alongside a copy which had been touched up. He studied every building contained by, and bordering, the area, from Pittencrieff House down to dilapi-dated workmen's cottages, and argued for conservation and reconstruction wherever these were not totally impractic-able. He observed privately, however, that it seemed to be the policy of the trustees to "breathe out threatenings and slaughter against their old buildings" and had been told that one of them "hoped to live to see every stone of them carried away". (This was to some extent understandable when one remembers that civic pride was then conventionally expressed in the erection of grandiose new buildings rather than the loving preservation of old ones.)

Having decided which buildings should remain and how they might be improved, Geddes drew up an ambitious outline scheme for the whole eastern side of the park, showing how the old structures would be adapted and new ones erected to form a complete culture complex. This would include a zoo, nature palace, history palace, crafts village, an open-air arena and music hall. It far exceeded the terms of his brief, but he explained that his scheme took "full note of places and things as they stand, of people as they are, of work, family, and institutions . . . then it boldly suggests new and practicable developments . . . not only for the immediate future but for the remoter and higher issues which a city's long life and its correspondingly needed foresight involves".[2] The trouble with "remoter and higher issues", such as a history palace which was to contain a "stair of spiral evolution" based on a stair design by Leonardo, was that for many people they tended to remain remote. However, Geddes's suggestions for the park itself were in the main eminently straightforward, and started with proposals for purifying the stream which runs through the Glen. One of the photographs in the report showed how higher up the stream beyond the estate a sewer was leaking into it, and another illustrated the piles of ashes regularly deposited by householders on its banks. Each area of the park was minutely analysed, and appropriate sections allocated for recreational activities, formal gardens, botanical gardens, rock gardens, animal paddocks, and flooding to create lakes. The Glen was to be kept as a wild area, but discreetly landscaped and planted to make a rich, arboreal environment, punctuated by simple bridges and a summer house, but no "subaqueous grottos or other costly conceits".

Geddes's whole aim was to show how a small town could avoid the degeneration and stultification that affected the buildings and institutions of larger cities. It could provide its citizens with a satisfying regional background that was not narrowly provincial, where their daily working lives might be extended to include leisure, beauty, recreation and culture—thereby following but enlarging Andrew Carnegie's intentions. In his report, Geddes asked: "What is to be hoped for this little Dunfermline? Has it any future beyond that of provincial mediocrity at best?" and was able to show how it could aspire towards the highest civic ideals. In the preface he explained one of his most fundamental concepts: it is not with Utopia (no-place) that planners should be concerned, but with Eutopia (good-place), so that rather than "imagining an impossible no-place where all is well" they should be "making the most and best of each and every place", and that applied to Dunfermline as much as to any other town.

Once he had completed the field survey work, circumstances dictated that he had actually to write the report in London. He had already undertaken to give various courses of lectures there during the winter of 1903–4, and Victor Branford, from his office in Westminster, was in the process of founding the Sociological Society. It was Branford's association with Geddes that inspired him to embark on this venture, and once again Martin White lent his support, acting as honorary treasurer, while James Bryce was the first president. The aims of the Society were

scientific, educational and practical. It seeks to promote investigation, and to advance education in the social sciences in their various aspects and applications. It aims at affording common ground on which workers from all fields and schools concerned with social phenomena may meet—economist and historian, psychologist and moralist, anthropologist and archaeologist, geographer and naturalist; as also physician and alienist, criminologist and jurist, hygienist and educationist, philanthropist and social reformer, politician and cleric.

During this winter, Anna and the children remained in Scotland and Geddes stayed in Harrow at the home of Lady Victoria Welby. A widow aged sixty-six, and one-time maid of honour to Queen Victoria, Lady Welby was a notable personality whose encyclopaedic approach was a match for Geddes's own. During 1902, while writing her book *What is meaning?* (Macmillan, 1903), Lady Welby wrote to Anna:

> I went to Oxford in March in order to submit various points to experts in anthropology, "pedagogy", philology, history, science, philosophy, psychology, logic and mathematics; and was much encouraged by the amount of sympathy I found even among those very conservative teachers.

She gave a good deal of support to the Sociological Society, and, as she explained to Anna, liked people to stay at her house.

> I am only 16 minutes by rail from London and people who have work there often come and make me their home for a time using the library for their own business . . . my great desire is to make my house of use and its garden and splendid view a refreshment.

Geddes admired her very much, and wrote a paragraph describing her for inclusion in his and Thomson's Home University Library book, *Sex*. (The book was published in 1914, two years after Lady Welby's death.) The paragraph, quoted below, was in fact deleted from the book at proof stage. Geddes had been developing a theory of the relation between the different ages of woman and figures from Greek mythology, paralleling old age with the nature of the sibyls "whose wisdom penetrates beyond even that of the sages":

that such genius is profoundly normal, we both not only believe on general grounds, but have learned from the sibyls themselves. Thus the late Lady Welby (sibyl and white witch if ever there was one), was wont to teach, as in her own life to prove, that this highest phase of life, despite its present rarity of attainment, is yet the normal culmination of the woman's life—so that to its possibility, and even hope therefore, no rightly educated girl should remain uninitiated.

Geddes did not work in isolation on *City Development*. He was assisted by professionals with the preparation of plans and drawings, and talked over his ideas with friends such as Lady Welby and Victor Branford, as well as writing frequently to Anna. He also canvassed by letter over two hundred people whose opinions he thought might be relevant to deciding the best ways of using Carnegie's gift. While probably few of the replies had a direct practical influence on his report, their scope and seriousness strengthened his belief in his own synoptic approach. Among the replies he received was one from Alexander Graham Bell, who declared he would "take pleasure in bringing the matter up at one of my Wednesday evening smokers". William Tolman, director of the American Institute of Social Service, went so far as to collect suggestions into a "Special Report", handsomely set out and pinned together. Dr Robert Felkin, in a paragraph headed "Education of Mothers", wrote: "So important do I think it to train all children from the day they are born to the use of both hands, that I would give prizes of £50 to each child (put £50 in the post-office savings bank) at birth to become its own if it were found to be ambidextrous at the age of 10." Perhaps the nicest reply was from Mr W. H. Cole, conductor of the Dunfermline Orchestral Society and Bandmaster for the 1st Lanark Volunteer Royal Engineers, whose memorandum paper carried an imposing portrait of himself, and who began: "Your letter of the 9th inst fairly took away my breath," but then recovered it sufficiently to make some very sensible remarks about the practicalities of light musical entertainment.

As soon as sections of the report were completed, Geddes dispatched them to the trustees. A letter written by him to Beveridge on 15th February 1904, shows that already his proposals were causing a good deal of dismay and displeasure.

Of course I recognise the disaster of sending off my unfinished Report in driblets and chapters finished piecemeal, instead of insisting, as the wiser Mr Mawson has done, on keeping back everything till he was ready. But it was done in response to requests; and no doubt I was a fool to do it. Nobody should see half-done work, and especially the less intelligible half first.

It seems that the trustees were dubious about Geddes's practice of getting accomplished draftsmen to develop his own rough sketches. This was no doubt because the practice would add to Geddes's fee, since he would have to pay for such services, and also because it appeared that the men so employed might expect to receive commissions for buildings which the trustees had no intention of erecting.

That the invaluable artist-draftsman-architect, who carries out the rough yet distinct designs of his chief—no doubt sometimes improved, though at other times against his own ideas—should be frankly recognised, and should sign along with his chief, and be recommended by him, is, I see from your letter, being ingeniously misconstrued; but I cannot help it.

There also appears to have been a complaint by the trustees that Geddes was already incorporating his Dunfermline experience into the sociology lectures he was giving at London University.

You know too how I have been working out the History of Dunfermline for two years past, just like the Nature Museums, History Museums, Exhibitions, and so on for many; and you are getting the cream of all these years' work in my plans and report. No wonder if there are more points than were expected. For this particular business of the lectures, I think it is not I who have anything to withdraw; it is for my critics to withdraw this, as really too ungenerous.

The multiplicity of suggestions in the report had indeed been causing alarm, and this final extract from Geddes's letter to Beveridge is all too explicit:

You at least know how I, like every investigator, have spent three-fourths of my life working for nothing, and how people, as in every age, suspect one as a kind of warlock in consequence. The other point is still plainer: just as my photographic survey disclosed a hundred usually unsuspected beauties, so every other of these dozen surveys of my chapters bristle with unexpected points, too often unfamiliar, and therefore undesired ones.

But our winter's propaganda must have helped to save Pittencrieff House, even the good old houses near the Abbey, and so on, just as in time my protest for purified stream and beautified glen from St Margaret's Cave to the Town Loch [both these locations were well outside Pittencrieff estate and therefore the terms of his brief] will be recognised as the best feature of my whole Report, by the trustees themselves.

. . . Finally, you remember the day I was suddenly called in to a meeting of the whole Trust, and heckled a little about my Report—did not Dr Ross say that I had insisted upon taking a strong line of my own, and must now, he supposed, be allowed to state it?—or words to that effect? Of course that is what I like and respect in Dr Ross: though I do not think we ever agreed at first sight upon anything, he has some of that judicial fairness which lets you state your argument; and that is all I am doing.

Dr Ross was one of the most ardent supporters of the demolition of old buildings (fortunately Pittencrieff House remained unharmed, and today is a museum), and his illness at this time tended to exacerbate his relations with Geddes. Characteristically, the one person with whom Geddes was on perfectly friendly terms during the whole period was his rival Thomas Mawson, as this letter to Anna shows:

Mawson and I dined together very amicably the other night. His plan is a very American and Haussmann one, so I don't feel crushed. He also won't be finished for a month! The job is a gigantic one for both of us—not even he with all his experience . . . had realised it. Least of all do the trustees; that's what makes them so horrid as they have been to us! Yet after all, I don't think there's any permanent harm done to speak of, though it's annoying they should put up that

shelter instead of one of Mawson's, or my pretty pavilions!
They may very likely make a mess . . . it's all the guilt of
refusing Sir Christopher's plan for rebuilding London after
the 1666 fire!

By June 1904 the entire report was in the hands of the
trustees. At Beveridge's request, Geddes emphasized that it was
of course perfectly "possible to carry out those parts which may
recommend themselves without the others". On 23rd June, at
4 o'clock, the trustees met in the council chambers. The minutes
of their meeting state:

The Trustees, having received from Professor Geddes the
report entitled: "Parks, Gardens and Culture Institutes,"
resolve to record their high appreciation of the fulness of
knowledge and the great talent which he has brought to bear
on the subject and the earnest desire he has displayed to
render the future action of the Trustees beneficial to the
community. They further resolve to award him their best
thanks for his labours, and their acknowledgement that he
has furnished suggestions which may prove to be of much
value to the Trustees in their future work. The report will
have their earnest consideration.

There then followed six observations:

1. They are of opinion that it would be unwise to adopt any
plan, however attractive in itself, that would greatly alter the
present aspect and character of the Park and Glen. They
recognise that at present the Park and Glen are characterised
by great natural beauty and are singularly adapted to form
desirable resorts for public recreation, and they are strongly
of opinion that they can best conserve these advantages by
limiting themselves to such alterations as may be necessary
or desirable in a place of public resort.
2. They realise that much may be done towards intensifying
the beauties of the Park and Glen, and, while recognising
that it may be necessary in the near future to adopt a general
plan of operations, they are of opinion that for the present it
will be sufficient to continue making such improvements as
from time to time may be found desirable.

3. They place on record their sense of the necessity of taking steps to secure the purity of the water of the Tower Burn, and of resorting to such measures as the law prescribes to prevent its pollution; also, their sense of the desirability of acquiring from time to time, if obtainable at market prices, properties which may not only give them control of the stream, but may also provide additional recreation grounds for public use.

4. In carrying out the work of the Trust they resolve to adhere to the principle of limiting themselves in their expenditure, unless in very exceptional circumstances, to the ordinary income of the Trust funds.

5. They deem it inadvisable to embark upon more schemes than they can personally and efficiently supervise by committees of their number, aided by other public-spirited citizens.

6. They consider that the scheme which at present most urgently calls for their attention is the provision of further library and reading-room accommodation, including the enlargement or the rebuilding of the Library, and the provision of a Reference Library and Reading-room such as will meet the educational requirements of the young people of the town. They also deem it advisable that the proposed Reading and Recreation Room at Townhill should be proceeded with forthwith.

And that, really, was it as far as Geddes and his plan for "this little Dunfermline" were concerned. He was neither invited to implement any of his own proposals, nor consulted in the future about any that the trustees might have contemplated. Thomas Mawson's efforts were no more successful—he was thanked for his report which, too, was retained "for after consideration". Indeed the only aftermath, perhaps inevitably, were the wrangles which both men had with the trustees over fees, Geddes finally receiving £750 in settlement of his bill for £798. McGegan, who in July was staying in Dunfermline with J. H. Whitehouse, the Trust's secretary, wrote to Geddes that the trustees were going to query his accounts because they had got more than they asked for in their brief and therefore felt Geddes had asked for more than he was entitled to in his accounts. "This," wrote McGegan, "and also the fact, now evident, that Mr Geddes need hope for no work from the trust as

at present constituted, is really the gist of what I have to say
to you."

City Development has 232 pages and 136 illustrations, and
Geddes had enough copies printed to circulate to friends and for
review and limited sale. It received some extremely favourable
notices, but perhaps the most significant reaction came from
Thomas Whitson. Not normally noted for his whole-hearted
enthusiasm for his friend's broader schemes, Whitson wrote to
Geddes:

> To me it seems astonishing that Carnegie Trustees did not
> adopt the major part of the Report at once. One cannot help
> feeling that even should the Carnegie Dunfermline Trustees
> not adopt the Report others will and must and it is well that
> such a Report has been written—the result, someday, will be
> great and lasting good.

However, for the present, Geddes was once again under-
employed. Without a great deal of enthusiasm he applied, on
28th September 1904, for the principalship of Durham College
of Science. It was to be his last unsuccessful attempt of this kind.

Having time on his hands, he was able to spend more of it
than usual with his family at the house near Dundee, and tried
to take stock of his position. His students at the university had
all passed their botany examinations, but an attempt to run the
Outlook Tower as the "Edinburgh School of Sociology for
promoting the study of Ethical, Social and Economic subjects"
under McGegan's stewardship had failed, and the latter was
shortly, and regretfully, to depart to work in Bournville.
Geddes's recent lecture courses and his talks at the Sociological
Society had not been widely well-received; people who were
used to the more incisive methods of thinkers such as Shaw and
Wells were bemused by his "radiating paths of knowledge" and
took a positive dislike to his charts and graphs. As he worked in
the autumn garden with its "sad asters" and "flaming torch
lilies beneath the withering woods", he was further depressed
by the building of a nearby railway line which meant that "this,
one of the loveliest shores of Scotland, will be destroyed for good
and all". He was engaged to lecture in London and Oxford
during the Lent term of 1905, and was "reluctantly forced to
think more seriously of making London our headquarters—

probably from next autumn". He did not dwell on Dunfermline, but the missed opportunity to realize his dream "to rebuild and re-educate" a town, and preferably a Scottish town, remained in his thoughts.

His report was not entirely without effect. Today Pittencrieff Park does in fact incorporate some of the less ambitious details to be found in *City Development*. The benches around some of the trees, the rustic summerhouse, the preservation of the old dove-cot, much of the tree-planting—all echo suggestions in the report. And in the area which he allocated for a zebra pad-dock, there is, more modestly, a rabbit-house. But it is the formal gardens and, above all, the Glen—with its varied planting and romantically wild effect—that most closely reflects the spirit of Geddes. Almost everything he felt about gardens is embodied there, and hopefully the children who follow the nature trail set through the park by its present superintendent, will catch a glimpse of that spirit. The final words of *City Development* are that hoary quotation from Emerson, "Hitch your wagon to a star". The Dunfermline trustees felt unable to take such a problematical step, despite Carnegie's dictum to "remember you are pioneers", but at least their gardeners have created in the Glen the "Paradise and groves Elysian" mentioned in the penultimate quotation of the report.

Chapter 15

CROSBY HALL

ON 18TH JULY 1904, 23rd January 1905, and 19th March 1906, Geddes delivered three long papers on civics[1] to the Sociological Society. These meetings were held at the London School of Economics, and on the first two occasions Charles Booth was in the chair, while James Oliphant took it on the third; Ebenezer Howard led the discussion which ensued after the first lecture—which he described as "wonderfully luminous and picturesque". In the papers Geddes developed his basic theme of the need for comprehensive regional survey in order that we might understand our cities, educate our citizens, and plan towards the highest civic ideals. All his most familiar thought-patterns reappeared as he tried to demonstrate how "our everyday experiences and commonsense interpretations become more systematic" and "assume a scientific character" while "our activities, in becoming more orderly and comprehensive, similarly approximate towards art". Some members of the audiences were put off by the exhaustive form of the talks, but others shied away from the idea that the muddle of life might be systematized into something approximating a science. His Herculean effort to persuade his listeners that society must study the whole of its past and its present in order that the shape of its future might be beneficially influenced, tended to dull people's perceptions. They were used to ideas being disseminated within recognizable categories, and they were not used to the notion of finding benefit in the study of every back street, waterway and open space in their own neighbourhood. Geddes had a holistic mind, but to more limited thinkers it appeared undisciplined. (The word "holism" had at that time yet to be invented, and when J. C. Smuts did so and published *Holism and Evolution* (1926) Geddes read the book with approval.) His work with the Sociological Society, and especially with the

Cities Committee that he formed within it, did not immediately have the impact that his supporters had hoped.

He was lecturing very frequently in various places during this period, and still not earning enough to pay off debts and plan a less peripatetic life. He tried to interest Town & Gown in schemes for developing a small garden suburb at Roseburn Cliff, Edinburgh, as well as a university hall in Cheyne Walk, Chelsea. The directors baulked at both schemes, and Geddes went ahead on his own with the garden suburb, involving builders, backers and would-be buyers in his accustomed manner. It was not a scheme which ever earned him much credit. In 1902, when the value of the shares which he had bought for his children with the remaining Burton trust money had suddenly dropped, he had sought permission to sell them. He had then persuaded the solicitor concerned that a piece of land on the main road to Corstorphine, just west of the centre of Edinburgh, would be a good investment, and the Roseburn Cliff project was the result. Nine villas were planned, but in the end only seven were erected, and as the scheme dragged on, Geddes lost a sizeable portion of his children's money. Also the siting and design of the villas themselves were not particularly remarkable.

The Outlook Tower was in an almost continual state of crisis now that McGegan had left, and when Geddes was away in London in 1905 it was only the efforts of Anna that saved it from being closed down altogether. (She was not aided by the fact that the Tower's caretaker had taken to drink.) A committee of interested people existed to run the Tower, but with little income from visitors, and less help from Town & Gown, they seemed unable to take a definite initiative. They appealed to Geddes for guidance, and during his 1905 summer session at Dundee he wrote them a long account of what the Tower was not, and what it should become, but without including much practical advice as to how to deal with it in the here and now.

While lecturing in London, he had been invited to advise on the design and planting of various gardens in the suburbs, and perhaps because of this, Norah suddenly decided that she wanted to be a landscape gardener. Her relationship with her father had continued to be rather strained, and this decision, at the age of nineteen, carried the signs of being a definite attempt to please him and to try to share his aims. He wrote to her in December 1905:

Do you know I think we could devise between us the finest gardens in the world! With wonderful pagodas—each great window looking over flowering shrubs and trees and herbs! So be designing and painting for all you're worth—and we'll perhaps try it next spring, who knows—if I can only find a client or two!

During 1906 he made a more concerted practical effort to help the Outlook Tower committee, sorting and tidying the display material and papers, organizing new shelving, and asking members to contribute "books, magazines and papers, woodcuts and photographs, engravings and pictures, scientific apparatus and specimens of all kinds". As part of an effort to drum up "a client or two" he had some elaborate writing paper printed on which he sent a letter to Norah, who was spending six months in Montpellier with old friends of the Geddes's as part of her education. (Alasdair was later to spend a similar period with another French family.)

Patrick Geddes & Colleagues	Outlook Tower,
Landscape Architects, Park and	Edinburgh.
Garden Designers, Museum	5th January 1907.
Planners, etc.	

City Plans and Improvements
Parks and Gardens
Garden Villages
Type Museums
Educational Appliances
School Gardens

Dear Lassie,
Since you ask for a serious letter from each of us, saying what we'd like you to think of and prepare for, here is mine; or at least an instalment of it. The very paper will show that I mean business—and of the largest kind. Lately I have been in correspondence with various people in Canada. Mr Hooker, whom you may remember, suggested to Mr Mackenzie King, Deputy Minister of Labour, lately in London, that he should recommend me to the Grand Trunk Pacific Railway (now building a line from Nova Scotia to the Pacific, north of the present Canadian Pacific and Grand Trunk and Canadian

Northern Railways). Their line will come out at Prince
Rupert, their new terminus on the north of Canadian Port
and south of the Alaskan U.S. border. This is the last great
city practicable northward on the line from San Francisco
through Portland (Oregon) and Seattle to Vancouver. I
might be of use laying out this and other cities. The upshot
is that they ask my suggestions and terms. Re: the former I
have written broadly but carefully suggesting that I go out
next summer for three months or so to prepare a report,
which could of course be finished on my return. . . . This
means a lot of work as well as thought. I have set about
learning to draw! and after a few trials on different evenings,
generally after work, I feel something coming back. The
enclosed is of course from a p.c., but it is helpful and gets the
form and proportions of this timber architecture—the thing
for timber countries like Canada. I have been stirring up
Alasdair and he is going to try too. . . .

Of course this job may not come off, but this will at least
show you that I mean business, and that on more ambitious
lines than ever; so the more and the sooner you and Alasdair
are ready to be colleagues, the better! It is a great pleasure
to think of you both being associated with me in these
endeavours, and I'll be able to work with far more
enthusiasm if I can think of myself as beginning a business
which will not end with my years—now necessarily few, at
best—of active life. It is in West and North-west Canada
that the next great development of a new country is beginning,
comparable to that of the Middle and West of the U.S.A.
in the last generation, and seems to me to offer very
interesting careers to you all. It is more attractive than
finding here and there a rich man's garden in the country, or
even on the Riviera. . . .

I won't attempt to go into the ways in which this might
affect your studies: I rather ask you to be thinking of this,
and to write me when you have done so. But rest assured that
I won't ask you to take too narrow or utilitarian a view of
these: on the contrary, the more wide and general your
culture the better. . . .

Your expedition to Corsica will give you a glimpse of
Italian architecture . . . you can make some sketches: I
think the pen is a good instrument, better than pencil and

with no nonsense of rubbing out! Try it and let me see the result. Trees in winter or something.

. . . I have been making some progress with Outlook Tower this autumn, you will know quite a difference. Be gathering interesting references as far as possible on slips— anything you think of use. In fact I want you and Alasdair and by and by Arthur to *collect* slips just as Branford and I (and of course such an increasing number of workers throughout the world) are doing. I enclose sample also for size: you can cut them out of anything, near enough—though the nearer the better. Or if you prefer I'll send you a packet . . .

Your affectionate Daddy.

Your portrait now hangs in a nice plain little oval frame over our bedroom mantel . . . as the best evidence it is appreciated. You are growing quite mature and thoughtful it says, (or going to be is it, for every artist idealises a little!). And we like your letters very much. Write often, not like me. But answer this at such length as a week's reflection may suggest.

Norah's reactions to the prospect of spending a lifetime planning half a continent do not seem to have been preserved. The opportunity in any case never materialized—partly, according to Geddes, because he was too busy to go to London to meet a particular Canadian whose approval of his approach was essential. As well as his lecturing and various activities in Edinburgh, he was always weighed down by a huge volume of correspondence. Friends wrote to him frequently for advice and comment, and the Dunfermline report in particular had sparked off long postal dialogues on the implications of regional development. He was always unreservedly generous with his correspondents, and would answer a complete stranger's questions with total dedication, producing letters that must have sapped hours rather than minutes of his time. Nor did he mind if other people then presented his ideas as their own. "I am like a cuckoo," he used to say, "who leaves her eggs in other birds' nests, and is only too glad to have someone else feed them and care for them till they are ready to fly by themselves."

Early in 1907 he employed a press-cutting agency to send him news items concerning gifts of land to municipalities. On learning of such a gift, he would write to the Mayor or Provost of the town concerned, drawing attention to his Dunfermline report, and offering himself "as of possible service as regards the laying out of the grounds in connection with recreation purposes and general amenity". These approaches yielded no positive result, though nearer home he was hoping to organize the reclamation and planting of disused plots in Edinburgh to be used as open spaces and playgrounds. He was also spending time among his charts and papers in the Outlook Tower, enlarging his thinking-machines to include the areas of Greek myth which were to concern him for the rest of his life. The following paragraph from a letter to a friend describes this development:

I am really, I think, gradually working off the scaffolding of diagrams and schemata which I have had to spend most of my life erecting, and coming to the actual towers and statues of my thought palace itself. It is like a chemist who begins with common things like air and water, then passes through long technical studies of compounds and series of merely technical interest, but at last emerges to the synthesis of familiar, wholesome and delightful substances like the starches and sugars. Or putting this more definitely still, my diagrams have been working out now into the very map of Parnassus with the Muses, and again of Olympus with the gods; and again those diagrams of the city, which you may have looked at in the Sociological Society's papers are now developing into presentments of the historic city, each surrounded by its appropriate fairyland of childhood, and elfland of poetic adolescence—its Inferno, alas, also; its working Purgatory too; and I trust some glimpse at last of its Potential Paradise beyond.

At this time the Sociological Society established premises in Buckingham Street off the Strand which were recognized as an extension centre by London University, and rather than publish their papers yearly, they started to bring out a monthly journal—to which Geddes frequently contributed. Worried by their friend's continued lack of established full-time employment, a group of people centred around Victor Branford and John Ross set up a Geddes Lectureship Fund, for which they collected £500. The terms of this were suitably vague, enabling Geddes to run courses of lectures at the Outlook Tower, with a view to collecting them in book form in due course. Ross and Branford were also involved in implementing Geddes's project for establishing a university hall in Chelsea, and by the beginning of 1908 a group of flats known as More House had been opened in Cheyne Walk. This gave Geddes a London base from which to operate, and for a time he was given the official position of Warden. The students living there mainly worked in the various South Kensington colleges, as he had done thirty years earlier, and he was encouraged by London University's official recognition of More House as a hall of residence. (Edinburgh had never granted similar recognition to University Hall.) Recognizing the need for student residences all over London to cater for the widely-flung institutions of the University, he had started, in 1907, an organization called the University and City Association of London, to foster fruitful relations between civic and academic bodies. The first meeting had been held at the Chelsea Town Hall with the mayor in the chair, "and hearty Alderman and Councillors, local magnates, ex-Chairman L.C.C.,* all speaking" in favour of the Association, and Geddes was able to claim that "here in the borough the watchword of 'Chelsea a Collegiate City' has caught on". By the summer of 1907 a further meeting "had the Mansion House overflowing, with Lord Mayor in Chair, City Magnates and Borough Mayors, University authorities, Bishops, keen and all". Similarly, Geddes claimed, there was support in the "House of Commons: liberal and conservative, society and labour—Burns and Keir Hardie equally—and so on, all sorts join our Committee or help otherwise".

Early in 1908 a coincidence occurred which enabled Geddes to instigate a grand symbolic event of the kind which he loved. More House occupied a portion of the land originally included in Sir Thomas More's Chelsea estate (he had built the first house of note in the area, but it had been pulled down in 1740), an estate which he had acquired in order to escape from the narrow confines of the City. And the house which he had owned in the City before moving to Chelsea was now threatened

* London County Council.

with destruction. This house, Crosby Hall, had been built in
1470 by Sir John Crosby M.P., and at the time it had been the
tallest in London. Crosby's widow sold it to the Duke of
Gloucester (who became Richard III) and Thomas More
probably acquired the lease in 1514, and then owned it outright
for a few months between 1523-4. It had escaped the fire of
London, but a disastrous fire of its own had caused severe
deterioration and it was in turn used as a post-office, grocer's
warehouse, religious meeting place, restaurant and wine
vaults. It was saved once from demolition by a subscription
fund, but the money ran out and in 1908 the Chartered Bank
of India, Australia and China bought the land in order to
build new offices. There was again a public outcry as demolition became imminent, and the new owners agreed to have
the stones and timber of the most notable part of the building,
the great hall, taken down, numbered, and put into boxes at
their expense. These boxes they presented to the L.C.C., who
accepted the gift on condition that a site and funds for re-
erection were provided. Gordon Selfridge, who was in the
process of building his great Oxford Street department store,
considered incorporating Crosby Hall on its top floor. But
Geddes insisted that it should be incorporated into a new
University Hall—and what site more appropriate than another
portion of Sir Thomas More's Chelsea estate? After much
urgent negotiation, and strong support from the Earl of
Sandwich, the L.C.C. leased Geddes some land (which had
been part of More's garden) on the Chelsea Embankment on
the west side of Danvers Street, on condition that "Crosby
Hall was erected thereon".

A large hut was built in the garden, the boxes of stones and
timbers were stored there, and Geddes launched into a cam-
paign to raise funds for the hall's erection. Walter Godfrey, an
architect experienced in restoration, drew up a scheme to show
how Crosby Hall could join with a new hostel building, and
Geddes gave fund-raising lectures all over the country on the
necessity of respecting the past in order to prepare for the future.
By 26th October 1908, he could write to an Edinburgh friend:

We begin re-construction of Crosby Hall after New Year,
and this will give us a character architecturally comparable
to that of one of the great Oxford or Cambridge Colleges

from the very start, and even Associations no less eminent than theirs. But better still this old Hall where More's "Utopia" was partly written, re-erected upon More's own garden here, gives a kind of centre for Utopia-making which has to be taken more seriously than people generally incline to do.

The construction was completed by the summer of 1910—Crosby Hall thus paradoxically becoming the oldest building in Chelsea.

With Geddes's life split between London and Edinburgh, plus his perennial shortage of money, the idealistic educational programme he had planned for his children became somewhat impaired—particularly for Arthur. Anna was mainly based in Edinburgh and in 1905 Arthur had been able to attend the home school run by Mrs Whyte, but as he grew older this was not suitable and there was not enough money to pay for him to have tutors. So for the two winter terms of 1906 and 1907 he somewhat miserably attended the local Board school—where there were sixty pupils in each class—while in the winter of 1908 he went to a slightly better secondary school, the summer term being spent at Dundee High. A friend of the family described Arthur around that time as a "brilliant and promising child—with nerves", adding succinctly that his father did not understand nerves. In adult life, when people listened with rapt admiration to Geddes as he expounded on the ideal education he had mapped out for his children, Arthur, not surprisingly, used to feel somewhat bitter.

Norah returned from her period in Montpellier to help with the projects organized by the Open Spaces Committee which Geddes had set up at the Outlook Tower, and whose Secretary was a young architect called Frank Mears. The first project which they completed was in Castle Wynd and was opened by the Lord Provost on 7th May 1907. As part of the ceremony, the children of Castlehill School, led by a somewhat stolid Alasdair in pied-piper smock, hose and feathered hat and playing the bagpipes, carried a tree in procession to the open space, where it was duly planted and a maypole dance performed. Later on, the nearby slopes from the Grassmarket to Castlehill were laid out as vegetable plots for the school-children to use to plant produce for their cookery classes.

However, the open space work was not always exactly easy, as extracts from two letters which Norah wrote to her father reveal:

19th October 1910
This afternoon Miss Le Maistre and I and two helpers were working at the Open Spaces. While I was alone in the King Wall, hordes of boys came in and made a regular bear garden, watering the soaking ground, tying the hose in knots, scraping up the ash, threatening each other with the dangerous ends of the hoes, and swinging on the posts. They declared at intervals that they were all on strike. I took it more or less as a joke and got them off in a little while to the West Port carrying some tools. Of course the problem is a difficult one. Where enough to give so many to do in a small garden?

20th November 1910
I am very tired of grubbing in the Open Spaces and count on this next week being the last—one thousand small bulbs, at 50 for 1/–, have just been landed on us and I wonder how many of the miserable things will flower . . . Mr Mears seems very active just now and sends me strange diagrams, and discourses on art and symbolism.

The work did, however, seem to bring Norah into a smoother relationship with her father. In an undated letter of about 1909 he had written to Anna:

And I am very sorry indeed to leave the dear Norah, who has written me one nice letter after another, still unanswered. But I somehow feel it more difficult to write to her than to you or to the boys. . . . But I am much pleased to feel from her letters the quiet and steady growth of professional competence, artistic originality and promise, and developing personal character.

And in January 1910 he confessed to Norah:

I have often feared I had nearly lost you, and the feeling of half estrangement which came or seemed to come sometimes between us . . . has grieved me more than it deserved.

Anna and Alasdair both tried to alleviate the awkwardness
between Norah and her father. Anna once wrote to Patrick:
"I can see from her sensitive face how much she admires and
loves you, and I sometimes think you are a stupid old father
not to be more satisfied than you are!" And Alasdair suggested
to Norah: "I think Daddy would be very pleased if you told
him sometimes how much you think about him!" It was not
until she was married and in her early thirties that Norah was
able to explain to her father how inadequate she had felt during
these years. She had tried to live up to his ideals and principles,
while half-resenting the force that propelled her to do this.
Geddes, who was then sixty-six, replied to her:

> I very much appreciated your loving letter. Yet I was also
> taken aback by your disclosure of how you had felt as if
> judged only by your performance of tasks, and not loved
> more simply—for yourself. Since my readings of the
> Freudians . . . I understand better how I must have seemed
> to you, as no doubt still more to Arthur. But now that you
> are older and know something of life's anxieties, you can
> form more idea of how much I had *la mort dans l'âme*, with
> the struggle of insufficient income and increasing debts,
> interest compounding at the banks, all these years of your
> youth, and perhaps all the worse because I tried to consume
> my own smoke and not cloud others, yet anxious to see you
> all ready to survive. Mother was *very* brave and encouraged
> me to go on thinking instead of pot-boiling, in faith that that
> was best . . .

Alasdair, too, had a not altogether easy time when, at the age
of sixteen, he decided to attend Edinburgh Academy for a
year—two terms as a day boy and one as a boarder. His level
of achievement was very different from that of most of the other
boys, and although he could climb, sail, garden, build and,
above all, think, subjects such as trigonometry and cricket were
something of a mystery. However, he worked diligently, and
came top of his class in several subjects. He had wanted to
make sure that he would not be disadvantaged by his lack of
conventional teaching, and his father was quite proud of his
prowess. He was hopeful of Alasdair's support in the future,
and found it easier to show affection towards him, as this

letter (written while Alasdair was at Edinburgh Academy)
shows:

> . . . your idea of your parents—of your father especially, has
> to change at your age, in these years anyway, from the
> child's to the man's. You have been a dear child, and I am
> sorry that amid my many cares and pre-occupations I have
> not been a better daddy. Still I hope you have felt yourself
> loved, and that is after all the main thing.
>
> But now you are no longer a child—or I the child's daddy.
> But I don't want simply to be "the governor", the "pater",
> the old boy, or whatever the slang of the moment may
> define—nor yet—(my real danger, I suppose) to drop very
> much out of your life—into the merest background of
> consciousness—or at least as too remote and too literally
> erratic—or errant—to count very much. Or may I hope for
> something different. Are you coming with me to the wars?
> If so, for a time at least, I can really be, I hope, something
> of guide, perhaps more of philosopher, and assuredly
> friend. . . . Mind you, I fully and warmly sympathise with
> your present need . . . of attaining a manly competent
> productive level in something—rather than at present seeking
> for . . . such manifest interests as mine.

In the spring of 1910 Norah was ill, and in the early summer
Anna took her to stay with friends in France and Italy on a
prolonged holiday which they both needed. Geddes and the
two boys went to Dundee for the summer term (Alasdair was
to act as his father's assistant, and Arthur was being tutored in
woodcarving and other subjects), where Arthur contracted
scarlet fever and was taken to hospital. Patrick wrote to Anna
in Florence to report:

> 10th May 1910
> Dearest,
> Since I wrote last night, I need not add much—save this
> that Dr Templeman has just been in, to tell me all he could.
> The great fact is that "it is quite a mild case" and that "there
> is no danger, no, no, none at all"—that "he is doing quite
> well"—that "we can see him whenever we like"—"at the
> window of course"—"no, no, not inside!" and that "his
> mother need have no anxiety": that "the matron is very

nice, very nice indeed, and will take every care of him."
"I've given him the little end ward to himself"—"Of course
the only thing is that it's rather tedious. I've to keep him a
good while." How long?—"Oh six weeks, very likely, till
there is no danger of infection."

"Well, I told him he was going to the school of patience,
and the school of imagination." "Yes, that is so; he has
already called for paper and pencils and is busy drawing."

"Can he have his fiddle?" "No! You see disinfection
would spoil it." "Well," said I, "what of his getting his old
one, and leaving it to the hospital? Would you like that?"

"Certainly," said the Dr., "that would be capital—it
would often be a pleasure, if you don't mind leaving it."
(Where shall we find it? Perhaps Alasdair may know, or
Miss Galloway get it for us? Don't you bother.)

Similarly for books.

Any explanation of how he got it? "No," said the Dr.,
"None! A certain number are just sporadic, without milk or
other discoverable cause. We always have some going about.
But it's a mild case, quite a mild case." So he bustled away.

There now dears; the next letter (tomorrow or more
probably next day) will no doubt tell you that we've seen
him, and had our talk through the window.

I forgot to say that I asked if there was any bill to pay.
"No, certainly not" said he, "we make no exceptions."
"Well," said I, "all the more you'll allow me to send some
little things?" "Oh certainly, all right," said he. I'll send
our publishing books, for instance, at least all that Arthur
would care for, like *Evergreen* and *Lyra Celtica* and *Ossian*.

No other news really—save that I have found a capital
book and had a good going over it—Macdougall's (Social)
Psychology—the theme being that the organic instincts and
their emotions develop into the life of society, and this is in
some respects admirably traced. Quite a book for each of
you to find worth reading. Alasdair is flourishing. We had
a walk before breakfast and a talk after.

Love again as always,

P.S. Saw New King* proclaimed at Cross yesterday, and
sailors' band going off after, to merriest airs. "Le Roi est
mort: Vive le Roi!"

* George V.

Reporting to Anna a few days later on Arthur's progress, he added a more personal note:

... you ask about myself: I answer quite truly, I have as in so many previous years and perhaps a little more than usual felt that depression which you remember—but that is wearing off decidedly, and I feel and see I look more my old self. My brains too seem partly returning! Partly to aid this process, partly and primarily for intrinsic reasons, I have been reading some psychology, and thinking over that translation of all things that way which is so plainly needed, and for want of which our biological, evolutionary and educational movements have all as yet so largely failed; I mean those of the great world as well as the small Tower.

By 7th July he was back in Chelsea to see the completed Crosby Hall, and wrote to Anna one of his periodic love-letters:

Dearest—dearest indeed,
    I stop in the middle of a morning's endeavour of synthesis and write you a bit at least of the long-dreamed love-letter, and to tell you how I think of you and long for you, and starve for you, and worship you in my day-dreams from morning to night, and so—beg you to come home! Since writing last night my ideas have cleared up. I can't leave this place at present: it would in no way be the right thing to do; so the other suggestion that I cross [the Channel] if need be in a fortnight or so is plainly the best. I'll ask Branford for his flat which he is not using, and we two can stay there I daresay, or failing this some other arrangement will be found, and so we can have a little honeymoon together, and yet do some of our best work together as well!
    So far then the practical arrangement. I hope you approve. Now returning to the love-letter; as I grow older I don't grow colder! All we have ever thought and said and done together is true and right and "il faut le dire bien souvent". And I have been thinking how I can again be your lover, and more than ever—your champion too, delivering you from the tangle of cares you have so long and bravely borne. More and more I see that the best of life for man is the worship of woman, the service of woman, the deliverance of

woman too from all the dragons which beset her! (I've been making you a triptych in my symbol-graphic way!) And since the great success of life has come to us—and soon once more I may sing (to myself) "my love has come", I am indeed resolved in the speedily coming renewal of our too short and too broken times together, to live more fully than ever in all these ways until your daily habit and not simply your occasional ecstasy shall be to sing aloud that living song of life!

Yes, dearest, you are always young and beautiful to me, and have grown fairer through the years, sweeter, wiser, and all. I am glad to have the sense to know it, the eyes to see it, the heart to feel it. Come then, as soon as you may!

Four days later, Alasdair joined his father in Chelsea, and reported to Norah on the day's events and his first glimpse of the completed Crosby Hall. He was "obliged to write in pencil as Daddy has run off with both my pens and my ink-pencil!"

We dined at a little restaurant close by (saw Mr Scott Moncrieff of Lister House there!), and then walked up and down Embankment talking—looked at Crosby Hall in the dim light—too dim to see it well. I was a little disappointed with the Danvers St. view, but from Beaufort St. it looks very fine; and D. says inside is most striking of all. I couldn't see this in the semi-darkness; and it smelt depressingly musty and damp and like a new unused church!

Chapter 16

CITIES IN EVOLUTION

THE FIRST TOWN and Country Planning Act, promoted by John Burns, was passed in 1909. Its object was "to secure proper sanitary conditions, amenity and convenience in the laying out and use of land",[1] and it empowered local authorities for the first time to prepare town plans. In the same year, a Department of Civic Design was founded by William Lever (Viscount Leverhulme) at the University of Liverpool, and the following year he provided extra funds for the Department to launch *The Town Planning Review*, edited by Patrick Abercrombie. 1909 also saw the publication of *Town Planning in Practice* by Raymond Unwin who, together with his partner Barry Parker, had designed the first garden city at Letchworth, and was in the process of building Hampstead Garden Suburb. Both Unwin, who was then the leading English town-planner, and Abercrombie, who became best known for his planning work in the 1940's, were sympathetic to the Geddesian theory of survey. It fitted in with their desire to create attractive living-spaces for all members of society, and their dislike of mean dwellings erected out of financial greed, which were the main-springs of the new, idealistic, town-planning movement. Unwin in particular became friendly with Geddes, who some-times stayed at his house in Hampstead. His preliminary training as a mining engineer, his early appreciation of the social significance of Ebenezer Howard's garden city theory, plus his ability to evaluate and instigate the political and aesthetic skills needed to realize that theory, made him the ideal practical planner with whom Geddes could discuss his ideas.

During the summer and early autumn of 1910 they saw a good deal of one another, for Unwin was the prime organizer of the first British Town Planning Conference, to be held in October, which was being sponsored by the Royal Institute of British Architects and in which Geddes was extremely interested. An exhibition at Burlington House was planned as an adjunct to the Conference (in those days the R.I.B.A.'s offices were in Conduit Street, not far from Burlington House), with contributions from Germany, America and Italy, and a special Garden City room to display designs which included Letchworth, Hampstead, the Co-Partnership Estates, Port Sunlight and Bournville. More particularly a small gallery, known as "the black and white room", was set aside for Geddes, in which he was to demonstrate his method of city survey by displaying some of the contents of the Edinburgh Room at the Outlook Tower.

These contents had recently been revised and added to, and had benefited from the 1903 Summer Meeting, but there was still a great deal of work to do to get them into shape. Frank Mears was Geddes's chief helper in this, and he also made some fine drawings for the exhibit. The aim was to make the display easy to assemble and mount so that it might travel to various centres, and this aim must have been achieved. For on 9th October Geddes gave a lecture in Edinburgh on the exhibit, with the Lord Provost (who "was most eulogistic") in the chair, after which it was packed up and taken by Mears down to London in time for the opening at Burlington House the next day. Geddes was rather disparaging about the Edinburgh "City Fathers" taking note of his survey work only when it was wanted in London, having, he claimed, held an "indifferent, unsympathetic, distrustful, puzzled, half-contemptuous attitude" towards it during all the years it had been on their own doorstep.

On 10th October he wrote to S. K. Ratcliffe, Secretary of the Sociological Society, explaining how he felt the exhibition to be a culmination point in his work, and outlining what combination of influences he thought should influence the sociology of the future. He was clearly stimulated and gratified to be contributing to an important, practical development like the new planning movement, and to be working alongside colleagues of stature who appreciated his philosophy.

At last your exasperating convenor of the Cities Committee has ceased simply to ring the bell and run away, as has been too much his forte, and is occupied at length in delivering the goods. At last I can face the Cities Committee in particular, the Sociological Society in general, and its long-suffering secretary above all. I want to talk of this, in my paper on the 18th, and practically to say—here at length, after all my talk about cities and city development there emerges a fairly orderly and even lucid outline survey of a great city, with some illustration of all these aspects I have so long talked about—industrial and artistic, hygienic and educational, social and moral. And all this not only considered as a development in the past, or even as a heritage in the present, but as a momentum of the future; a mighty pressure, a complex resultant which it is now possible to analyse into its main factors of good and evil, better and worse. Hence from all this sociological survey there emerges at every point, elements for a corresponding practical report, and I was able to lecture yesterday not only the Lord Provost, but the Town Clerk (a tougher customer) and his colleagues, on the weaknesses of a publication they emitted two years ago, entitled: "A Preliminary Memorandum for the Increase of Industries in Edinburgh", and in which after courteously bowing out the education and art and beauty and civilisation, for which our city has stood in the past, they proceeded essentially to pray for blacking and matches and patent inventions in the future—developing all this ideal industrial quarter of theirs straight in the face of the South-west wind, so as to blow all the smoke of this torment upon their existing citizens.

. . . Here again is the justification of the idea I have so often brought up to the Sociological Society's Council, viz. that the Society should not only *permit* our Cities Committee, but develop it to the utmost. Of course the comparative clearness of this exhibit—still far from what it should be— makes me feel how indefinite I must have seemed to you all, and I quite see that I ought to thank my stars and your patience for having been granted these years of grace. Here is *some* fruit anyway; so I should like to get the Council, indeed the Society, to visit this exhibition. . . . For there I think I could make you and everybody—not simply long- enduring friends like Martin White, but those who see nothing at all in Civics, at least nothing but gas and drains— see, well, here is a concrete sociology, a description of human hives a good deal more interesting than those which biologists make for simpler species.

Beyond that even, I have to get you all to see that just as a biologist derives his theories from this concrete observation, so must the sociologist. Spencer's sociology is excellent, so far as it goes, and Haddon and Westermarck are his prophets. But this is all too anthropological. Bentham, Stuart Mill, and the Liberals generally, have also their place and gospel, and most other sociologists, e.g. Hobhouse, are their prophets. Yet (a) Darwin, with his direct observational science, and his direct interpretations of this into world theories, (b) Le Play, with his corresponding concrete studies of the simple and the developed occupations, as in his arrangement of international exhibitions, his social economy exhibits and his social development theories, and (c) Comte, with his concrete historical knowledge, and his interpretations of this heritage as phases of a great evolution, a great transition from the old order before the political and industrial revolution, towards a nobler and more concrete utopia than that revolution has ever seen—these are all better doctrines. And with all modesty, our city surveys and exhibitions are the beginnings at any rate of the needed exposition of these main teachers, the delivery of their message, the justification of their great previsions.

There then is my point, broadly and roughly expressed (in the midst of constant interruption and pressure), yet I hope intelligible enough till we meet.

I get to Chelsea tomorrow, Saturday night. Will you send a note there saying what afternoon you are free to go with me to the Exhibition? On Tuesday I have to lecture on the City Survey at the R.I.B.A. Conduit Street. Can you come, and let us go to tea afterwards, and talk things over?

In his book *Town and Country Planning* (1933), Patrick Abercrombie recalled the effect of a visit to Geddes's room in the exhibition:

The survey first emerged into public view at the great Town Planning Exhibition of 1910 at Burlington House, and it is safe to say that the modern practice of planning in this country would have been a more elementary thing if it had not been for the Edinburgh room and all that this implied. It was a torture chamber to those simple souls that had been ravished by the glorious perspectives or heartened by the healthy villages shown in the other and ampler galleries. Within this den sat Geddes, a most unsettling person, talking, talking, talking—about anything and everything. The visitors could criticize his show—the merest hotch-potch—picture postcards—newspaper cuttings—crude old woodcuts—strange diagrams—archaeological reconstructions; these things, they said, were unworthy of the Royal Academy—many of them not even framed—shocking want of respect; but if they chanced within the range of Geddes's talk, henceforth nothing could medicine them to that sweet sleep which yesterday they owned. There was something more in town planning than met the eye!

However, the reporter from the *Evening Standard* did not encounter too much difficulty, claiming that the exhibit was "of quite extraordinary interest and value", and saying that "it, so to speak, explains the whole exhibition, and prevents it becoming for the unprofessional visitor a collection of unrelated facts and illustrations". A perspicacious comment, which must have pleased Geddes.

After the close of the conference, Geddes gave a course of lectures on civics at Crosby Hall, and prepared to transfer an extended version of his exhibition there in February. This was to be a complete Cities Exhibition, showing their development from Valley Section to Garden City, and including sections on Medieval Cities, Renaissance Cities, and selected Great Capitals. John Burns presided at the opening, and S. K. Ratcliffe gave this summing up of the exhibition's effect:

His collection of historical, architectural, and imaginative material was a remarkable expression of his mind and method, and I would assert that no interpreter of our age, in the wide province of social evolution and institutions, was in the same class with Geddes as, accompanied by a group of students, he made his progress along the road of civilisation as it was illuminated by the maps, plans, and diagrams on the walls and stands.

A letter sent to Geddes from Edinburgh by Norah, just as the

Crosby Hall exhibition was due to open, includes an affectionate tribute to his teaching method:

> In the evening Mr Holborn lectured on Art in Daily Life. His style is almost too perfect—I didn't know whether he was most like a minister or a variety entertainment man, but thought he would do well at a street corner. It was very good of course, but as Alasdair and I agreed, we are more accustomed to following helter-skelter as best we can, than to feel we are treading on the lecturer's heels.

In March the Cities Exhibition transferred to the Royal Scottish Academy galleries in Edinburgh—where it was opened by Lord Pentland, the Secretary of State for Scotland. Branford wrote to Geddes:

> I have been wondering how the Exhibition was getting on in Edinburgh. I augured well from the fact that Ross told me you had a column of appreciation in The Scotsman—it is a great sign of changed times!

17,000 people visited the exhibition during the three weeks that it was open, after which it toured to Dublin and Belfast. The Viceroy of Ireland, Lord Aberdeen, together with his wife, were deeply impressed by Geddes's whole approach, and talked with him at length about the problems of Ireland, particularly the poor housing and run-down cities. Raymond Unwin used his influence to try to persuade the authorities in Canada to sponsor a tour of the Cities Exhibition, and also made suggestions for standardizing the size of the screens and pictorial items so that it would be easier to assemble and pack. No other invitations were forthcoming, however, and when the exhibition closed in Belfast it showed a total deficit of £500. An appeal was made to cover the debt, towards which Unwin and George Cadbury each paid £50, Neville Chamberlain five guineas, and Geddes himself £20.

An immediate result of the impact of the Cities Exhibition was that Lord Pentland approached Geddes to find out if he would like to be recommended for a knighthood in the forthcoming New Year's honours list. Geddes talked the matter over with Anna, and decided to decline: mainly for "democratic reasons", but also because it might interfere with "peaceful 'hermitage' thinking" and force them into "Society and new demands on time and strength", and, too, might prove expensive, since in most people's eyes knights were supposed to be rich.

Throughout his mature life, Geddes depended on skilful shorthand typists to capture his flow of rhetoric for the production of his lecture papers, books and many longer letters. The particular combination of patience, education and quick wits needed for this job was not always easy to find, and he used to bemoan its scarcity. In particular he once said that the existence of *Cities in Evolution* owed much to a particularly good secretary. This book was largely drawn from the lectures on civics he was giving during the first decade of the century, and it was originally prepared for Williams & Norgate to go into their Home University Library series. Together with Gilbert Murray and Herbert Fisher, J. Arthur Thomson was editing this series, and had no doubt been instrumental in pushing Geddes to get his city lectures into book form. The manuscript, then entitled *Evolution of Cities*, was submitted to the publishers, and on 8th March 1912, Thomson had the unenviable task of writing thus to his friend:

> On my return I found a letter . . . saying that Murray and Fisher had taken fright at your book and had strongly advised postponement. . . . I have in the meantime written to say that I am entirely of an opposite opinion except as regards some verbal blemishes (like "conurbation"*).

This was not a convenient moment for Geddes to have a setback. In order to celebrate the twenty-fifth anniversary of the founding of University Hall, he was in the process of organizing a masque involving 650 participants, to be performed at the Synod Hall, Edinburgh, on 14th, 15th, 16th and 19th March. Entitled *The Masque of Learning and its many meanings, a pageant of education through the ages*, it was a feat of compression and imagination. Like most amateur pageants it must

* The only one of Geddes's verbal innovations to find its way into the *Oxford Dictionary*. It reached the Concise edition in 1964, and the Supplement in 1972.

have had its comic side, but it is impossible not to admire Geddes's endeavour as he proceeded to involve such a large section of the community in a celebration of the cultures of the world. From the list of helpers named in the text which he published to accompany the masque, it appears he found a Dr C. C. Wang to organize the Chinese section, a Mr M. L. Banara for the Hindu and Buddhist ones, a Mr M. M. Gandevia for the Persian, a Mr S. El Azim for the Moham- medan, a Mons. M. Tirol for the French, and a Herr Hopp for the German. Rehearsals can barely be imagined. . . . They were conducted by a "Stage Manager and Marshal" called Mr T. Duncan Rhind, A.R.I.B.A.

Geddes replied to Thomson that he hoped that Williams & Norgate were not going to renege on their contract, and on 17th March Thomson wrote: "they are in a difficulty because of 'the strongly-expressed opinion of Murray and Fisher' " and "are going to propose another mode of publication". On 18th March, G. H. Perris, the assistant editor of the series, wrote to Geddes from the publishers' offices in Henrietta Street:

I am infinitely sorry to say that, against Thomson's opinion, the other two Editors strongly object to the inclusion of your volume in the Library, and that the publishers agree with them in this objection. As I do not agree, I find it difficult adequately to represent to you their position, especially as it has in part been put to us verbally; but they think that the book, although containing valuable passages of vivid interest, is not well designed for our public and is quite too individual a pronouncement to stand beside the body of volumes, which they regard as impartial and objective reviews of various subjects. They had anticipated something quite different— something, perhaps less stimulating to the exceptional mind, but more useful to the humble individual who is looking out for a short and matter-of-fact explanation of how cities grew to what they are, and how he or she can help to make them what they ought to be. They feel—and here I cannot disagree with them—that you have been cramped for space, and that your volume would be more satisfactory, would attract more attention, and would probably remunerate you much better as an independent volume.

Messrs. Williams & Norgate, for their part are very willing, and will be greatly interested, to publish it independently, and would be glad to do so at the earliest moment that you can make it possible for them. They would ask you to bring the total quantity from the existing 50,000 words up to 60 or 70,000 words, and to provide them with a few plans and illustrations for it; and they would then rush the book out without any delay. They would pay you the stipulated £50 upon the book being passed for press, so that you should not suffer in that respect. In view of the heavy cost to which they will be put for double setting—for the book will have to be completely reset in a larger type and page—they can only offer you a 10% royalty on the first thousand copies, after which it shall be increased to 15%. The price of the book would be five or six shillings. Directly you intimate that you agree to this, Mr Williams will send you a form of agreement embodying these and other usual details.

He has read the book carefully himself, and has been much interested in it; and he asks me to add the following message. No doubt, you will be able to insert some of the matter which you had to cut out. But he thinks that there should be two more chapters added, dealing with two essential points, as to which he fails to find any guidance in the book as it is, namely (1) the effect of communications upon city-planning—especially, of course, of railway communications, the provision of goods services as well as of passenger services; (2) how city-planning schemes are to be paid for.

On 28th March, Geddes replied:

I understood from Thomson . . . that the book was accepted, and to spring on me, at the close, that it is rejected, and by editors who have not had the courtesy to write, explain, or otherwise appear, is the most amazing combination of nonchalance and of insult.

The book, somewhat enlarged—though not in the region of goods services—finally appeared in 1915. To the "humble individual" looking for "matter-of-fact explanation" it is indeed a non-starter. Its virtue is to make the reader consider the immense sweep and value of the civic fabric into which such things as goods services have to be fitted. It is an affirmation of civilization and a negation of industrial greed. But it is never elitist, theoretical or merely rhetorical. Much of it is concerned with the need for regional survey. Geddes has been criticized for encouraging people to collect thousands of items of information in the name of survey, and then omitting to lay down how this would lead to enlightened town-planning. But it could not be as simple as that. The survey was not intended just to facilitate good surface urban planning; it was a whole process of re-education. Once one had undergone the process, had gleaned at least a partial vision of the implication of a citizen's evolution and potential, one would be equipped to take up a place in the team responsible for planning that future. But it was no good inventing utopian drawing-board blueprints. The future grew from understanding of the past, and integration of its methods and achievements with the new discoveries of the present. Then, Geddes felt, when proper understanding and education existed, free of superstition, bigotry and specialism, all political and economic rivalries would be seen to be unnecessary and destructive. To most people that still seems Utopian rather than Eutopian. But with our diminishing resources and increasing weapons, to a growing minority it simply appears as true.

1912 was, of course, not an auspicious year to be writing of the disappearances of class and nation rivalries. In fact by then Geddes and Branford were already convinced that war was inevitable, and in connection with the Cities Committee they embarked on planning a series of books called "The Making of the Future", which would analyse the real causes of the conflict and help people to think constructively about international regeneration. The credo headed "What To Do" which summarized the objects of the series, appears in Appendix III. Many of its comments, particularly concerning direct action, seem familiar today.

Added to the probability of war, was Geddes's continuing insecurity about his own livelihood. The Roseburn Cliff scheme was still dragging on, and he needed financial help if he was to salvage anything from the project. As usual, he appealed to Martin White. Drafts of two letters headed "destroy when read" which he wrote to John Ross about this appeal have survived.

The following extracts do not show Geddes in a particularly good light *vis-à-vis* his benefactor. However, it was perhaps inevitable that when lack of money incapacitated him, he would attack the one person able and likely to help him should he fail to do so.

21st October 1912

I have never found White in a more disagreeable humour— or a more muddled and irrelevant style of talk, cutting across everything with weary wails . . . the scoldings of me— on every subject but the present one—e.g. Roseburn Cliff— then of you and back to me again and so on. . . . I came away but told him at door that if 3 flats could be kept we'd retrieve matters. He said he was going to Whitson and Methuen tomorrow in Edinburgh! I said they had no powers to bargain, and wouldn't, that he'd better take it from me that I'd be prepared to recommend a definite shift of next break of lease from 4 yrs to 2.

. . . but he was not going to put up any more money—and so on. I came away.

Now note this: after this fit will come the cold one; he will repent.

24th October 1912

JMW is full of ideas of "running this thing himself" and "if he is to pay the piper, he is to call the tune". . . . My feeling would be that you might well have things out with him on first occasion—and give it to him hot and strong, yet quietly and decidedly, with just a touch of conciliation too: that may be dangerous (and then lead to a final rupture)—but it may also be the best way to heal the difficulty.

White was clearly genuinely worried about Geddes's whole future, and it seems he approached the university authorities at Dundee about the possibility of increasing Geddes's teaching commitment. On 12th December he wrote to his friend advising him to "take the Dundee £600", pointing out that in ten years' time it would lead to a pension of £3–400 p.a. (Geddes was fifty-eight, with no visible means of support for his and Anna's old age.) White confided his worries to Thomson, who wrote from Aberdeen trying to persuade Geddes to accept the offer:

I had a talk with Mr Martin White about a fortnight ago. Of course it is not my business, but surely there is much to be said for settling down at Dundee for a few years at an increased salary and getting some collaboration done. Dundee is only two hours from here. Besides, they would not seek to imprison you too much this time of day. I was impressed by the touch of real affection for you in Mr Martin White's expostulation, and I gather that he was prepared to clear some Chelsea business up a bit if you would fall in with desires at Dundee. But I am urging it rather on the ground that though you are youngest of us all, you can't go on very long with your tremendous rush, and that I should like to see two or three books out. Forgive me, however, if I am meddling.

(The collaboration to which he referred was further scientific books which they were jointly planning.) But this advice, however well meant, did not incorporate the wider fields that had opened to Geddes through his experience of the cities exhibitions, and their impact on men like Unwin, Cadbury, Pentland and Aberdeen. He did not accept the Dundee offer. The support of loyal friends had helped him to reach his present level of achievement, but it could not carry him through to ultimate recognition. Of those loyal friends, none had been more effective than Thomson and White, and it must have been sad for them to watch their mentor floundering out of reach. But he was out of reach: Scottish waters were no longer sufficient to contain him—if, indeed, they ever had been. He returned for help and renewal (often an exhausting process where Thomson was concerned), but his mind restlessly searched wider horizons.

Inspired by *The Masque of Learning*'s success in Edinburgh, he decided to remount the pageant in London in order to raise funds for improving and extending Crosby Hall. This time the number of people involved was over a thousand, and it was staged at the Imperial Institute, South Kensington; the planned five performances held in March were so successful that they were repeated in April. Geddes himself acted as the Prologue, dressed as a medieval scholar in a large velvet cap, and one of the performers remarked that in rehearsal he would move from group to group, demonstrating how parts should be played "with complete absorption" and "the dramatic force and finish of a fine professional actor". Anna worked behind the scenes, checking lists, answering questions, and creating an impression of calm amid chaos. The masque received, on the whole, very enthusiastic press notices, including the following in the *Manchester Guardian* of 12th March 1913:

> Professor Geddes knows how to avoid the vice of most pageant-makers, who smother action in a fuss of costume. Violin music sounded softly from somewhere behind the curtains; there was little speaking, and what there was was significant; everything was given up to the delight of the eye. The performers were people who could move with dignity and grace, and what one remembers afterwards is not the story but just the vision of tall, fair women and the dancing of children.

Gremlins crept into the press responsible for printing *The Gentlewoman* of 29th March, and produced this splendid item:

> The most striking costumes were worn by the following ladies: The Marchioness Townshend, the Lady Holden of Alston, Mrs Marigold, Mrs Basil Gill, Miss Holman Hunt, Miss Marrow, Miss Cynthia King, Miss Diehl, Captain Egerton, Mr Heslewood, Mr Detmould, and the Rev. Dr. Walsh.

The Lady, however, refused to be carried away by spectacle, and delivered the following reprimand:

> One would like to know Professor Geddes's authority for giving a monk a maniple when he is not vested for mass, and for putting a bishop performing the function of opening a college into a chasuble.

Geddes would not wittingly have included inaccuracies, but he certainly was not aiming at text-book realism. He saw the masque as an opportunity to convey the spirit of culture, the life that is in learning. It was his supreme gesture against the "mouldering hay" approach.

Earlier that year he had been invited to make designs for the new zoological gardens on Corstorphine Hill in Edinburgh. The extended run of the masque inevitably meant that he was separated from the day-to-day detail of this work, and Norah was deputed to advise on the landscaping and planting. The animal quarters had been planned with careful concern for their occupants' needs and comforts, and the whole design had a pleasant, almost domestic atmosphere which would particularly appeal to children. Much of the original layout still survives, and while some of the animal spaces now appear rather restricted, the paths and bridges, trees and shrubs (particularly when planted in the enclosures, so that a wild cat may be seen asleep in the sun under a brilliant yellow forsythia), ponds and stream, make an effective landscape. Even Geddes's predilection for small-scale castellation and balustrading fits quite well into the invented landscape of a zoo.

While Norah was occupied with Corstorphine Hill, Alasdair was enlisted to help get together an enlarged version of the Cities Exhibition. Geddes had decided to participate in the "Exposition des Villes" which was to be a feature of the international exhibition due to open in Ghent in July. He himself was committed to spend the summer term in Dundee, and after a brief visit to Ghent in May to see the gallery, he left Alasdair to supervise the erection of the exhibit. Amelia Defries, one of Geddes's pupil/disciples and compiler of *The Interpreter Geddes* (1927), was one of several friends who helped Alasdair, and in her book she gives an account of what it was like to participate in such an event.

Two days before the exhibition was due to open, Geddes had still not arrived. Paul Otlet, one of the exhibition directors, came to ask Alasdair where his father could be.

Alasdair shrugged his shoulders, spread out his hands like a Frenchman, and said simply and smilingly, as if it were a joke: "Il n'est pas encore arrivé." . . . My general impression was of frock-coated gentlemen, top-hats in hand, decorations in buttonholes, rather excitedly exclaiming: "Mais Monsieur Geddes, où est-il donc?"

Then the next day Miss Defries arrived at the exhibition to find the workmen in a frenzy, most of the pictures and diagrams— which had been hung so carefully—scattered about the floor, and a shirt-sleeved Geddes maniacally redirecting everything.

> For the first and last time I saw Alasdair in a rage. But no word was said; he was obeying orders like a conscript and it was towards the middle of the day, when helping him to get a great map of Paris into place, that I asked him if we had really made so many mistakes as to hang all those things wrongly.
>
> "No," he said quietly, with tight lips and almost on the verge of tears. "No. Daddy had an inspiration in the train last night. He saw all at once a way to make things clearer."

Anna had also arrived in Ghent, and Amelia Defries found that she created quite the opposite effect to her husband:

> Mrs Geddes found time, while sorting books and jotting down notes, to inquire as to my health and living arrangements; and a few days later she had me in better rooms, working shorter hours and living more normally than during the last three months.

Their labours were rewarded. The Cities Exhibition won the *grand prix* awarded by an international jury for the best portrayal of civic development and planning—despite the fact that the German exhibit was government-subsidized and meticulously mounted. Many visitors praised the way either Geddes or Alasdair would conduct them round the exhibition tirelessly explaining the unfolding philosophy behind the charts and pictures. Emile Claus, the painter, went round the exhibition alone one evening, and was observed to take off his hat and bow low several times. After asking Miss Defries who was responsible for everything, he said: "I take off my hat to the genius whose thoughts are here. I take off my hat to him."

Despite the public acclaim, it remained a difficult experience for Alasdair. He was staying in the same lodgings as his father, and remarked that "no human being could live as well as work with P.G. and survive". By 15th October, when the exhibition was nearing its end, he wrote to his mother:

> I have been feeling the awful demoralizing side of international exhibitions. Here are crowds of people (*guardiens* to

curators) hanging around their exhibits which are not permanent enough to make it worth while perfecting them. Here they are, I say, hovering about, waiting for interruptions and losing the habit and the satisfaction of creative work or of study. Degeneration results—it is a miserable atmosphere. No one—even Daddy less than usual—is having *good days*. Life has no continuity or regularity. We have fallen back to days anterior to invention of the one day of rest in seven, i.e. before the creation, and in our chaos we await in expectation the day of judgement when our false world here shall be destroyed and we set free to face real life once more. Amen.

As soon as the exhibition closed, Geddes took Alasdair on a tour of German cities, and in the train on the way to Cologne on 25th October he was able to write more cheerfully to Anna:

This trip will be most interesting and will, I feel sure, leave me with an impulse towards thought for the winter and will wash away the dregs of unpleasant memory which this on the whole good summer has left in me and which otherwise might clog me.

Daddy will be telling you of the results of his strenuous day, of which I am not *quite* informed yet (in detail). I'll try and send him back to you in as good preservation as possible. It won't be long before we're all together.

How is Arthur getting on? Is he taking more kindly to his maths, or is he simply dogged? What regular exercise is he having? This I feel more and more important.

One of the results of the Cities Exhibition's visit to Ireland in 1911 had been Geddes's continuing friendship with Lord and Lady Aberdeen, together with the establishment of an Irish National Housing and Town Planning Association. Norah spent the best part of three years working in Dublin organizing play spaces for children, a scheme which was incorporated into the national health policy promoted by the Aberdeens. They invited Geddes to visit them early in 1914, and together they planned another exhibition and discussed a thorough-going policy of civic and social reform. Geddes had already met Jim Larkin, the militant union leader, and discussed with him "the idea that 'housing' is fundamental to the problems of labour, since the house is the central and fundamental fact of real wages". Home Rule was being debated yet again in the House of Commons, and the industry of Ireland was half paralysed by the strike which had spread under Larkin's leadership. Geddes remarked that "the Irish difficulties are not a little due to their keen and bright intelligence which ruthlessly exposes the imperfection of every hopeful bud, and indignantly pecks it to pieces". Having planned the outline for the exhibition, decided that a competition for the best Dublin improvement scheme should be held, and asked Branford to involve members of the Sociological Society in a School of Civics within the exhibition, Geddes left the Aberdeens and went to Cardiff to fulfil a lecture engagement. After that he returned to Edinburgh where a vacation course on regional survey had been organized at the Outlook Tower. There was particular significance attached to the leading participant in this course, but first brief mention should be made of future arrangements which Geddes clinched at this time.

He accepted a lecture tour offer from America to start at the end of the year, which he then immediately cancelled because he had received a subsequent invitation to take the Cities Exhibition to Madras. Lord Pentland, who had opened the Exhibition in Scotland while Secretary of State, was now Governor of Madras and he wrote to Geddes urging him to come and "enlighten the municipal administrators of India". Geddes agreed to go in October—after the Dublin exhibition had ended. A decision that was to change the course of his remaining life.

Meanwhile the regional survey course flourished—under the able guidance of Mabel Barker, the now grown-up child of Harry Barker, and Geddes's god-daughter. In 1909 she had written to Geddes asking advice about her education and development—a letter which had prompted a prolix reply, similar to when Mrs Whyte had enquired whether her son might act as a Saturday apprentice. The long-term result had been that in 1913 Mabel had become established at the Outlook Tower, and she was instrumental in organizing the 1914 vacation course—which in turn led to the founding of the Regional Survey Association and the promotion of survey as an educational method. She was a girl of great energy and strength

of character, whose commonsense was a boon to the muddles
that beset the Tower. Geddes often wrote praising her efforts,
and soon began to confide in her in the kind of easy manner
he found so difficult to achieve with Norah.

Mabel was among the party that went to Dublin to help
with the Cities Exhibition and School of Civics. Also included
were Norah, Alasdair and Victor Branford. But when the exhibition opened, Archduke Franz Ferdinand had already been
assassinated in Sarajevo. It was staged at the great disused
Linen Hall, which had been especially restored for the occasion
as a symbol of Irish regeneration, and included a section of
exhibits from many local towns. The work so far achieved for
the Dublin survey organized by the National Housing and
Town Planning Association was also on display. And there was
a pageant: somehow Geddes managed to organize a procession
of eighty Irish mayors who, Patrick Abercrombie later recalled,[2]
"were all in their robes and marched to the Civics Exhibition
in the Linen Hall". Abercrombie also remembered a specific
incident which occurred at the exhibition:

> . . . one Sunday afternoon the only person left in charge of
> it was Lady Aberdeen herself. An enormous flock of people
> from the Dublin slums came to visit the Show that Sunday
> afternoon. After they had had a look round and found only
> Lady Aberdeen in charge, they began one by one to remove
> the chairs and the tables and carry them off home. At the
> end of the afternoon the Exhibition was not quite empty, but
> a large number of exhibits and the whole of the furniture
> had disappeared. The late Lord Leverhulme was very de-
> lighted when he found out what had happened to the model
> of Port Sunlight, saying it was the greatest compliment that
> they could have ever paid him. Each thief would have a
> model of a little cottage on his mantelpiece and that would
> show him the sort of place he should be living in, instead of
> in the slums. Geddes of course was delighted too.

As Geddes discussed with Jim Larkin and others a plan for
building a garden village for the dock labourers, Austria-
Hungary declared war on Serbia, and within a week Germany
was at war with Russia, France and Belgium, forcing Great
Britain to join the hostilities.

Geddes and Branford seized the opportunity to lecture even more passionately on their beliefs. War was a symptom not a cure. When this one was over, Britain had to learn what true peace was all about, and had to remodel her cities so that no one was excluded from the benefits of a neotechnic society. Geddes elaborated his concepts of Wardom and Peacedom. (Very much as Buckminster Fuller was later to work out similar concepts of "livingry" and "killingry".)

> Where Wardom is destructive of cities in war and careless of their life and growth in what it calls peace, Peacedom is reconstructive, in both the rural and urban order, recovering the concept of industry and of economics from their patent misuse, as dominated respectively by mechanism and by money. . . . War, among its superiorities to the peace of Wardom, is undeniably neotechnic where the latter is still little save paleotechnic; but the neotechnic character of Wardom is too much concentrated upon weapons, while that of Peacedom rises into all the arts.

The entries for the competition to improve Dublin could not be judged as the American assessor had cancelled his passage to Ireland. (When the three judges finally met in 1916, the prize was awarded to Patrick Abercrombie, though little of the work was ever carried out.) As the exhibition closed, the Linen Hall was immediately requisitioned for use as a Red Cross training centre, and the exhibits were duly packed, ready for dispatch to India. Because for him the actual declaration of war was simply one event within the general state of Wardom, Geddes had no intention of changing his plans. If he had a message to give to people, then it was as valid now as it had ever been.

Alasdair, who was to accompany him to India, was in a much less certain frame of mind. In Belgium, places and people that he loved dearly were being destroyed. Many of his contemporaries were enlisting. Following his father on to the S.S. *Nore* was not easy. For a young man of twenty-three in 1914, no matter how unorthodox his upbringing, the outbreak of war could not be viewed simply as a symptom of society's unsatisfactory condition. However, once aboard ship, Geddesian life continued as usual. While Anna remained behind at Ramsay

Garden, her husband noted: "the fine landscape of the Canal after passing the great Bitter Lakes, to the oases of the plain under the precipitous hill front towards Suez, and there came to me a vivid feeling—What a splendid work it would be to extend these oases and multiply them!" He wrote to her:

> Our journey is mainly occupied with quiet grind at papers brought—with a considerable (yet, alas too inconsiderably) clearing out of rubbish, and a refreshing of one's general grip of the civic ideas which have so long been fermenting and yielding the confused skimmings of these many bundles...

The bigger bundles containing the Cities Exhibition were travelling on another vessel, the *Clan Grant*, along with a thousand cases of whisky. And a German cruiser, the *Emden*, was approaching the Indian Ocean.

Meanwhile Geddes pondered on ways in which the "European mastery of nature" and "the Mohammedan acceptance of things as they are" could combine to make a flourishing "spiritual brotherhood".

Chapter 17

PASSAGE THROUGH INDIA

DESPITE THE WAR in Europe, there were aspects to Geddes's arrival in India that made it seem like the start of a promising new era. He had celebrated his sixtieth birthday on board ship, but he had the vigour of a much younger man and his stamina was unimpaired. He was to receive consultancy fees for any planning proposals he might make in the Madras presidency, and his Cities Exhibition was assured of a welcome both there and, later, in Bombay. But first he and Alasdair were to travel right across India, from Bombay to Calcutta, and would be invited to make some brief city reports *en route*; after which they would journey south to Madras.

On 22nd October they left Bombay and went to stay at Government House in Poona. Geddes reported to Anna:

His Excellency [Lord Willingdon] especially quite in love with India, and Indians—and thus much more to Alasdair's and my mind than all the other people we have met, nice to us though all have been.

It was the middle of the Hindu New Year holiday, and they accompanied Lord Willingdon on a visit to several temples. At the City temple the crowds wore flower garlands "beyond description exuberant and fine" and "in this supposedly most disaffected of cities were mostly more than cordial". The next day was spent with an agriculturist and "a thoughtful peasant member of Town Council" poring over a plan of the city. Then, Geddes wrote to Anna, they

Got back well pleased with ourselves, to find news of *Emden*'s exploit. Are we downhearted? NO!

The *Emden* had sunk the *Clan Grant*, whose crew and cargo were lost without trace. The Cities Exhibition had not been insured against war risks.

A letter written to Anna a few days later indicates the desperate straits their finances were in before Geddes received the first of his Indian fees. Nevertheless, he had reverted to his youthful habit of smiling in the face of calamity.

Dearest,

This difficulty shall be made an opportunity.

As to your personal cares, I only send £20—and have had to draw £15—but by next week's mail I hope to do better. I enclose note for Bank; and shall I hope be able to pay Whitson rent* before long also tell him—though this loss is serious for the time.

How lucky we had some pleasure in foreseeing relief of cares, though now not assured! But Sisyphus is working his shoulder under the stone again, as so often before.

Always your loving,

P.

P.S. I shall have better economic conditions for you than you will expect from this!

About a week later, he received the following cable:

Emergency Committee Lanchester chairman endeavouring collect and forward within fortnight small representative Exhibition replace loss. Have you any instructions?

Partially inspired by Geddes's ideas, H. V. Lanchester, the architect and planner, was already involved in city survey work, and the emergency committee which he set up acted with impressive swiftness. Burns, Branford, Unwin and George Pepler all helped, Anna and others searched the Outlook Tower for items, and a smaller replacement exhibition was packed and shipped to Madras in time for the scheduled opening in January.

Meanwhile Geddes and Alasdair continued their travels through Agra, Delhi, Lucknow, Cawnpore and Allahabad. By the time he reached Delhi, Geddes's remedies and propositions for Indian town-planning were already well-formed. They had

* The lease of 14 Ramsay Garden had been sold to Town & Gown.

little to do with the formal municipal architecture of Europe
that the British Raj was gradually imposing on the old cities,
but took cognizance of existing structures and social patterns
—however humble. This was the period when Lutyens's designs
for New Delhi were being built, and they did not meet with
Geddes's approval. Early in 1915 Lutyens wrote from New
Delhi that he was wildly angry

> with a certain Professor Geddes who has come out to lecture
> on town planning—his exhibits were sunk by the *Emden*. He
> seems to have talked rot in an insulting way and I hear is
> going to tackle me! A crank who don't know his subject. He
> talks a lot, gives himself away then loses his temper.[1]

By 1st December Geddes and Alasdair had reached Benares,
which they found "quite the most vividly pictorial city in the
world". The contrast between the absolute religious devotion
of the people, and the dilapidated buildings shattered by
the violence of the sacred river when it flooded, fascinated
Geddes:

> Contrast of cosmic indifference and human religions can go
> no further! Yet the religions too are right; and in the main
> they hold back the cosmic stream, and make it the human
> one it is. Yet how simply!—that nature is sacred, that sex is
> sacred, that creatures are sacred, life sacred, and that even
> out of destruction comes new life. . . . It is a great relief, after
> the totally materialistic character of our civilization, and of
> most of that of Mohammedan and Hindu life also, in the
> cities we have come through, to find ourselves in a world
> where ideals, and meditations on them, are recognized as the
> main business of life.

He reported to Anna that Alasdair was going to stay behind in
Benares on his own for two days, thus shortening his visit to
Calcutta, "for this is one of the great experiences and uplifts of
his life".

In fact Alasdair was tormented by his dilemma as to where
his duty lay: to his country and her war-ravaged allies, or to
his father's work. He loved the Indian landscape, and had
already formed plans for touring the Himalayas the following

year, but he was not comfortable in his role of Geddes's aide. He had written to Mabel Barker about his anxiety, but she had replied firmly:

> Surely you . . . would not desert from that army (which needs you so badly, and seems so small, though its force need bear no proportion to numbers) even if you were *not* in India? You, who see things so quickly and clearly as a rule—do you not believe that you can work for something better than even the prevention of ravage spreading over French and English and Scottish earth? Give the Earth real Peace, and she will heal even the wounds in time. And if you would really have run away to bombard Belgian cities and shoot Germans— well, never would I have thought to be so glad that you are far away my friend!

Nevertheless, her letter also contained the news that a mutual friend was seeking a commission, on which she commented: "I feel that he, with his education and outlook on things, has taken the right and only course open to him. . . .". Alasdair, modest, good-natured and painstaking as he was, did not share Mabel's conviction that his qualities singled him out to fulfil quite different ideals from his contemporaries.

While in Calcutta, Geddes was invited to bring the Cities Exhibition there the following October, and he wrote to Anna asking if she would accompany him for his second visit. A slightly moody Alasdair was no substitute for his favourite co-worker and companion. They left Calcutta on 9th December, and had five towns (populations *c.* 50,000) to report on in the north of the Madras Presidency before arriving in the capital in time for Christmas. This sounds a ridiculous programme if the advice in the reports was to be of any value, but in fact Geddes was quite capable of getting the feel of a place after spending two or three days walking through all its districts— well-to-do and squalid. He would then visit the town's planning offices and pore over old maps and new designs, spending hours in deep concentration. The two main bugbears which he found kept reappearing in the Indian planning of the time, were the desire to develop modern communications by driving broad roads (far broader than were needed) right through poor districts, heedless of the displaced inhabitants and their social function, and the insistence on filling in the village tanks (reservoirs) because they were insanitary. Time and again he would point out how roads could be gently improved, a little widening here, a milder curve there, so that the intervening shops and dwellings were only disturbed where necessary, and the infill of city fabric was only demolished when it was quite beyond renovation. As for the tanks, so valuable to cool the air and water the vegetation, they could be kept virtually free of malaria-bearing mosquitoes by cleansing out and re-stocking with fish and duck which would eat the mosquito larvae. In all, during his periods in India, Geddes made about fifty town reports.[2] Some were just preliminary observations, but others were full-scale affairs and were printed in India. Copies of the latter were circulated among architects and planners in England, and their ethos had a marked effect on some of the architects invited to design new buildings and communities in countries where the culture was very different from their own. Geddes was among the loudest denigrators of those who tried to impose western patterns on the defenceless cities of the British Empire. Nor was he greatly impressed by the local officers who undertook to implement these patterns. "There seem to be comparatively few really live people about, whether among officials or Indians—that is the disappointing element in this otherwise most fascinating and delightful journey." In Bellary, he wrote to Anna, his fight was to be

> with the Sanitary Authority of the Madras Government, with its death-dealing Haussmannising and its squalid (Belfast 1858) industrial bye-laws, which it thinks, enacts and enforces as up-to-date planning; and, for the least infraction of these mean, straight lines it scolds, abuses and delays this poor municipality, and at length not only bullies, but threatens it with extinction altogether! From the callous, contemptuous city bureaucrat at Delhi, I have now to tackle the well-intentioned fanatic of sanitation . . .

He and Alasdair spent Christmas in Madras, where Lord Pentland gave them "thoughtfully chosen presents—to each of us the right book, etc.". Geddes found the people "more open-minded than at Delhi" and the head of the municipal department accompanied him for two days on his tour of southern cities: "Fancy the head of the Home Office coming on tour, . . . !" Best of all the reconstituted Cities Exhibition had arrived, and Geddes later explained that: "No youngster ever put his hand into a Christmas stocking with such excitement as I did into those cases from home." Alasdair was set to work to mount the exhibition, while his father travelled south to make further reports. In the Dravidian temples of southern India he experienced what he felt to be the apotheosis of design. "What astounding magnificence of architecture! What a stupendous magnitude, intricacy, exuberance, variety of design and of execution!" In the plans he sensed the complexity and completeness of the spirit behind them, which perhaps found an echo in the completeness he had tried to aim for in the arrangement of the Outlook Tower.

> Sriringam . . . that is the true masterpiece of style; destitute of the European and Tanjore unity effect though it be. The masterpiece, indeed, of all the planning I have seen, whether religious or lay, and here both are together.
>
> Imagine the succession, here seven-fold, of temple-court outside temple-court, all in "concentric rectangles", as somebody, inaccurately yet vividly, first expressed it to me. First the small ancient shrine, now the Sanctum Sanctorum, built, they tell us, long centuries before Christ; then this, an altarspace, henceforward widened and lengthened by a foretemple of no mean dimensions, and around this cloister, a wall with its four oriented gateways, each a Gopuram*—the magnificent invention of its day. Then beyond this the piety of a later age creates a new court, and new gateways: and so again and again, each a new ring of the tree of evolution, and like many a tree growing most towards the sun and south.
>
> Realise too that in the great outer courts there grows up the City. First the priests and the levites—then their overflow, with the patricians, the other high castes; then, in the large outer city the lower ones—outside all, alas!—"the untouchables", the pariahs.
>
> But now we climb the east Gopuram and look over it all.

* gopura: "a vast, towering, many-storied sculpture pile" (Geddes); "towering gopuras like the mythical mountains rimming the Indian world" (Wu No-sun).

Fifteen towers from South to North, nine at least across, all
rising around the central holy place—a low dome, ablaze
with beaten gold!

Despite the speed with which the replacement Cities Exhibition had been collected, it nevertheless contained about 3,000
items when it opened at the Senate Hall of Madras University.
Geddes was able to incorporate into the course of lectures which
he gave to accompany the exhibition many references to the
Indian towns and districts which he had already seen, and he
made a strong impact on the Indian intellectuals. Lord Pentland had deduced that he might provide an authoritative link
between the Britons who were sympathetic to Indian culture,
and the Indians who were anxious to improve the condition of
their country; and so it proved to be. As previously arranged,
Geddes then took the exhibition to Bombay before he and
Alasdair returned to Europe.

Although he quickly became very involved with India's planning problems, Geddes had not pushed the war to the back of
his mind. On 14th January 1915 he wrote to the university
senate asking if he might be excused from his summer duties
at Dundee. His plan was to spend the period organizing interested people to visit those parts of Belgium "as may be free of
the Invader" in order to plan the reconstruction of her towns
damaged by the war. Early in February he wrote to John Ross:

Now about Belgium. I want to be in this job, as doubtless
do others. I have applied for leave of absence for Summer,
as I think I told you; and have little doubt but that I'll get it.
    Now I have been having the time of my life as a Town
Planner here in India; and am incomparably the better for
it: more able to undertake responsibility, alike of repairs and
reconstructions and general improvements of cities; and more
able too to take in situations rapidly; and I can and will work
with anybody who will work with me. Hindu and Briton
alike are in different worlds from mine, but I have got on
wonderfully better than I anticipated with them both; and
though I have given them both as plain speaking as I ever
used in my life, I think I am leaving many friends and few if
any enemies; (though some of course are a little sore, and
others dubious what to make of me, as always).

Now I want your friendly aid, and that promptly, in this matter. The Sec. of Belgian Embassy has not answered my note suggesting assistance. . . . Perhaps that was politic, of course, but it does not matter whether we go officially or unofficially. Will you talk this over with Branford, and Ratcliffe, etc. . . .

Try to get a message from me through to Professor Cloquet, of Department of Architecture, University of Ghent . . . a delightful and scholarly man, though not quite a great architect—but conciliatory, etc. You see I had better not write him lest a letter get him into trouble. Tell him that is my only reason; *but ask how we can help?*

I have written also, some weeks back, to Otlet, Waxweiler and Vinck; (also to De Vuyst, Director of Agriculture, though in more general terms of sympathy, etc.). If you come across them raise the question. (Should I stump American cities for a month or two before returning home? Would that not help the reconstitution?)

Returning to London—the Garden Cities people on one hand and Lanchester on the other, seem specially active. I am, therefore, writing a line to each and I'd be glad if you'd phone them a day or two after receipt of this and ask them what they think as to whether any use can be made of Al and me. (Did you see too that Norah is at organising women gardeners towards help in Belgium as soon as may be?)

Ross forwarded the letter to Branford, with the following message added to the bottom.

The above received this week. Have been unable to do anything about it so far, but will see Culpin and Lanchester. I doubt, however, whether they are very keen to have Geddes on the war path, possibly upsetting their plans for them! As usual, however, he leaves one to imagine what line he is proposing to take—whether entirely volunteer and unpaid or at someone else's disposal or on his own with a comprehensive scheme for the various persons and bodies concerned!

After a lot of bother have settled up Town & Gown affairs today—in the end a liability of well over £800 settled for £290 cash!! So much for corporate consciences! You will be amused to hear that I was approached today to know if I

would, if asked, undertake executive responsibility for the
Hall in its new abode when found and for Crosby. For the
moment at least I don't think this will materialise, but it
caused me to smile inwardly! No further progress re Crosby*
scheme but I still hope something will come of it.

In the end Geddes did attend the summer session at Dundee,
though he and Anna were in contact with European friends
planning a future *Exposition de la Cité Reconstituée*, and
instigating a war-time Summer Meeting to be held in London.
They were also involved in closer family matters.

While he was in Bombay, Geddes had heard from Norah and
Frank Mears that they had decided to marry. Mabel wrote to
Alasdair:

Isn't it lovely that they are really engaged at last? I am so
very glad. Although it is not exactly a new idea, their new
relation is very interesting! Our walking tour à trois last
September went off very well, but that couldn't be done
again—even with the experienced gooseberry that I am
becoming!

Geddes himself was pleased, though he proceeded to place the
forthcoming event into the kind of wider context that Norah,
not surprisingly, found difficult to live up to:

I was indeed sorry to write so briefly and weariedly last week:
but your letter only arrived on a Friday, and we post on
Saturday morning. Even now I have too many things on my
mind unfinished to feel fresh and free enough to write as I
would wish, and as—believe me, darling—I feel!
I often like to think of you continuing our home, with a
place in it now and then for the boys when they return for
brief visits to the stern old mother, Scotland, which is so
reluctant to employ her sons—other than with sordid labour
or futile words! Yet are not we first of those most concerned
with the renewal of the mother city to Art and thought once

* During the war Crosby Hall was used as a centre for Belgian
refugees. After the war the Crosby Hall Association Limited was
founded and it became, and still is, an International Club House
and Hall of Residence for University Women.

more?.... Your mother and I have made now and then some
beginnings of salon and centre, of which so many are needed;
though our life has been too much interrupted by long
absences, and by cares and difficulties and overpressures and
what not, to give us the restfulness needed. Perhaps you may
be able to carry this on better than we?

Or will you be swept away into the London vortices—
which ever so allure, and which often and deeply drown? I
wonder indeed. There are attractions and compensations and
influences—pressures too of sheer need of work—and as you
know, I have felt them all, and had to yield to them. . . . The
intense feeling of the deteriorative influences of London upon
the bodies and souls, the minds and spirits of its children,
which I have had all my life since I first came to it more than
forty years ago . . . has always made me keep up the Edinburgh
or neighbouring home for you young folks—despite the facts
that I have failed to earn anything appreciable there, and
that I necessarily fail to take root in London effectively also.

You think London will be *different*? I doubt it. Its sheer
magnitude will take an uplift after the war, its magnificence
also; and I feel, like you two, the attraction of helping in this.
But won't it be, Prussicated, more than ever? Gross-
Prussiburg-am-Thames! I much fear so—and to help with
the minor cities attracts me far more. To restore the vision
of Cities, in place of these dreary abstractions of State, and
hideous Blood-altars of Empire, on which France, Germany,
Russia, Austria, Turkey and we, too, sacrifice so much—in
short to escape from Rome and her megalomania to Hellas
and her ever-renewing civilisation, that seems to me the
political ideal. . . . To break up Germany into free city-states
once more, that is the true way of defeating her, of ensuring
all communities against the Berlin sword, the Essen gun, yet
also of enabling her to find again her true greatness in the
world. . . .

But you are at a very different viewpoint in your life-curve
than this? True, so far, yet the great world-currents fight for
us, and sweep us to one goal or another.

You, however, have to build your nest!

I am only disappointed not at all in India to have come
across the sort of shops I care for—either of old or new.
Artists seem as inconspicuous as tigers or snakes in one's

ordinary course, much though one has read of these as characteristic elements of town and country respectively, and though I doubt not they will exist—but out of my sight!

Must close for urgent appointment—motor waits.

The marriage was planned for July. But a month before that, Alasdair had made his decision to enlist. Geddes's initial reaction was one of sorrow tinged with anger, and he asked Alasdair to reconsider accompanying him to India again in the autumn. Alasdair, who was in London, wrote to his father:

Suppose I am a poor swimmer, but the finest fiddler in the world; my friend, skating, falls through the ice, or falls overboard from a ship. Am I not to do all in my power to save him? despite my powers of swimming being far less important to humanity than my fiddle-playing? . . . No, it is not for nothing that you have given me Highland blood and name; the clan feeling will not be merged in foreign empire when the clan is pressed. Now, the clan is France, is Europe; when these call, let the East wait.

Your brother was a banker against his will, in violation of his call, and Walter* a soldier, and what did it profit either? And so I feel that if you take me to India I shall go fettered and broken and blighted, for I shall not have been true to myself (and after that of what use shall I be to the Future?)

Geddes replied:

I am sorry I have caused you pain; but you for your part will see it best that each question should be clear. . . . while I feel it right not only to go, but also to have asked you to come, I recognise it also right, for you, feeling as you do, not to come: and you have accordingly and henceforth my approval in staying, and this without reserve.

Alasdair's answer began:

My dear Daddy, Many thanks indeed for your truly magnanimous letter, so living and understanding in its response to mine.

* Robert Geddes's son. Robert had died in 1909, and Walter in 1907.

He arranged to learn to drive motor vehicles before joining a course at the Roehampton School of Aeronautics. From there he was commissioned into the Royal Naval Air Service.

The Summer Meeting which Geddes co-organized with Dr Gilbert Slater, principal of Ruskin College, was held at King's College, London, from 12th to 31st July, and had as its theme: "The War: its Social Tasks and Problems." Lecturers came from many countries, and included Herbert Hoover, Lanchester, Unwin and L. T. Hobhouse. Following his procedure at the Edinburgh Summer Meetings, Geddes opened each morning with his own lectures, this time on "The Sociology of War and Peace", and most afternoons Dr Slater talked on "The Economic Aspects of War". These lectures were duly collected for a volume in "The Making of the Future" series under the title *Ideas at War* (1917), though not without difficulty. Geddes's lectures were stenographed; Slater incorporated the drafts with some of his own material, but before he had finished took up an appointment in Madras. Geddes was also in India at the time, and the book finally went to press without either author having seen the final manuscript.

The Cities Exhibition was due to open in Calcutta in October. Anna and Patrick travelled via Paris and Marseilles, arriving just in time to organize its erection. Accompanying them was H. V. Lanchester, who aided Geddes in some of the planning projects made during this trip and who had already carried out various planning schemes of his own in India. The Geddeses stayed with Dr and Mrs Jagadis Chandra Bose—Dr Bose being the bio-physicist whom Geddes had met in Paris at the 1900 exhibition, and who was doing pioneer research work in plant physiology at Calcutta University. The two couples became very close friends, and while Geddes was lecturing at the university and making proposals for a railway workers' housing scheme, Anna accompanied the Boses on a holiday in Darjeeling. She had not been entirely well, and after the strain of doing much of the organization of the Summer Meeting, travelling to India, and helping set up the exhibition, the Boses no doubt thought a quiet period away from Patrick would do her good. She must also have been worried about her sons.

Alasdair was about to be sent to France—where he was transferred to the Army Balloon Corps. Ironically, his education had admirably fitted him for some aspects of war, and his colonel remarked that he had "a genius for observation". He became an unofficial link between the British and French air services, and incorporated the improvements to kite-balloons worked out by the French into the British models. He was soon made a field instructor and promoted to the rank of captain. For much of the time he was happy. He wrote to Norah in March 1916:

> We've had another two or three really good days or half-days. Last time we registered "direct hits" on two different houses which we were ranging for two different batteries. It is very exhilarating after straining to see whether the little puffs of grey-black smoke are over or short, to see the target go up in huge clouds of smoke and red brick-dust. . . . I continue to find it very difficult to have any thoughts or anything to write to India about. . . . I have been practising signalling pretty steadily for one or two hours daily, so as to be able to work without telephone.

Arthur had also experienced a dilemma concerning what he should do during the war. At its outbreak he had been only eighteen, and not nearly so strong and confident as Alasdair. He was a pacifist by nature, but wished to contribute positively to a constructive cause. For a time he worked on a farm, and then volunteered for the Army Field Ambulance Unit, but was turned down on health grounds. He nevertheless joined the Society of Friends War Victims Relief organization and was sent to France.

On New Year's Day 1916, Geddes was in a train bound for Nagpur in central India, where he had been invited to take the Cities Exhibition and to make planning proposals. He took the opportunity to write to Norah and Frank, who despite its "vortices which ever so allure" were living in London (in Putney, scarcely a vortex of urban evil). He told them that he was trying to persuade Dacca not to spend a quarter of a million pounds "on absurd sewage schemes" but "to regenerate the town with perhaps a third of this and save the rest". (Geddes believed in making use of human manure; in his report on Lucknow he wrote: "Now, since a large proportion of the community do not and will not use latrines, but insist on communing with nature after the manner of the ancients, how much healthier to have their daily contributions absorbed by the cultivated land, as in the ordinary rural village. . . . No fact is more frequently forgotten in India than that the wealth and permanence of China depend profoundly upon its economical use of manure . . . whereas the poverty and instability of India are deeply associated with her wholesale waste of human manurial matter.") The Calcutta railway workers' scheme was as yet unfinished: "You have to come here to realise the wild and wasteful ways of engineers", and he wanted to make another visit to Jabalpur. He asked for "any news you hear about those at war"; "one poor fellow I hoped to meet has been killed. . . . He was 6 ft 3 or so, and they made him an officer of Ghurkas who average 5 ft 2 or so: he was of course picked off at once." There was a chance that he might be invited "to plan the new Hindu University at Benares, but the trustees are divided: as a leading one fears, 'Geddes is an idealist'. They have asked me to hold forth on *University Ideals* at the approaching foundation stone-laying, so that may wreck my chances!" With such possibilities in view, India continued to be a long-term prospect:

> I feel more and more that I am not likely to have so much work as here (nor any chance of pay!) at home, and so must keep to this, winter after winter, as long as strength may allow. It is a great satisfaction to have something over to pay off the Bank etc. by degrees, though that will take a long time. And it agrees with both of us: Mother has been all right since she had that stay at Darjeeling. Of course there is always a certain risk of fever, but coming home year by year we abate that.

In a letter Mabel chided him for committing himself too much to India when there were so many tasks for him to fulfil at home. He replied that he felt his Indian town-planning activities were effective in a way his home activities never were, and also he was allowed to participate in the thick of university planning and politics, which he never was in Scotland. Above all he was learning, "and if I stopped that, I'd become— respectable!"

He and Anna returned to Europe in April, and as the S.S. *Malwa* steamed up the Suez Canal, Geddes wrote a thirty-page document headed "Notes for Executors of P. Geddes" which was a kind of informal will. In it he not only listed his liabilities

and assets, but took the opportunity to explain what lay behind
them. The items covered included Roseburn Cliff, Town &
Gown shares, Patrick Geddes & Colleagues ("Here is another
of my as yet disastrous yet not ill-conceived endeavours . . ."),
and the Eastern & Colonial Association ("I regret that the £800
odd shares of my holding in this concern must be regarded as all
but valueless . . ."). The Cities Exhibition he claimed as his
main asset: a friend had "lately indicated a probable demand
. . . in Australasian cities when the war is over . . . also for
Canada.. Why not also later for S. Africa? It only requires some
fresh contact and co-operation for the organisation of a tour
through American cities." Just as he had once seen the opening
up of Canada as a family opportunity, now he tried to visualize
their future in terms of exhibiting and lecturing:

> To Alasdair I specially recommend this field of activity for at
> any rate a period, while Arthur may find it in both the edu-
> cation of travel and of city-improvement and design. Indeed
> should the war, or rather its consequences, render archi-
> tectural practice too scanty and unremunerative, why should
> not Frank, and Norah too, find congenial and varied work
> in this way?

Among his creditors he named Martin White and Victor
Branford:

> My oldest and greatest creditor is of course Mr Martin White,
> and it is with him . . . that the most serious settlement has to
> be made accordingly. With characteristic generosity he has
> again and again proposed quittance upon the most easy
> terms. . . . While health and working opportunities and
> powers continue, I hope to go on paying off liabilities . . .
> but if I disappear I can only ask my executors and family to
> meet the sum due to Mr White as fully as funds allow, and
> thereafter to place themselves unreservedly in his hands.
> Without his active co-operation I should neither have been
> in Dundee nor Edinburgh, and without making him in any
> way unduly responsible for undertakings which he often, and
> doubtless rightly, criticised they could neither have been
> undertaken nor continued without his active support and
> patient goodwill.

To my old and peculiarly esteemed and valued friend and colleague, Victor Branford, I also owe certain sums, viz. several advances, at crises of difficulty, each of £50. Of this something has been repaid; but the bulk remains.

Part of the Cities Exhibition (now duly insured against war risks) accompanied the Geddeses on the *Malwa*, as it was to form their contribution to the *Exposition de la Cité Reconstituée*. While Geddes went to Dundee, Anna took the exhibition to Paris and remained there in the combined role of organizer and guide. Geddes joined her towards the end of June, and Alasdair was able to spend a short leave with his parents. The latter then went to Putney to stay with Norah, while Frank was undergoing the same course of training nearby at the Roehampton School of Aeronautics that Alasdair had taken the year before. In due course he was sent to France to serve in the same unit as his brother-in-law. Norah was expecting her first child, Kenneth, who was born in the autumn when her parents were back in India.

The subject that was uppermost in Geddes's mind during this summer was the possibility of being involved with the planning of the new University of Benares. Although the university authorities had made it quite clear that they were not committed to the preliminary conversations which he had had with their governing body, he journeyed to Oxford, Birmingham, Aberystwyth and Bangor, lecturing on "Universities and their Replanning" and discussing his ideas with all and sundry within the context of the opportunity at Benares. At the end of his Oxford lecture, Sir Michael Sadler (then Vice-Chancellor of Leeds) said: "What we have heard today is pure gold; the concentrated wisdom of a life of toil, of travel, of thought and of high courage . . . I hope that England will recognise in him one who speaks with genius on university organisation."

In September 1916 Patrick and Anna returned to France in order to study some village reconstruction schemes engendered by the *Exposition*, before journeying on to Lucknow. Geddes had already done some preliminary work on a planning report for the city, and he continued with this while awaiting news of the Benares project. To his disappointment, owing to a change in the membership of the governing body, his involvement was no longer countenanced. Victor Branford wrote to him in

February 1917 pointing out that his vision of a great university, embodying the highest ideals, was still just as relevant, even though this particular opportunity had been withdrawn. Geddes replied:

The University Militant is all very well, and I am not going back upon it. But my work here, in the definite tackling of city after city . . . makes me feel that such sustained and concentrated effort is worth far more than the diffused literature and lecturing of my past endeavours in Civics.

In another letter to Branford, written a few weeks later, he commented: "I can but express my delight over the Russian Revolution. How glad I am old Kropotkin has lived to see this!"

During the months of February, March and April 1917, he was undergoing what he described as "a very distinct phase of intensified lucidity and reason". He called it "a life-climax" and found that it combined a sensation of intensified—even impassioned—will, with a "serener contemplation and passionless calm". It was almost as though his mind were preparing itself to measure up to the suffering which lay ahead.

Chapter 18

"CANNOT WE, WHO HAVE LOST . . ."

WOMEN AND CHILDREN were refused sea passages out of India by the spring of 1917 because of danger from submarines, and Geddes did not attempt to return to Dundee on his own. Anna, who must have longed to see Norah and her new grandson, went with him on most of his planning and lecturing visits, and together they began to make plans for a summer meeting to be held in Darjeeling. She undertook most of the organization, and the star visitors were to be Bose and Rabindranath Tagore.

They heard regularly from Alasdair. In December 1916 he had been made a major, and was awarded the Military Cross for his reconnaissance work. Earlier, when bad weather had prevented his unit from carrying out their observation duties, he went out foraging for something to occupy their time, and came back with a plough and horses. He then proceeded to teach his men to plough the nearby neglected fields. Frank, although he was eleven years older than Alasdair, served under him as captain and freely admitted that he could not work "nearly so strenuously and well". When the unit occupied a building with a garden, Frank reported that "Alasdair told them to take care of the place and they have dug around the gooseberry bushes and elsewhere". Once they were flying together in a balloon which was punctured by German incendiary bullets. They used their parachutes and escaped unhurt.

In the early spring Anna suffered from an attack of dysentery and was taken to Lucknow hospital. When she had partially recovered, she went to stay with friends a few miles outside the town, and there she continued with her correspondence for the Summer Meeting. But the fever returned and, seriously ill, she was once more taken to hospital.

While she was there, towards the end of April, Patrick received a cable saying that Alasdair had been killed. He felt he could not tell Anna lest the news endanger her life.

Alone in his room he faced the deepest misery he had known
since he lost his sight in Mexico. He tried to fumble for some
kind of positive response. Taking up a large crayon of the kind
used by school teachers to correct exercise books, red one end
and blue the other, he drafted a letter. Its proposed recipient
is unclear. The draft is not always decipherable.

Cannot we, who have lost sons . . . in the war, be now of some
help to those who have lost one or both parents? And so
renew what we can of our service as parents to the coming
generation which needs all we can do and give, and even
find some consolation for ourselves?

What I mean of course is the renewal of the good old
practice of adoption, or where that is not practicable in
view of the feelings of surviving parent of children left
fatherless, of some measure of fosterage and other semi-
adoption corresponding to godparentship, executorship,
uncleship and auntship and so on. . . . Life-help as maturity
or age may, and should, offer to children and to youth, and
so with mutually arousing love.

As an evidence of sincerity in the matter . . . my wife and
I, who have lost a son of scientific and constructive promise,
are willing to accept such responsibility as our age and
circumstances may allow, for a boy or youth of kindred
interests . . .

[Here a line is drawn across the page]

Better than stone, than brass or glass

Best personal monuments

Best way too of aiding the great causes—national, European,
human—for which our sons have died is to take our share in
preparing others to live further.

On his mantelpiece he made an arrangement to commemorate
Alasdair and his place both within the close-knit family circle
and the wider realm of the human spirit. Reading from left to
right he placed a vase of flowers; a picture of a group of
Sikh gurus; Norah's wedding photograph; a painting of "the
youth as sunworshipper, (who afterwards became Rameses
the great)"; photographs of Frank, Arthur and Alasdair—
with, in front of the latter, an Indian lamp "like the one he held
so sacred at Innesforth and wept over when broken", an Indian

brass bird of victory, and an Indian brass lamp of memory; a photograph of Norah and Kenneth; and a single flower. He wrote to Norah:

> I lie in bed and look at all this, and then past it to the vast Himalayan landscape he so longed to explore two years ago, and would have gone to but for the war—and above all this to the stupendous world-pinnacle of Kinchenjunga snows— and then back again, to sorrow, and memory:—and Hope:— and Love with all.

"My wife and I . . . are willing to accept such responsibility." Patrick could write this because Anna had never flinched from any responsibility he had undertaken. Indeed, it was so often she who fulfilled the "responsibilities" in the full sense of that word.

He still felt unable to tell her about Alasdair, even when she became slightly better. She was insisting that he continue with the arrangements for the Summer Meeting (due to start on 21st May) and asked to be moved to a friend's house in Calcutta, as this would be nearer to Darjeeling. The friend was a doctor whom they had known as a student in Edinburgh. Patrick acceded to her request.

During this time, Alasdair's last letters continued to arrive, the mail from France taking several weeks. Having the letters made it possible for Patrick to continue to conceal their son's death. Somehow he managed to read them aloud to Anna.

Not long before he died, Alasdair had been awarded the Cross of the Legion of Honour for his liaison work with the French. Then one day he was walking back to his unit from an observation post in front of the artillery lines and was struck by a shell fragment. He was killed instantly. He was buried on a nearby hill top. Frank destroyed some love letters which he found in his pocket without reading them, and sent Norah a few flowers from the garden Alasdair had asked his men to care for. A farmer and his wife on whom he had earlier been billeted, wrote to Norah asking for a photograph: "Notre cher Alasdair, il était comme le fils de la maison. Nous l'appelions le modèle d'officier—il était si gentil envers tous."

Settled in the doctor's house, Anna bade Patrick go to

Darjeeling. She was not much better, yet he feared that to stay with her and cancel his arrangements—an unprecedented action during their life together—would upset her. He left her, but wrote to her daily; sometimes twice a day.

The Summer School opened well, the botanical and geographical survey course taking on a very special character among such spectacular scenery and vegetation. Nearly all Patrick's letters to his wife were love letters.

But still dear I weary for you and we shall have a happy day when I have you in my arms. Though we be love birds caged apart, we are not quite out of sight and hearing—are we, with this daily post?

Then on 30th May, he wrote:

Yes dear, you and I have another chapter of our partnership before us, in which I hope to be more to you than ever, and console you for all your long separations from home and its love-ties to the utmost I can, and be with you more than I have. I have not *always* cherished you enough and my regrets for my omissions—when you needed me, yet I let myself get caught in work or thought, and left you too much alone to bear your cares and pains—will I hope make me henceforth a fuller and more constant lover than ever before. And so the evening of our lives will open into brightness, despite all clouds, and even gild and redden these with the fair colours of our morning when we were young, and so make us young together once more, And, oh dear wife, gather your strength together towards peace and hope and courage, and so to convalescence and recovery, for my sake as well as your own, and for your children and grandchildren and all those who love you.

Each day in early June he sent a letter, until on Friday the 8th there came a telegram from Calcutta. Anna's health was causing grave concern. The train journey took twenty-four hours. By the time he arrived at the doctor's house, she was dead.

He asked for her room to be filled with flowers. Sitting by her bedside he wrote to Norah:

We exchanged letters daily these weeks past; and as lovers ever. But what a hardship to have been separated! Yet each of us had been accustomed to that division of labour too, and I was carrying out what she largely had willed . . . and good work it has been. Our summer meetings have always been of use and happiness to many, and she was keenly interested in this even to yesterday. . . . She had no idea she was dying—indeed quite happy and hopeful—only needing to sleep—that is a comfort after so much pain, that her last day was peace. . . . You will I am sure feel the fitness of the Indian burial and cremation, since she gave up home, and health, and life as it has proved, to help me here with Indian civics and education—and this as fully and definitely as ever of old at home in our young days. And it is among the Indians, far more than among our countrymen here, that we have found our friends and fellow workers. I think I'll go back to Darjeeling for a time—though not to lecture again. Nature is the best anodyne—and I can be as free to stay alone with this new sorrow as I was with the first—and when I am fit for science or plans—as at times I shall be, just as since the previous blow—I have the conditions too. So do not be anxious about me. And now again to my vigil—of tears. Here again, now for the third time in my experience is the beauty of death as she lies among her flowers—and now with something of the youthful bride to which your Grannie Burton returned, and something too of the grave dignity of my mother—so that I can well believe how hopeful the Doctors were up to the last day . . . and as I watch her face, I see more in it than even I knew—or rather all at its finest—friend and lover, artist and workfellow, mother too; and matriarch beyond her immediate home from earliest days onwards; but all now with the dignity of silent repose—from which I too have so soon to stand back for ever—till my turn comes to share it.

And oh my poor daughter and wee grandson . . . the mother heart was often yearning for you both, and for Arthur too, as for Al. Only her love for me and all the fellowship it meant kept her far away from you, and I shall now often regret I did not come this time alone. Yet who knows! I am very sorry if I have done wrong, as I often have felt since this illness began. I have had forebodings and misgivings too, since Auntie Bex's death and Jeannie's illness—yet also hopes of longer life for her as well.

Anna was cremated later that day. "Student boys whom she had 'mothered' in Edinburgh, and those of our Masques, now public men in Calcutta, mustered to carry her to the crematorium—Indian (and Highland) fashion."

Arthur Thomson wrote her best obituary in a letter to Norah and Arthur:

The qualities I most admired in her were her power of cheering, her courage and her loyalty. Some people *try* to encourage others, but heartening cheer radiated from Mrs Geddes. She made one feel stronger and better, and partly because she had an overflowing reserve of faith in right things prevailing. It was often interesting to see Mrs Geddes convert men to some good scheme—not by argument and certainly not by wheedling, but by sheer cheerfulness of outlook.

I have never seen anyone excel her in courage—not even your father. For often as he burned his boats, he was less aware of the details involved; and then there is the reward to the initiator. Sometimes, if not often, the result of some decision meant years of frugality and self-denial. She seems to me in this way one of the most *heroic* people I have known. I don't think she could have stood some of the disappointments if it had not been for her music—which had religious value for her in the true sense, a sending out of tendrils into the absolute.

Thirdly, I was thinking of her loyalty to your father's ideals and schemes. No doubt there was also the devotion to you both and to Alasdair, but that is often highly developed in mothers. I mean rather her unswerving loyalty to your father's philosophy of life and his highest ambitions. Never, of course, would a noble lady murmur before an outsider, but she had a *positive* loyalty as well, extending, even, as I know, to the defence of schemata which were, I think, rather outside her province, clever as she was! I suppose it just meant that she loved him so deeply.

No doubt she had many other gifts and graces; she was wise, broad-minded, tolerant and forgiving: but I think first of her radiating encouragement, her courage, and her loyalty. I owe her much, and am grateful.

Patrick returned to Darjeeling. He stayed quietly with friends for a few weeks, spending much time alone wandering in the foothills of the Himalayas. Again his own room became a kind of shrine. On 5th July he wrote to Mabel:

I have periods of thinking clearly—both on the hill-side and indoors. I have made my room magnificent beyond its recent aspect of sad and happy photographs and the flower vases Mrs Das and her children fill so richly: for now I have bought Tibetan pictures of Buddha and his legends, and some of the strangely magnificent brass and copper work we meant to have bought together—and of course *her* photograph in the centre of all these.

Ten days later he wrote separate letters to Norah and Arthur in which he asked them to tell him about their immediate cares and future aims. To Norah, who was staying in Fife while Frank was in France, he said:

That you are in no need of counsel from me as mother and educator, as woman in the world, as wife in separation and anxiety, yet courage and hope, I know quite well, and don't intrude—but all the same I might be able to write to you on less immediately vital matters, albeit accessary to all these vital ones—if you care to give me an opening by writing of what must be to you a very significant time. I think I understand your view of solitude; I am appreciating and using mine here—but tell me what you can and care to of its interests, problems, perplexities, solutions, results? And of what you think I can write to you about?

He was lonely without Anna; a loneliness that lasted until his death, despite the many events the intervening years encompassed. Arthur had been invalided out of the Friends' Relief organization and spent his sick leave working on a farm. He was suffering from nervous debility, and it cannot have been the best moment for him to have been asked to think about his future education in terms of his father's all-embracing vision.

But Geddes wanted to keep the family intact—preferably with a shared purpose. Several days later, on 25th July, he wrote a semi-formal letter to Norah, leaving her the furnishings and contents of 14 Ramsay Garden. (These had previously legally belonged to Anna.)

> It is my ambition to preserve our old home as long as may be for the family and not to dismantle or abandon it, but keep it as far as possible in memory of your mother and brother and all our happiness together and to see it inhabited by you and yours, or by Arthur's family when it comes, and to go to Kenneth or other coming descendant who may remain attached to Edinburgh. For this purpose, it is my ambition, if I can so far retrieve my fortunes, to repurchase the flat from Town & Gown . . .

Both Norah and Arthur were to suffer from his need to keep the Geddesian ship bravely afloat as a family concern. Sorrow had aged him, and as he grew older his impatience was aroused increasingly quickly by minor obstacles. Family and friends might try to help, but often their efforts appeared to go unappreciated. Sometimes it may have seemed to them that no one was to be allowed to replace Anna and Alasdair. The truth was, no one could possibly have begun to fulfil Anna's role; and Alasdair in time, after his almost perfect apprenticeship, would have taken off to become his own man. As indeed he had done during those nine months before a fragment of shell killed "a son of scientific and constructive promise" who, as a boy, had been "a dear child".

Chapter 19

INDORE AND ISRAEL:
GANDHI AND ZION

BOSE AND TAGORE both gave comfort and friendship to
Geddes during his weeks of mourning. He found it impossible
to stop working completely, and used the summer in Darjeeling
to start writing an account of Bose's life and his work in plant
physiology.[1] Never a heavy sleeper or eater, he did little of
either and lost a good deal of weight from his already slight
frame. He also began to smoke heavily. Once or twice he
experienced an hallucination, seeing Anna standing vividly
before him.

When an invitation came from the Maharaja of Indore to
make a report on the re-planning of his capital city, Geddes
accepted. He attacked the work with a fervour that exhausted
his assistants and alarmed his friends. It was to be his longest,
fullest and best Indian report.[2] Well over a quarter of a million
words were expended in an heroic effort to bring the existing
reality, the future (economic and social) possibility, and past
history into a living synthesis, accessible to planner and citizen
alike.

The immediate reason for his appointment, he wrote to
Norah, was the springing up of a "new Cottonopolis and
Factory town" and "a certain vague recognition on the part of
the authorities that these are not satisfactory". Also three years
previously, Lanchester had made plans for the city which had
"turned out larger and more expensive than they can face;
though . . . doing the immense service of squashing the usual
wasteful super-blunder-bungle of a great 'Drainage Scheme'
such as that by which most cities are devastated and
defiled . . .". For the first few days while he surveyed the town,
he was accompanied by the Municipal President and the
Chief Engineer, and together they drove out into the country
to see

two immense reservoir tanks constructed some years ago . . .
at an expense of £113,000 or more, and which have yielded
no water as yet to the thirsty town; and we spent hours in
wondering how to make them do so!

I cannot discover that it has yet at all adequately been
grasped by women what an awful mess our masculine
division of labour—into mechanical stupidities and so on—
makes of the world!

Geddes had always emphasized the importance of the role of
women in society, but after Anna's death his estimation of its
value seemed to increase. He experienced a measure of guilt
concerning the burdens he had allowed her to bear, and as he
meditated on this and remembered their life together, he
perhaps completely understood for the first time the full value
and complexity of her part in his work. After describing his
activities to Norah, he ended:

> I don't like to lament, and sadden you; but once for all may
> I say to relieve myself, how different is the home-coming
> now—this home-coming that is no home-coming, but
> desolate. . . . What a contrast from our happy little bungalow
> at Nagpur, for instance, this is!

His work in Indore coincided with an outbreak of plague. As
he explored the poorer, dirtier quarters of the town, a rumour
started that "the old sahib" with the ravaged expression and
untidy clothes was in fact a malevolent sage with the power to
spread the plague. When Geddes heard of this, he made a
grandiloquent request. He went to the ruler and asked if he
might be made "Maharajah for a day"—the day in question
to be Diwali, a festival which celebrated, among other things,
the slaying of Rama's adversary, Ravana. His request was
granted, and with co-operation from the mayor he proceeded
to plan a great processional masque to illustrate that, far from
being a plague-bringer, his methods would show everyone how
to become a plague-killer. Rather than follow the traditional
routes through the city, this procession would go along the
streets whose citizens had made a good job of cleaning them
up and making repairs to their homes.

The theme of the procession was to be civic renovation with

special reference to the conquest of disease. The opening sequence was traditional: the bands, infantry, cavalry, artillery and elephants of Indore State, followed by the Maharaja's beautifully caparisoned horses. Then Geddes had organized chariots to symbolize agriculture and the harvest, ending with Lakshmi, the goddess of prosperity, riding an elephant. Traditionally her mount was supposed to be white, but the Indore elephants were grey, so one poor beast was given "two coats of whitewash from trunk to tail; what snowy brilliance in the sunshine—a paragon of a white elephant . . .!" After Lakshmi, the atmosphere of the procession changed, and there was the sound of "melancholy, wailing, and discordant instruments" as weird figures dressed as tigers, demons and disease danced and mocked at the crowd. They were followed by swordsmen and raiders representing the ugly aspects of war. Then came models of slum dwellings, "well-caricatured with their crumbling walls and staggered roofs, broken windows and general air of misery and dirt". The wicked Ravana came next, presented in the guise of a "Giant of Dirt—a formidable figure some twelve feet high"; he was accompanied by the Rat of Plague (six feet long and "quivering all over with rat-fleas"— "locusts dipped in ink and mounted on wires") and huge model malarial mosquitoes. Cheerful music followed,

heading the long line of four hundred sweepers of the town, two abreast, all in spotless white raiment, with new brooms, flower-garlanded. Their carts were all fresh-painted, red and blue, and their big beautiful white oxen were not only well-groomed and bright-harnessed for the occasion but had black polished hoofs, blue bead necklaces and golden flower garlands, with their great horns gilded and vermilioned by turns. Every sweeper too was wearing a new turban, and of the town's colour—as were all the employees and higher officers of Indore, as well as the mayor and myself: this had been arranged with his warm approval as symbol of the democracy of civic service.

Just as the sweepers were about to begin their march, Geddes greeted their leader and took a marigold for his buttonhole from the old man's broom garland. The other sweepers cheered. To the Brahmin officials they were Untouchables, but Geddes had emphasized "the democracy of civic service" by his actions. Indeed he had placed the sweepers in the procession ahead of all the civic dignitaries that followed—including himself and the mayor. After the dignitaries came a newly-created goddess, "Indore City", carrying a banner with a large outline of the new city-plan. Behind her on floats were models of proposals contained in the plan, including the workers' homes that were to replace some of the slum dwellings. Floats representing the crafts came next—masons, potters, ironworkers, carvers—and finally fruit- and flower-laden drays whose contents were handed to the children. The last dray carried thousands of tiny pots containing seedlings of the Tulsi plant, Hindu symbol of a well-kept home, and these were distributed among the households, hopefully to flourish and remind their owners of the pageant and its theme. At evening-time the procession wound its way to the public park, and there the Giant of Dirt and Rat of Plague were burned on a great bonfire, and a spectacular firework display ended the day. These final events were well within the spirit of the Rama legend, for he slew Ravana with a "deathful weapon flaming with celestial fire" and afterwards "heavenly flowers in rain descended".[3]

Norah's second son, Alasdair, was born in January 1918, several weeks after the Diwali festival, and she wrote to her father on 4th February:

I had been waiting and waiting for the letter that should tell me you had heard of your second grandson and rejoiced thereat. I do miss "my ain folk" as well as my man. I think of the two boys as being as much Geddes as Mears. . . . You will greatly rejoice at Arthur's news of himself—his escape by release to Liverpool. . . . He is not fit for full time work yet, but much better for the military interlude, it would seem. [Arthur had had a brief spell in the army.]

Two months before Alasdair was born, Norah had expressed some of her frustration at the conflict between her role as mother and the expectations which she felt Geddes had of her:

You were holding before me the ideal of accomplishing great park and garden schemes for cities and slum clearances. I may return to that work which I began on a smaller scale.

Meantime I cannot live fully and happily with a divergence between my ideals and the work in hand—which is the care of Kenneth. If I think in terms of "making cosmos" of "reconstruction", then my work now appears in its trivial and monotonous aspect. To see its beauty, happiness and importance my mind must always be tending thereunto. This it does eagerly. There is a time for everything as you yourself would say. Other work seems to me onerous and barren while I enjoy this.

Do you know, I have too, many bitter memories of those years of struggle with professional work. So often a master's responsibility with the experience only of the apprentice; so often most difficult and adverse conditions with no memory of past triumphs to carry one's confidence through.

A week later she wrote:

After a good free walk I come back perhaps a little impatient of Kenneth's small tyrannies. I need someone to magnify my office to me—the office of acting mother. To say, "yes, it is quite hard work and does demand a sacrifice of other things other sides of oneself but it is worth while over and over".

As Geddes weighed up the pros and cons concerning whether he should return to Dundee for the summer term, some discomfiture over Norah's feelings may have helped to influence him to stay in India. Though the over-riding reason for his decision was the fact he was offered reasonably congenial, well-paid work there. In March, as his involvement with the Indore report drew to an end, he accepted an offer from Bose to lecture at Calcutta University during the summer. He wrote to the Dundee authorities requesting leave of absence for a second year, knowing that this would inevitably lead to his retirement from the chair. He agreed to return for the summer of 1919 for a final session. Bose was anxious about his friend's future, and wrote to him:

I am also personally attached to you, at the same time a little afraid of the intensity of your temperament! You are fiendish in your activity, that I like. But if you find any delay or obstacle, you are likely to grow very impatient and impute coldness or apathy. . . . It will make me very unhappy if you come to think that you've burnt your boats and people here did not appreciate you. Weariness and illness are apt to make us impatient. I would have wished (if it was possible for you to get extension for one year from your university) to try one year and see whether things would suit your convenience. If you would in spite of uncertainty like to cast your lot with us, then I would say stay! and share with us all the hardships and uncertainties.

Norah in the meantime cabled an offer to move to Dundee with her children for the summer of 1918 in order to look after her father, even though it meant being separated from Frank, now back from France. Geddes replied, on 25th March, that he "was indeed touched by your cable, and I feel a keen regret that I am to miss your offer. . . . But I am also glad not to take you from your man!" Some of the Indian friends he had made in Indore, he wrote,

are really interesting—more than I can say, alas, about most of our countrymen and women one meets. But I dine regularly every Sunday night ("Dobsonday" my assistants Paul and Sinha call it) with Rector Dobson of the big High School here, an unfrocked and married ex-Jesuit, of culture and sympathies of many kinds . . . [the principal] of the University College is unapproachable, in his well-starched Cambridge don-ship.

In the same letter he told Norah about the forthcoming All India Hindi Conference and Gandhi, whom he had previously met at the Boses' home:

A huge temporary building of bamboo and matting, to hold 10,000 has sprung up in the last fortnight in the park opposite—with help of 600 volunteers, students, etc.—with a village of tents for the 700 guests not otherwise lodged, for the All India Hindi Conference, to meet at end of week and boom Hindi as the lingua franca of India again. The famous Mr Gandhi—a quite remarkable person, at once apostolic and fiery, as per his South African and other adventures, is to be President; and writes that he wants to come a day earlier to tackle the Town plan.

Mr Gandhi did indeed come and look at the plan, and four days later Geddes reported to Norah:

> President Gandhi . . . is a fine spirit, half saint, half warrior—or rather both in one keen little body and face. If I can turn his politics to town planning, it will be an event.

In fact the Conference itself did not meet with Geddes's approval, and in a long letter to Gandhi, which is worth quoting in full as a typical example of Geddes's somewhat high-handed but sincere application to any new subject that chanced his way, he explained why. (Being a politician, Gandhi never really rose to the top of Geddes's esteem; he preferred Tagore.)

> Dear Mr Gandhi,
>
> As President not only of the Hindi Conference here, but I presume until the next one opens, permit me the frank and friendly criticism, which you of all men will least deny is within the rights of membership—constructive criticism moreover!
>
> Now though I don't know Hindi, I know the value of vernaculars; and I have observed, and asked others about the meeting. Some are pleased, and found it "a complete success"; others disappointed, who found it "very dull"; and my criticism includes both views. For it was really *perfectly* English. Hindi apart, and as a Conference, it might have been in London or Manchester, for any political, social or cultural purpose. For there was the proper succession of decorous speeches, by the proper persons, in the proper tone, and with the proper conviction.
>
> But surely your real problem was not simply to reproduce the customary and orderly ritual of every British Congress? It was to revive, enrich, ennoble your language and its literature and thus more fully to extend it, and no great public Conference has yet given English a thought, or seen need for that. Yet at Stratford-on-Avon they play Shakespeare. But your theatres were silent. No sign of Tulsi Das.
>
> The Hindi Literature Exhibition was excellent; save that people were not allowed to touch the books.
>
> But since you do at present take your examples and methods from the West, why not now also consider the vital

and the relevant ones? Though it is still too much unknown in India, you must have heard of the Welsh "Eisteddfod"? At the one before last I heard good speaking: e.g. Lloyd George in his utmost vigour, his most flaming mood, since largely in his own vernacular. He was telling us why he had left his anxious and all-important post, as Minister of Munitions, and travelled to this far side of Wales. "I have come here—TO SING!" And how song matters for Victory, does not France teach the world with the Marseillaise?

Their great Pendal was a tent like yours; but it was divided into sections not by payment, nor by social status, and age as everywhere in England or here, but by grouping each quality of voice, for collective song. Rival and grouped performances of choirs and singers are also a foremost feature; and the whole function culminates, as in Athens of old, in the discernment, enthronement, and investiture of a poet—"the Chairing of the Bard". A noble ceremonial—an ancient sacrament of Peace—opens the meeting; a Bardic Procession expresses its purpose to the city; and they build and consecrate a great stone circle in the park, to keep up its memory for each return.

So the Irish, of late years reviving their language, might also give you points. One, for instance, is the establishment of small Vacation Gatherings in the little towns and villages where Irish is best spoken, and where the old traditions, folk-songs, and tales still linger. And the Irish Agricultural Co-operation paper is edited by the noblest of our living poets, not only of Ireland but of the English tongue today—George Russell, "A.E.".

Our Highland Gatherings, when I was young, were mainly Olympic games for athletic youth, and with splendid old Herculean feats, like tossing the stone, the hammer, and the tree. Dance too at its intensest ecstasy and skill, and pipe-music, the wildest, and the saddest, perhaps in the world. But now we are recovering the Irish and Welsh linguistic, poetic and choral elements.

Perhaps above all, look to Provence. Here a great folk-poet—Mistral, their Robert Burns and Tagore in one—has been the life long leader of younger poets, and of philologists, historians and antiquaries also, and their meetings were not merely oratorical, but poetic on one side, scholarly and scientific on the other, each marking the year's advance. For fuller expression and appeal, they re-opened the ancient Graeco-Roman theatre of their region, and brought from Paris Sarah Bernhardt and her Company—not simply to do their plays, but to start their own acting at its highest level. And when the Swedes gave old Mistral the Nobel Prize, he built the "Musée Provençal"; no mere glass-case museum!

In Denmark again, after its defeat in 1866, a bishop and a layman (their Shankara-Sankaracharya* and Gandhi) laid their heads together, and set about re-educating the youths and maidens of Denmark. And not with the "3 Rs", but with plough and cow, and tale and song; and since that generation has grown up, it has been leading in Europe, with all these alike.

On returning to the wide-spread languages, why continue to ignore the "Alliance Française", which has its meetings from St Andrews to Bombay.

Why not enquire into such real Language-meetings, and thence more fully into your own surviving and remembered traditions? Thus you will find—with your juniors' help mostly—and for your millions, how to rival (why not even surpass?) all these examples; and so make the needed step, beyond your present enlarged edition of the English Public Meeting, successful, dull, or both.

Yours faithfully,
P. Geddes

P.S. Now, since you think me a little mad about Town Planning—(which your progressives don't yet quite see as the beginning of the more Ideal City which you seek to evoke and guide) let me add a word on that.

Your town-planning was all right so far: Pendal, tents, etc. So think of it as a good example of how all movements spiritual or social, as they seek to reach the objective and public plane, have to find, or create, the needed material environment for effective action—the fulcrum for your lever, before you can move the world.

But what you need for all such gatherings is no mere transient Pendal, and with its poor acoustics. It is the Open

---

* One of the four Patriarchs of Shivaite Hinduism, with whom Geddes had recently become friendly.

Air Theatre of the Hellenic culture; and it is still to be seen almost from one end of the Mediterranean to the other. Here it was that the Greeks perfected their language and their literature to its heights, still in so many ways supreme for us of the west to this day, and still fuller of suggestions to you in India than most of what we have been doing since. This was the very climax of the Greek City, at once its popular and its spiritual centre, surpassing all save the Acropolis, and in many ways even that.

Now to cut this out of a slope is easy; to heap it up on the plain is not difficult. It need cost little or not more than did your Pendal; often less, since more within the constructive powers of volunteers. Then and only then, all can hear and see; and people will speak, and sing far better.

Yet with a little care it will last for ages. Once made, it would soon come into use for all kinds of purposes; suiting as it does every size of audience, small as well as great.

Now you, as a leader and organiser of democracy—educator, moraliser, civiliser—must peculiarly see this. So why not, as a beginning, ask such an Amphitheatre to be made for your next Conference?

Soon every City in India, might make one: even the children will make theirs for the schools. Is it not the best of schools, and at all levels? Visualise these and as filled, their circles rising and enlarging together.

P.P.S. I do not need to tell you how strongly your plea for the Union of the Hindi with the Urdu vocabulary may be supported from the history of English, with its gradually united Saxon and French vocabulary, yet these taking distinctive shades of meaning. English thus gained the best qualities of each; for it preserved the homely directness and force of the Germanic languages, yet gained a new precision and dignity also from the classical side. It also made all these languages less difficult for us to learn (badly though we may learn them still).

Again, you know, as well as I, how the maturation and mastery of this united language are expressed in the English Bible and in Shakespeare; and how it gives every poet more scope for his individual powers and temperament; and helps prose writers also to their varied styles.

To express this possible Union to Urdu and Hindi speakers alike will no doubt be a difficult task. Yet might not this theme be well worth working up, say by means of Essay and Poem Prizes for next Conference—written in that style?

                                                                    P. G.

Gandhi's reply was magnanimous. He was "truly thankful for your very kind letter" and claimed:

You could not be more pained than I am over our base imitation of the West. . . . I tried last year to do away with the Pendal for the congress and suggested a meeting on the maidan early in the morning. That is the Indian style and it is the best. I wonder if the amphitheatre is an improvement. My ideal is speaking to the crowd from under a tree. Never mind if the voice does not reach the thousands, nay millions. They come not to hear but to see.

He ended:

But what is the use of my writing. Both of us are preoccupied. The wretched fever of the West has taken possession of us. We have no leisure for things eternal. The utmost that can be said of us is that we do hanker after the eternal though our activity may belie our profession.

I shall treasure your letter. May I make public use of it?

And do please tell me how I may build cheap and durable houses—from the foundation to the roof.

The last six months of 1918, which Geddes spent in Calcutta and Darjeeling, were, compared to the frenzy of preparing the Indore report, fairly quiet. He lectured at Calcutta University, prepared a scheme for "saving most of their principal business quarter—'Bara Bazar'—from extravagantly wasteful and destructive programme of the Government's 'Improvement Trust'", and wrote long letters to his friends in Britain in order to pick up the threads before his return in the late spring of 1919. To Mabel particularly he enquired whether she saw any results or growth in Britain of his and Branford's ideas and teaching. He also exhorted her, just before the armistice when the men were beginning to return from the war, to "choose you one of them! Your free life is all very well: but it is time now you took some decent fellow to work for you, love you, cherish you, honour you. . . ." Of the armistice celebrations themselves, she sent him the following vivid description. Reading it must have been one of his more poignant moments of exile.

Of course when the news of the armistice came, I was in Kings Langley, and we had to content ourselves with the rather subdued and tragic rejoicings of a little village, badly hit by both war and influenza epidemic—(the funeral bells of its old doctor—who had almost died on his feet of the epidemic he was trying to cope with, interfering with the joy bells). I went to Putney on Wednesday, and on Thursday and Friday nights mingled with the populace! I missed the rather rowdy outburst of Tuesday (fire in Trafalgar Square). The crowd was all in Trafalgar Square and the Strand and soon—the happiest thing. Really most people were perfectly quiet, hundreds not even talking—just glad to be there— then a shadow lifted. They were like happy children, and some played with toys and flags and danced in the streets, and men went about openly hugging each other and they got a few poor little fireworks and let them off with great glee: and kept this up all the week! Very few drunk or really disorderly considering the thousands involved. Tragic too of course— grave faces behind the smiles. The hospitals seem to have emptied themselves of wounded who were all over the space, all radiant: and as one put it to me "The sky is full of those for whom the way to Tipperary was too long . . .".

She was unable to reassure him very much over the growth of his influence in Britain, and he wrote to Victor Branford discussing the various strands of his activities, and speculating on the reasons why they had not taken root. The fundamental one, he said, was that while they had both "ploughed and sown for ideas—and are not unsuccessful in that way—we have alike had less time, and still less inclination" for organizing the gradual acceptance and implementation of those ideas and "*making*" them become successful.

My Dunfermline plan was not carried out. Why? Simply— and here I come to the point—just as I was asked to do this through friendship with Beveridge, and acquaintance with

Ross, I fell out with Ross's views, but above all, I socially neglected the Dunfermline people, and was friendly with Whitehouse, of whom Ross was jealous.

There is no doubt some truth in this view. And perhaps the crucial point is, having once prepared such a report without then being given the opportunity to settle down to the bread-and-butter business of implementing it, it set a pattern for Geddes's planning activities. All the Indian powers-that-be, it seemed, were content for Geddes to lay his egg and fly away. Nor did this state of affairs seem to perturb him. It is outside the scope of this study to explore, as far as may still be possible, what effect the reports had on the cities concerned, or the young planners and engineers who read them, though it has been suggested that the latter effect was quite considerable. But his Indian peregrinations, with their subsequent sheaves of comments, plans and ideas—some not even printed, but left behind, no doubt, in dusty files—were an amazing manifestation of his powers of creative integration with a community. The three doves on the title-page of this book are the motif that used to appear on the Outlook Tower publications. They represent Sympathy, Synthesis and Synergy, and these qualities were perhaps never better realized during Geddes's career than in the reports he produced for cities as disparate as Dunfermline, Indore, Amritsar and—his next, and greatest, commission —Jerusalem.

Despite the diversity of Geddes's life, it has a symmetry: one of the fortuitous associations in the pattern being the link between his childhood in a cottage named Mount Tabor with a father who joyously recited the Old Testament, and an invitation he received in his sixty-sixth year to plan the new university and environs of Jerusalem. First, however, he had to return to Britain: a sad home-coming in many ways: and before his return, he had already committed himself to arrangements that led to him being offered a specially-created Chair of Sociology and Civics at Bombay University.

Arthur joined his father at Dundee during the summer of 1919, and acted as his assistant. Amelia Defries was there to record her impression of Geddes's farewell lecture.[4]

Arthur and I had helped the Professor to carry plants and range them on each side of the lecture desk, before his farewell to his students—his valedictory address after thirty years of work.

Slowly the people filtered into the lecture room, a miscellaneous audience, dotted with many sturdy, khaki-clad figures.

The chair was taken by a splendid young fellow, who—my neighbour told me—had won the Military Cross in France as the surviving officer of a Black Watch attack.

A good many townspeople were there, but the faculty of the College was absent, and its governing body, too; and this was commented on around me. I got no clear reason, but I gathered that Geddes was felt as a sort of truant professor, who ran about the world and only returned in Summer-time; and then more to lead his students through gardens and woods, than to lecture indoors with customary propriety.

The title of the lecture was "Biology and its Social Bearings: How a Botanist Looks at the World", and, like most of Geddes's lectures, it was long—corralling in all the issues and main activities that had absorbed his life, and finally urging the students before him to see "beyond the attractive yet dangerous apples of the separate sciences" to where "the Tree of Life comes into view". An old lady sitting next to Miss Defries said: "He has been talking to the next generation—it is too much for us."

During that summer, Geddes also gave some lectures in London and visited Dublin to see how the activities he had started there in 1914 had developed; but by July a proposition was put to him that outshone any he had ever had before. Through his friend Dr M. D. Eder, the psychologist, he was introduced to Dr Chaim Weizmann with a view to his being engaged by the Zionist Commission to plan the new university in Jerusalem and advise on the city's wider rehabilitation problems. Palestine had been freed from the Turks by Britain during 1917–18, and under the Balfour Declaration was shortly to become a British mandate. The immensely complex racial and reclamation needs of Jerusalem were ideal grist for Geddes's city development mill, but the political power-struggle was not. Dr Weizmann found his outlook sympathetic, and on 21st August signed a contract for him to prepare a preliminary design and report during an initial period at a salary of £400 a month. Geddes rearranged his schedule, and was in Jerusalem by mid-September. There he stayed with Eder, who wrote the following description of his activities:

> The first two weeks Geddes prowled around Jersualem at all hours of the day and night. To my wife and myself, who accompanied him whenever possible—and often, because he insisted, when it was impossible!—he would say no word of the planning of the university or the town. As he went to this hillock or that, examined a sukh, peered into a house, reverently touched a tree, Geddes had no set plan in his mind but he followed some inner vision. Ideas, too formless yet to find expression, were brooding in his mind. It was the period of fecundation—not a note was yet put upon paper, not a line drawn. On any other subject he conversed freely and gaily.

By 4th November Geddes could report to Weizmann that

> My preliminary report on city improvement and town planning of Jerusalem, as desired by General Watson as Chief Administrator, and General Storrs, Military Governor of Jerusalem, will shortly be in your hands. The corresponding preliminary report to you on the University is also in progress.

The latter was to be completed on his voyage to Bombay, and Frank Mears, who had joined him in Jerusalem, was to complete the designs for the university.

Extracts from a letter which Geddes wrote to a friend on 5th November, just before he left Palestine, give an impression of his activities there:

> I have had a very interesting six weeks or so in Palestine, of which fully five in Jerusalem, where I have had the double task:
>   (1) of improving the very crude Extension & Improvement Plan, recently prepared for the Military Government of occupied territory, and
>   (2) of planning the University.
> It has the most magnificent site in the world—the crest of Mount Scopas . . . immediately north of and continuous with the Mount of Olives, and thus overlooking Jerusalem, old

and new, to the westward, and on the east the vast descent of mountainous country to the Dead Sea and the Jordan Valley. . . .

As you can imagine, I have worked more intensely than ever—(always from sunrise, and generally for an hour or two before), and I have (broadly) solved both problems. The City problem indeed is manifold:—

(a) the old buried city of David, (of which my archaeological programme has been successful in eliciting the enthusiasm of the archaeologists here, so far as I have met them).

(b) the picturesque old Jerusalem within the walls, with its strongly marked quarters, Moslem, Jewish, and Christian.

(c) The existing modern town—a vast spreading suburban area, not well planned, but capable of improvement, and

(d) the future expansion of this on better lines, a matter of practical certainty so far as any can be.

The University too raises all the problems. My first question to my clients—the heads of this Zionist Commission—was this: "Is this University to be the 244th or so in the list of Universities in *Minerva* (the *Jahrbuch des Universitaten*), or No. 1, the first of a new order?" "Certainly if possible that latter," replies Dr Weizmann and the other chiefs of this movement, one after another. "Very good," say I. "But do you realise to how much you are committing yourselves? and on what a great scale you are thus instructing me to plan?" . . .

The great *Unity* discerned by Israel first of all peoples—and this at once in the cosmic order . . . and also in the human and moral order . . . needs again to suffuse the whole range of studies. See Psalm 148, with its expression of this, for a single instance among many. That was the vision of old Jerusalem, and its permanent glory. . . .

Hellas failed—and modern Universities do so too—for lack of the Hebrew wisdom—of that close inter-connection of the cosmic unity and the moral and social order. . . .

Here then is our problem, for this University of Jerusalem, to relate its ancient synthesis to the Greek and modern analysis of Knowledge—and so to become Jerusalem-Athens. . . .

Recall now my Tower in Edinburgh, with its combined Outlooks—synthetic and ethic from the Turret and camera,
range of co-ordinated initiations into the sciences. . . . Now
imagine all this raised into the great Central Hall of the
University, upon its hill-top—and around the base of its
great dome a double ambulatory—one for the general view,
. . . and the other immediately below equipped with all the
essential . . . instruments of each of the sciences from astro-
nomic to social.

Then around this Central Hall . . . there will run the main
buildings of the University—and these again sending out
along the ridge of the hill, the great ranges of buildings for
the special sciences, . . . with ample space for their extension
in the future. I think then we may claim to have solved the
problem essentially—of uniting the unity of the religions and
moral spirit with the progressive researches of the scientific
world. . . .

Similarly a great range of Museums is getting into plan—
and these nearer the City, in fact continuing the perspective
of the wall. School of Medicine, Music, etc., in the city, and
much else—perhaps a High Street of academic houses and
college halls of residence, recalling in some ways Oxford, in
others Edinburgh, but of course Jerusalem in style. To distinguish and develop the Jewish style from the Arab or Sara-
senic is of course a great problem—and I think we are suc-
ceeding. Frank Mears is surpassing himself, and his beautiful
sketches have just been carried off to Cairo by Dr Weizmann
to show Marshal Allenby today. . . . I am off to Bombay by
first steamer, for since the University has not only founded
this chair of Sociology and Civics, but given me my own way
and terms for it, I must not be late. I hope, however, to be
back here in April. So far then my news of which, as you
see, I am full: (you can imagine my one and two-fold regret).

He was, of course, referring to Anna and Alasdair. It would be
the first time he had sailed to India alone.

The Chair which had been specially created for him in Bombay only absorbed him intermittently. His students were apt to
be passive and deferential, seldom engaging him in real discussion, and this lack of equal opposition tended to encourage
his increasingly short temper. Also there was a wide gap be-

tween the traditional Indian mind and his own philosophy of
civic endeavour, in which the spiritual and poetic elements
were tempered by a puritan practicality. He wrote to a friend:

> Indian philosophy seems strangely mingled and contrasted:
> the highest vision of the abstract—Idealism and Infinitude
> imaged most abstractly—yet with elements of the fatigue,
> neurasthenia and malaria, as well as the resigned falling
> asleep, of the last senility distilled into the worst poison for
> youth and maturity; and taking advantage of their rever-
> ence for age at its best to inoculate them with age at its
> worst.

When the winter term was over, he accepted an invitation to
go to Ceylon and make a city report on Colombo. Bose, on
hearing of this, wrote:

> I wish I could induce you to take one year somewhat less
> arduously. What is left of you physically is but a few bones,
> and the diabolic intensity with which you are working can-
> not possibly last.

Just as he was about to leave for Colombo, Geddes received a
cable from Weizmann saying: "Agree your proceeding Palestine twelve months expenses paid. Inviting Mears also." He
replied:

> . . . you may depend that no other commission whether in my
> life or in my dreams, could give me so much pleasure. . . .
> But I cannot manage a continuous twelve-month, being under
> formal agreement with this University. . . . Moreover I have
> already found it impossible to arrange a passage, applied for
> several months ago, before the end of May; and I have hence
> been obliged to accept commissions here meantime—viz. to
> the town-planning of Colombo for which I leave tomorrow
> . . . but I shall decline further possible invitations.

His plan for Colombo included suggestions for enlarging the
postal system and an engineering scheme to combat the river
floods. He took a short holiday at a hill station nearby, but even

there made some plans for extending the station. It seemed necessary for him to keep up a merciless tempo of activity.

He returned to Palestine in June, and was there for five months. A summary of what he did during this time is contained in a letter he wrote to Harry Barker in January 1921, telling his old friend how his recent expatriate years had been spent:

I had to hurry off to Palestine again, where busy all last summer. Partly with Haifa—the future big Seaport—and (I trust) replacement of Admiralty plans by far simpler and cheaper ones. Then Tiberias, with big garden village schemes and renewal of famous baths of Herod, etc. (still going hot and strong!). Back to Haifa to plan garden villages on Carmel Top, and start "Pro-Carmel" Society like "Pro-Jerusalem" civic organisations of great promise, since uniting representatives and public of all faiths and classes, in city betterment of all kinds. My "grateful patients" (as the Edinburgh Doctors say) surprised me by the gift of the finest site on Carmel, to tempt me to build a house; but I have had to make it a camping-site for Boy Scouts and holiday-makers.

Then a great fight at Jerusalem; first with one General, who wished to make a vast military camp on Scopas (Titus' site for the destruction of Jerusalem, and now for spoiling both University and City) and next with a new General, who chose instead to evict Mears' and my best garden village on hill by Bethlehem Road planned for 1,000 houses to cost (say) two millions! However a cable has just come in to say he has given in, and accepted my plan for him on the plain (far more practical too—with railway siding, etc.). So this double saving of the New Jerusalem proper, of which I hope Mears will have time to make the fine perspective he can do so vividly and truly in time for next Academy perhaps. But to this I must return this coming season, unless (as I am trying to arrange) Mears can go on there, as I am wanted again at one or two States in India.

Which seems to confirm that by this time Geddes definitely preferred to make his plans and reports and then leave all the implementation and politicking to others while he entered the more exciting vortex of a fresh challenge.

He left Palestine in November 1920, and in a breathless letter to Eder, written on board ship and recording all the problems and loose-ends he was leaving behind, he said:

I am again unluckily late for my Bombay term! but I have done what I could to start my class by cable. Only heard of this boat (transport for Government) afternoon before last train to catch it, but just got away by sitting up all night, getting motor to Ludd, etc. and with various other adventures just managed (though there may be another passage, which had to be taken prudentially, by later boat to pay!).

During the journey he also wrote rather wistfully to John Ross: "I can't say whether home next summer, or Palestine, or planning in India—I'd like to be home—but no potboiling there, and I'm still paying for the dead horses!"

In fact he did return to Scotland for the summer of 1921. He was supposed to be completing a report on Bombay, but it was the one city which defeated him. Sprawling, disease-ridden, and with an infant mortality rate of 50 per cent, it was impossible even for Geddes to image Bombay in terms of concrete civic hope. His social life at the university was restricted and quiet, and once again he found his warmest contact with Roman Catholics—this time the Jesuit professors at Xaviers College.

On his way to stay with Frank and Norah—who had just had their third son, John—at 14 Ramsay Garden, he travelled via France. He wrote to Norah on 22nd April:

. . . through the extraordinary kind and efficient offices of the British Army Graves Bureau . . . I found Alasdair's grave. As you know, it was at first alone, but 30 or 40 more now surround it, in a little enclosure. . . . Need I tell you how I sobbed over it, as the day of news 4 years ago. Hardy* too could not but join me; and our good chauffeur broke down too when we came back to the road and he saw our faces.

While in Scotland he visited Arthur Thomson in Aberdeen for discussions about future collaboration, and afterwards Thomson reported to Branford:

* Marcel Hardy, an old botanist friend.

The proposed book is quite in the air—suspended between heaven and earth—as Geddes left it after his comet visit to these realms. Not a page of it was written—not by me, for I *could* not, not by Geddes, for he *would* not. . . . I was greatly enriched by his visit; I never saw him in better intellectual form; I never admired his intellectual system more. . . . Another wave has swept me away for a year; a greater wave bears Geddes.

Before the "greater wave" took Geddes back to India, he visited London and lectured at the Town Planning Institute and Sociological Society. He also saw various old friends and acquaintances, including a Scottish lady of considerable means in her early fifties called Miss Lilian Brown. Originally from Paisley, she was a member of the Brown family that comprise one half of Brown & Poulson. After seeing her, he wrote to Mabel:

When you go back to town, I want you to make acquaintance with Miss Lilian Brown—3 Netherton Grove SW10. . . . She frets her heart out—over old loves and sorrows—but has I believe violin talent and outlet accordingly, I want you to take her out to Priory to play to Miss Cross, and the children too.

This time he did not return to Bombay alone, but was accompanied by Arthur. He was to have three more winters at the university, but the hectic periods in Israel were over—apart from a brief return in 1925 for the opening of the new university. But it was not the university dreamed, conceived and drawn by himself and Mears; only the library building was to the latter's design. Their plans had fallen prey to the various power-struggles and ever-changing needs, and their employers learned to grow wary of the Geddesian ideal. "It was not," wrote Eder,

wholly due to want of money, for Geddes was an economical builder and planner . . . I do not want to be drawn into hard words and judgements. Suffice it to say that there are few who could rise to the lofty heights of his imagination and practical knowledge.

Weizmann, in his autobiography, said: "I wish that at least we could see Geddes's great dome." But even the dome itself was subject to contention, some feeling it would be taken to symbolize a political affirmation rather than a spiritual and intellectual expression of unity. Geddes himself commented privately: "There is no doubt in either of our [his and Mears's] minds that at bottom the difficulty is that we are Gentiles."

Working in Jerusalem at the same time as Geddes was an old friend, C. R. Ashbee, who, in *A Palestine Notebook, 1918–23* (1923), summed up perfectly the continuing clash in Geddes's life between the ideal and the real:

I have become the residuary legatee of the work Patrick Geddes has been doing here, for he, too, has had a hand in the shaping of *Civitas Dei*; and for all his failure his work has ever a touch of prophecy. We have worked together now for many years and shall never fall out, but when it comes to editing hundreds of pages of crabbed, mercilessly written manuscript, and still worse typing, on Palestine cities, I tell the Administration, for the love I bear Pat I will do it but on one consideration only, that if they publish they will allow the coloured plans, on which all turns, to be published also. As this will cost several hundred pounds, the Administration antennae instantly retract into their financial shells. "Files—Bureaucracy—Yes, as much as you like! Straightforward town surveys—No!"

Geddes's chief work out here has been the plans, *en ébauche*, for the Zionist University, a magnificent scheme and a wonderful report. But it has cleft Jewry in twain. The orthodox and the ritualists have no use for a *Universitas* in the real sense of the word, such as he desires, nor have the political propagandists for the scholar and the man of science.

Geddes's great achievement in life has been the making of a bridge between Biology and Social Science, thus giving a fresh clue to reconstruction, to civics and to the town plan. His, I think, is one of the synthetic minds of our time. But he is very tiresome about it, and always when you think you are just going to get something done, when the thing is within your grasp, you hear the mocking chorus of the birds. The reality escapes you. You lean back and listen to Aristophanes.

The children parody his wild way of combing his snuffy, smoke-like hair, outward through his fingers into space infinite. It is indicative of the perpetual radiations going on in the man. His talk is wonderful, when you can follow it, for the ideas tumble out so fast that they trip each other up, and at times lose themselves in his fuzzy beard before they have a chance to seminate. He maddened us one evening when we were discussing the language difficulty and the Zionist University.

"You and I . . . and the rest of us will be invited to lecture there, of course!"

"But in what language?" I asked. "Because if it's going to be Hebrew I can employ my time more profitably."

"The language difficulty will settle itself," he said airily.

"Of course it will, and we're here to help settle it, but . . ."

Followed a periphrasis brilliant and partially audible, but No, my dear Pat, you blinked that question shamelessly. Will it be a university or only a Zionist university? Geddes has thrown down the glove to Jewry. It is another challenge to the theocratic state and the old devil of sectarianism who stands between us and our search for truth. Will the challenge be taken up?

We were mocking at the derelict site on Scopas one day— the University in the clouds. . . . But when all's said and done, Pat is right. His prophecy is likely to sound the farthest. You can have no sectarian university.

Chapter 20

"...THAT OLD BULL OF THE HERD"

WITH ARTHUR'S HELP, Geddes was able to install the Cities Exhibition as a permanent feature of his department at Bombay. Writing to Tagore, he described it as "a long picture book of cities covering a quarter of a mile and more of screens". This was one of the many tasks that Arthur undertook in a brave attempt to combine both Anna's and Alasdair's roles as Geddes's helpmeets. Geddes had previously discussed with Eder the possibility of his younger son's having a "father complex", but did not extend his concern into judging it best, therefore, not to put him in a situation where he might feel undermined by the past prowess of his mother and elder brother. In the summer of 1922 they both went to Patiala, the capital of the chief Sikh state of the East Punjab, and prepared a report on the city, for which Arthur provided the drawings. They also visited Tagore's college settlement, Santineketan, which Arthur described as a "ramshackle institution". But he enjoyed the atmosphere, and spent periods on his own there, undertaking some teaching. In November, when he was back in Bombay, Geddes agreed to make some suggestions for extending the college, but the member of Tagore's staff concerned failed to send on promptly the photographs and plans he needed in order to undertake the work. When they finally arrived on 26th February 1923, Geddes wrote to the college:

. . . last November I was then free of other planning, and until Xmas—a very rare opportunity for work on your problems, and on which I was then fresh, as well as keen.

But I had in the Xmas vacation (of less than a fortnight) to go and tackle (1) the Lucknow Zoo, and also the Osmania University at Hyderabad, each, and especially the latter, on large scale and needing much work. They thus pledged me to my remaining free time—(after term here closes on 10th March until sailing for home and U.S.A. on 31st).

One of the reasons he had decided to spend part of the summer in America was in order to meet Lewis Mumford. As a result of reading the Dunfermline report, Mumford had become interested in Geddes's work, and in 1916 (when he was twenty-one), had written to the Outlook Tower enquiring about any courses run there. At the time, Geddes was *en route* for India, but they later fell into correspondence, and by 1919 Geddes was considering Mumford as a future collaborator. In 1920 Mumford went to England for two years, and for a year was acting editor of the Sociological Review; he got on extremely well with Branford, whom he both liked and admired. However, by May 1923 he still had not met Geddes. It was to be a traumatic experience.

A full account of their meeting is contained in Mumford's brilliant and revealing essay *The Disciple's Rebellion* (*Encounter*, September 1966), which is the source of quotations used in this account. The plan had been that Mumford should organize a full-fledged lecture tour for Geddes, but this proved impossible so near the close of the academic year. In the end it was decided simply to announce a special course of lectures at the New School for Social Research in New York, and to arrange a few nearby visits: "to Washington for a social workers' conference, to Worcester to see his old friend Stanley Hall, to Cambridge to lecture for the landscape architecture students" and "to Woods Hole, for a week with his scientific colleagues". In advance of his arrival, Geddes sent $200 to Mumford "so that I might devote myself to him during the next few months". Before going to New York, Geddes travelled across Europe and stayed with Norah and Frank in Edinburgh. Seeing Norah, now aged thirty-six, with her young family around her, he was forcibly reminded of Anna at the same age, and their life together at Ramsay Garden. He was particularly moved by her singing one evening, and wrote to her while he was sailing to New York saying that Anna's failure to educate him to music, and hers to educate Frank, was due to his and Frank's inhibition. "The shaking off of mine, as by versing last summer, would now make it possible for me (could your mother again now take me in hand) to join a chorus and even to sing (to my-

self!)." The "versing" that he referred to was a sudden impulse
to express his feelings, and even write letters, in (very) free,
and usually execrable, verse. One of his first attempts at a
verse-letter had been to Anna's old friend Marjory Kennedy-
Fraser and contained the following lines which describe how,
after a period of fatigue, he began to write in this way:

> But still blood waxed; so suddenly—just a few days ago—
> I found
> It true—what I remember skimming long ago, and had
> forgotten—
> The vivid guess, if not clear-evidenced theory, that speech
> came
> To man, and grew to language—not as we speak it now,
> in plain prose—
> But rhythmic cry, then call, "Arbeit und Rhythmus!" That
> Had place, and service manifold; even soon, as you know
> well,
> 'Twas Song! So I—after a life of thinking—all plain prose
> Or technical, oftenest graphic (thus so far *mathetic*)—yet
> Of working too, and only by rarest impulse scribbling a
> rhyme—
> Suddenly found myself aroused anew, to write, as if by
> Caedmon's call!

It was perhaps the final signal that Geddes's papers, charts,
thoughts and dreams never were going to be collected by him
into that elusive major work, his *opus syntheticum*. He was sixty-
eight and a portion of his brain had slipped into a free-wheeling
state that permitted an old man to indulge his continuing
energy and creativity in whatever eccentric way he pleased. It
did not, however, augur very well for Mumford, a young man
of twenty-seven, waiting in keen anticipation to meet the crucial
influence on his working life. He had been forewarned. His
friend Dorothy Loch, Branford's part-time secretary, had written to him and his wife Sophie, about Geddes:

> Geddes must be accepted as a good Catholic accepts grief,
> with an open heart and no reserves, *if* he is to benefit those
> whom his presence scourges. He will brook no reserves. . . .
> I have lost much of Geddes from my flights, fears, and

reserves. Stop dealing with him when you (or if you) must, but when you may, go with him fully. Don't forget he is an old man and lonely, and the very-most-vicious-cave-barbarian when sad, angered or thwarted.

Mumford had reserves right from his first sight of Geddes:

> My first glimpse of Geddes was at the White Star pier near 23rd Street, on the other side of the customs' barrier: a little, narrow-shouldered man, frail but wiry, with flowing, gesticulating beard and a head of flaring reddish-grey hair, parted in the middle: hot and impatient that warm morning, vexed that I had not got a ticket to take me past the customs' barrier, talking in a rapid stream whose key sounds were muffled by the grey thicket of moustache and beard. To my still adolescent horror I realised, as he turned his head, that he wore no necktie under his beard. I feared it might be his regular costume: but discovered later that in the haste of a belated packing that morning he had dumped all his neckties into his bag before he realised that he had not put one on.

However, Geddes's lack of convention in matters of dress was only of momentary significance. It was the emotional demands he made on Lewis Mumford that turned the whole visit, from the younger man's point of view, into a period of frequent frustration and tension. The worst demand came first:

> On the day after his arrival, in the basement lounge of the New School, which gave out on the garden, he took me squarely by the shoulders and gazed at me intently. "You are the image of my poor dead lad," he said to me with tears welling in his eyes, "and almost the same age he was when he was killed in France. You must be another son to me Lewis, and we will get on with our work together." There was both grief and desperation in this appeal: both too violent, too urgent for me to handle.

It was a totally false claim that Geddes made. Mumford was an intellectual, on the threshold of a long career devoted to deep and true expression of thought—a solitary activity; whereas Alasdair had been a man of action, a man of the people. And physically they did not resemble one another at all. As Mumford ascertained, Geddes *was* desperate, desperate to find someone "to transform the accumulated seekings and findings of a lifetime into an orderly, readable form". But Mumford quickly came to realize that, even if such a person existed—which seemed unlikely—he certainly was not the man. They used to meet at the New School before ten in the morning, and by the time Mumford left at four or five in the afternoon he was

> usually in a state of fatigue approaching exhaustion . . . somehow this daily intercourse did not bring us closer; and I was never alert enough at the end of the day to put down even a fragment of all that he had told me and taught me, though I had had the ambition, before we met, of using this period to gather material for his biography. He did, of course, tell me much about his past, as he might tell any chance acquaintance in a railroad train or a restaurant; but he was averse to making any systematic effort to review his life: "Time for that later," he would say, and by later he really meant after he had died.

There were brief moments, however, when the two men made real contact, one of those moments even stretching into an "illuminating, almost ecstatic day". And Mumford found that Geddes's actual presence "shook my life to the core". Although old, "he conveyed what it is to be fully alive, alive in every pore, at every moment, in every dimension".

When the time came for Geddes to leave, the bales of charts and diagrams which he had sent over to New York in advance, were spread over many rooms in the New School. He was due to sail at midnight and had made, inevitably, a dinner appointment. Mumford writes:

> ... he left to me the dreary task of packing his bags and papers —those heaps of clothes, those middens of notes and charts, those shelves of new books! An English artist, Stephen Haweis, who had long been influenced by Geddes, dropped in for a last chat, and he too was disappointed at finding the Master absent. Years later Haweis recalled to me the remark I had made in the midst of my packing: that it was like putting the contents of Vesuvius back into the crater after an eruption.

In a letter[1] to Frederic Osborn, written in 1944, Mumford described Geddes as "that old Bull of the Herd", and commented: "he was too old and I was too young for there to be any real partnership. . . ."

Arthur clearly experienced similar difficulties, but he continued to fulfil his father's needs. While Geddes was away, he had started to write up the notes he had taken down the previous winter during his Bombay university lectures, delivered under the general heading of "Contemporary Civilization". He continued and completed this work after Geddes arrived back at the end of October. Then, shortly after his return, Geddes became seriously ill. When an attempt was made to take his temperature, he bit the thermometer in half. Finally he was sent to a nursing home and attended by an excellent and firm doctor—described by Arthur as "Colonel Carter, head of chief Bombay hospital (demoted for his exposure of the medical débâcle in Mesopotamia after siege of Kut)"—who diagnosed colitis.

While in the nursing home, Geddes occupied his time by trying to write a paper on "International Intellectual Co-operation" for Henri Bergson. He had known Bergson since the 1900 exhibition, and had seen him in Paris on his way back from America in order to discuss the work of the League of Nations Committee of International Intellectual Relations, of which Bergson was an active sponsor. Previously he had spent a week in Geneva, mainly at the League of Nations, and on the boat back to India he wrote Raymond Unwin a long letter expressing his concern for the way the League was functioning:

Just as with National Governments, the bureaucracies come to rule—and to wither up (or get rid of) their live spirits. For the short life of League of Nations they are already going wonderfully in that line; and I feel that unless organisations like yours for supporting the League can be roused to this danger, it will grow past their powers of keeping it in their service!

He also criticized the plans for the League's new offices:

A symbolic expression of their limitations was in the new plans for a vast new office to be built shortly. . . . Ably

planned, so far as it goes; but no space for graphic illustrations . . . and no outlets to the roof—and thus to magnificent
Lake and Mt. Blanc views—for cooling and refreshing the
tired heads of either Governing body or staff. Yet so absurdly
easy to supply for both of them! So too in existing L. of N.
building. I insisted on getting on to the roof: and my
friendly guide discovered the way for the first time. This
blindness to outlooks—to synoptic vision—is symbolic indeed.

The doctors advised Geddes that he should not spend another
hot season in India, and Arthur set about helping to nurse him
well enough to return home. His bowel complaint was an unpleasant one, and it did absolutely nothing to improve his
temper. However, at last, on 13th March 1924, Arthur was able
to report to Norah that he had seen their father off on the boat:

He has *no* fever, and has his sterilised milk for the voyage.
The season is pleasant and I think he may be really well
again by Genoa. He's not allowed to eat any solids it's true,
but he can rest, and so the doctor has no anxiety.

In fact Geddes became acutely ill during the voyage and had
what he described as "a full experience of advanced old age as
never before". He disembarked at Marseilles and went straight
to friends at Montpellier. By Easter Sunday he could write to
Norah that he was gradually getting better, partly due to a
course of injections. He was also reading a lot and enjoying
going to church. (He had always taken pleasure in Roman
Catholic church services.) Above all he extolled to her the
superiority of French culture over all others. Victor Branford
arranged for him to go to a Swiss sanatorium as soon as he was
well enough, and joined his old friend there for a brief rest.
By July Geddes had recovered sufficiently to attend the International Town Planning Conference in Amsterdam, and from
there he went to lecture in London at the Conference of Living
Religions.
    The doctors in Britain advised him that just as the hot
weather of India would harm his health, so would a cold northern winter, and so, in the autumn of his seventieth birthday,
he repaired to the place for which he had only ever felt affection, and where he (and Anna) had always derived comfort—

Montpellier. There he purchased a plot of land and an old cottage on a stony hillside, with no piped water supply, outside the town. By 4th November he could write to John Ross:

> This adventure is prospering, and my old cottage is growing on each side and back, and quite as a small chateau with its Outlook Tower on quarry cliffs and future rock garden below. . . . Paul Reclus has got for me the place I told you of, at Domme in Dordogne—the windmill and site—for under £100, and yesterday I bought at auction a cottage of 4 rooms near this, in good contition, with ample annexes, etc., and cistern and well, with 7/8 acre of meadow, for—exactly £50. . . . I am offered an intermediate house, on next hillside from this . . . with some 7-8 acres of good land for £400, and wish I had it handy.

Why did a septuagenarian in supposedly poor health need all this semi-derelict rural French property? Because Geddes was about to make manifest a microcosm of all his ideals by creating an international residential college just outside his beloved medieval university town of Montpellier. (How a windmill in the Dordogne was to fit into this is unclear!) And he called his do-it-yourself institution Le Collège des Ecossais.

It was a venture that caused bother, muddle and exasperation to most of the friends, family (and sometimes students) who came into contact with it. Mumford wrote sternly in his *Encounter* essay of his own

> failure to be captured even for a moment by Geddes's plan for creating a series of residential "colleges" at Montpellier. From the first, that project seemed a folly. . . . This was his last opportunity to turn his dreams, his plans, his graphs into firm structures . . . the Montpellier project, I realised, was an evasion.

Well, yes—if Geddes is to be judged by the conventional standards of written western intellectual tradition, Mumford was right. But for a long time he had not observed those standards, and as his favourite Emerson said: "Words and deeds are quite indifferent modes of the divine energy. Words are also actions, and actions are a kind of words." Was Le

Collège des Ecossais a symptom of *folie des grandeurs*, or just another "*solid*, three-dimensional" expression of the Geddesian world? On 11th December he wrote to John Ross telling him more about his activities, and commenting, "It sounds like a repetition of the old days in Edinburgh when we used to buy houses knowing not where the needful to pay for them was to be found!" And indeed it did. But what might he have done? Lived quietly with friends and written books? Nothing so far in his life suggests that as likely.

Chapter 21

GEDDES-LAND

So you see I'm greatly pleased with the place and with
myself, because I'm again happily at real *work*—open air all
day long—and bed after a bread-and-milk supper—say
8 p.m.—to begin next day with a spate of thinking from
5, 4, 3 (or 2) a.m., as the case may be, before going up to
work at 7 or 7.30 or 8. . . . In short, I am again realising
vivendo discimus!

GEDDES WROTE THIS to Amelia Defries after he and a party
of workmen had begun to transform the old stone cottage. He
stayed during this time with his new neighbour, the owner of a
vineyard at the foot of the hill. In order to lay out paths and
terrace gardens leading up to the cottage, the stony ground had
to be literally blasted away, and topsoil brought from elsewhere.
Water had to be paid for and hauled up by the cart load.

The upper terrace garden was to become a botanical thinking-
machine: two plant-beds laid out in geometric squares. One
contained plants that were economically important, the other
ones that were aesthetically pleasing; specimens also had their
own symbolic significance related to classical mythology.
Geddes's aim was to encourage an ecological approach to
society: to demonstrate the parable that as a gardener must
nurture his plants and shape the development of his garden,
so a planner must understand how to sustain and control the
environment in order to enable society to flourish.

From the hillside could be seen the city of Montpellier, and
beyond it the flat plain and then the sea. To the east, though
too distant to be seen, lay Aigues-Mortes and the mysterious
lakes and marshes of the Camargue, while immediately north-
wards were the stony slopes known as the *garrigue*, with their
dry grass, brittle plants and dwarf trees. In the sunshine the
scent of aromatic leaves filled the air. When the mistral blew

relentlessly for days on end, the environment was less welcoming.

Le Collège des Ecossais had no set courses and, of course, no degrees. Some students used the opportunity to combine living in Geddes-land with studying at Montpellier University, or undertaking research for a doctorate. Geddes's old friends at the university gave practical guidance to such students, but there were never very many of them. Geddes's idea was that they should come from all over the world, and that their home countries might endow college buildings: one for America, one for India. . . . For a time, Norah found it hard to hide her impatience. Arthur reluctantly, and under pressure from his father ("you cannot desert me . . ." etc.), spent the best part of three years at Montpellier, and wrote a successful doctoral thesis on "The rural civilization of Western Bengal and its geographical factors". He also met his future wife, Jeannie Collin, niece of Paul Reclus, to whom he became engaged early in 1932. Mabel Barker came to take a course at the university and helped Geddes with the housekeeping. But Norah commented in a letter to Arthur: "Thinking machines for breakfast, dinner and supper bore her!" A handful of Geddes's Indian students, with time and money to spare, stayed at the Collège, and one, Gopal Advani, took over some of the administration. Geddes usually acted generously towards impoverished students who wanted to stay there. As Arthur had previously remarked of Tagore's college, it was "a ramshackle institution".

As soon as the hot weather started in June, Geddes would repair to northern Europe, making his customary whistle-stop tours of Paris, Brussels, London, Edinburgh and Aberdeen to see and talk to old colleagues. His visits to Aberdeen were mainly to discuss with Thomson their final, and major, work of collaboration, *Life: Outlines of Biology*, which was published in two volumes in 1931. It was the culminating product of forty years of combined biological and social thinking, and Geddes commented ruefully: "Cambridge and London, Edinburgh or where you will, have had very little use either for our ecstasies of nature-studies, or for our all-round surveys and interpretations." Everyone kept telling him not to over-work, but, as he wrote to Norah: "While it is very kind of all one's friends to want to take care of the old man, it's no use for 'Old-and-Bold'. . . . I'm still out for adventure, for all risks; and did not need Nietzsche to teach me to 'live dangerously'!" In the summer of 1925 he met Lewis Mumford again, who was on a five-day visit to Edinburgh. They both stayed at the Outlook Tower, described by Mumford as "an all-but-deserted place, kept going through the financial efforts of a small loyal group of supporters. . . ."[1] Everywhere there were dusty piles of manuscripts and "bins of teasing notes, mostly on folded paper".

In 1925 Geddes was awarded a Civil List pension of £80, and then in 1926 John Ross succeeded in getting him a sum of £2,000 in compensation for the loss of the first Cities Exhibition during the war. The Collège was still primitively equipped and needed some money spent on it; the rough-cast walls hung with oriental weavings and containing numerous niches filled with images of eastern gods were effective, but did not take the place of sanitation. But, as Geddes wrote to John Duncan: "though cautious friends think me daft, and uselessly expostulate, I can't help going ahead"—and he went ahead and bought the Château d'Assas, an eighteenth-century mansion, with medieval remains, six miles from Montpellier. As Craufurd had been to University Hall, so was this splendid white elephant to be to the Collège.

Many of his old friends, including Martin White, visited Geddes at Montpellier. And Tom Marr, now a successful business-man with a construction company in France, was persuaded down to advise on the management of the Collège. The terrace garden particularly took his fancy, and he offered some financial help towards it. The students, between their studies and private pursuits, and listening to Geddes, also helped with the gardens and the never-ending building projects. After Mabel had left the Collège, Geddes wrote to her describing how "the most literary imaginable of young Brahmins" and his English friend, son of a civil servant, had asked for a vacation building job, while a Bulgarian barrister was helping with the housework. When Harry Barker wrote seeking Geddes's views on age and immortality, he replied:

. . . anything I can say must be disappointing to you. For I have never had any feeling of immortality for myself or my dear lost ones, any more than for autumn leaves like myself, or those already gone. I just work away to do what I can with such days as may remain, and think of death as sleep . . .

Although he bemoaned to Norah that he could not get enough writing done for lack of a really good stenographer, this did not prevent him from entering into new contracts with publishers. He promised a volume on Sociology for the Home University Series, and he accepted an advance from the Yale University Press for a book entitled *Olympus*. Potentially this was one of his most exciting, and correspondingly most elusive, projects. It was based on the concept that

> Each goddess, each god of Olympus is the essential and characteristic, the logical and necessary, expression of the corresponding life-phase of Woman and of Man,

and was to explore the needs, expectations and potentialities of each life-phase in bio-sociological terms. He wrote to Amelia Defries:

> . . . we have to think out the possibilities of our own species, and of life in general, until these again intersect and combine in gods and muses. Mythologies of the past thus renew and reappear as mythologies of the future; and science is thus resumed into art.

He did not complete either book, though he did produce a considerable body of manuscript for each. However, it was not in a form that made it feasible for his executors to finish off the tasks.

A record of what it was like to be a student at the Collège has been written by Giles Playfair,[2] the author son of actor-manager Nigel Playfair. He left Harrow in 1927, and his mother, who knew Amelia Defries, decided it might be a good idea for him to go to Montpellier to brush up on his mathematics and French before taking an Oxford scholarship examination. Miss Defries wrote to Geddes:

> The Maths is the real trouble and they want to know if you can get him interested in this sufficiently, and in three months, to pass his Exam? At the same time they want him to have a chance to continue his organising and acting and French. Acting and Literature are his two main crazes and he also shows gifts for Leadership and Politics. They

are very broadminded but don't want him to be a Socialist
and they are anxious for him not to get "cranky" and
above all to take care of his person and have his trousers
pressed!

It seems that Geddes arranged for Playfair to walk down
through France to Montpellier with a vacation party mainly
of ladies interested in regional survey, for Miss Defries wrote
anxiously:

> Last week there was another development strictly entre
> nous. Giles was greatly disgusted and enraged on finding he
> has to walk to you with women—he expected to go with
> Arthur. He dislikes women unless beautiful and well-dressed;
> and the leader of the party was described as cross-eyed and
> wearing a round straw hat (out of fashion). Many people
> have been at his mother not to let him go at all—saying you
> are a crank.

These problems smoothed over, Playfair arrived in Montpellier
to find "Geddes disliked both Oxford and the examination
system with equal vigour" though "he did attempt to teach me
mathematics". However: "I found his method of instruction
so peculiar, so indirect and so incomprehensible, that I failed to
derive the vaguest practical benefit from it." Staying at the
Collège at the same time were "an American Professor, a
Scottish curate, a Hindu, a Parsee, three English girls" and
Playfair's painter friend, John Tandy.

> Despite the fact that my chances of a successful Oxford
> career were not materially advanced during my two months'
> stay in Montpellier, I could not have had a happier, a more
> interesting and a more enjoyable time. I do not regret a
> moment of it.
> I readily acquired a cosmopolitan attitude of mind. I
> liked all my fellow collegiates enormously. We were together
> most of the time when we were not engaged in our own work.
> There was an exceptionally harmonious and light-hearted
> atmosphere about the Collège des Ecossais.
> It is the trivial incidents which endear one's memory
> permanently to a period or an environment. I have memories

of regular afternoon meetings in the London Tea House, of bicycle trips into the country, of visits to the local Opera House, of the long luncheon table with its invariable first course of fresh hors d'œuvres.

We entered freely into the life of the University itself. We met many of the students. On Sundays some of the French professors and their families came to tea at the college and we were often entertained by them. . . . But it was Geddes himself, though he moved among us vaguely and almost aimlessly and though he never interfered in or cared about what we were doing, who set the real mark on the Collège des Ecossais and made our stay there so memorable.

Among the friends who visited Geddes was Lilian Brown, whom, several years previously, he had described to Mabel as fretting "her heart out over old loves and sorrows". Mabel was no doubt as surprised as everyone else who received the news when, in a long chatty letter from Geddes dated 8th February 1928, she suddenly observed the post-script:

P.S. Not forgetting the past—yet after eleven years nearly of solitude, I am being *married* tomorrow, at British Consulate, Marseilles, to my old friend Lilian Brown.

There was a good deal of disapproval among Geddes's friends of this latest proof that "Old-and-Bold" was still determined to live life fully. For although it could be seen as a *mariage de convenance* since Lilian put money into the Collège and tried to help with the organization, evidence suggests that Geddes was seeking a closer, more living, relationship. And by all accounts, well-off though she may have been, Lilian was a hopeless organizer. Arthur described her as a "very kindly and likeable but quite unbalanced and personally undisciplined old maid". And in his biography of Geddes, Philip Boardman, who stayed at Montpellier, recalled that "she carried to an alarming extent, the feminine weakness of mislaying pocketbook or vanity bag". In fact, for a lady of leisure nearing sixty, it must have been quite a formidable experience even to have attempted to deal with letters such as this one, which arrived from a lady organizing a vacation party due to stay at the Château d'Assas over Easter, 1929:

May I raise several points which have been brought to me by various members of last year's group:—

(1) The question of bed-linen and pillows. Some of the women folk last year said these were inadequate.

(2) The question of three of the rooms which were damp last year—will these be alright this year?

(3) Can you possibly make any better arrangement for the water supply in the lavatories? This seems to have been rather a vexed question.

The food supply last year seems to have been excellent, and Mademoiselle Tarame seems to have been a popular person. I conclude some one will take her place this year?

While Geddes continued to live almost as energetically as ever, time was catching up on his friends. Victor Branford died in June 1931, and Arthur Thomson, now retired, was beginning to suffer from angina. The co-operative work towards a better society which, despite distance, war, and clashing of personalities, Geddes's friends had undertaken for so many decades under his vital influence, was drawing to a close. They all admitted that their lives had been changed by him, and they never, however exasperated, left the compass of his friendship. But his own health too, despite everything, started to deteriorate. A doctor diagnosed the "beginnings of sclerosis", put him on a diet, and told him to give up smoking. He did not succeed in doing the latter, but used to cut all his cigarettes in half in an attempt to decrease his consumption.

As usual, he visited Britain in the summer of 1931, and on 11th August, from the B.B.C.'s Edinburgh studio, gave his first and only broadcast, entitled "When Scotland Wakes". He wrote to the producer: "My theme would *not* be the nationalistic one: that party seems to me starting to repeat the long line of political errors from Fenians of 1860 to Valera." He was going to urge Scotland to lead the regional movement of decentralization and avoid the sterile aim of separation. Other matters also took his interest, and he did not return to Montpellier in the early autumn as usual. He joined the English branch of the Adler Society, attracted by Alfred Adler's aim to help people to integrate with society. When the branch formed a New Europe Group to replace the international Adler organization that had been dissolved to avoid persecution by the

Nazis, Geddes was made its first president. On his seventy-seventh birthday he was staying at Lilian's house in Netherton Grove, and described contemporary London to Thomson as "this awful place, biggest of hells so far, yet *medleyed* with Purgatories and Paradises too—so far as this too often hellish atmosphere allows us respite from being literally *gassed*". He had just had an exhibition of his "Graphic Presentments" at the French Institute, and it was about to transfer to the London School of Economics. Commenting on this latter venue at 4.30 a.m. on his birthday morning in a letter to Arthur, he said:

> Great event for me to bring the Tables of the Social Law to the very heart of the Temple—the essential University Faculty of Divinity of the City where God is Mammon.

After Branford's death, he had been made President of the Sociological Society and later that day, he told Arthur, he was going to their premises in Le Play House, Belgrave Square, "to try if I can put some fire into them—(but I won't succeed)".

He stayed on in London, doing too much, and ignoring doctors' advice that he should go south for the winter as usual. Then, on 18th December, he wrote to Norah:

Dear Norah,

Tell Frank I have at last fixed talk with Weyman for tomorrow, Saturday afternoon, so shall report for Monday.

Now advise me. As you may know, my old friend Lord Pentland sounded me 20 years ago or so as to acceptance of Knighthood—but I declined, on grounds of lifelong policy and views of life.

But now Ramsay Macdonald repeats this for Xmas or New Year honours. Should I accept—as this time I am tempted to do on business grounds, though not from pleasure. It did not stir or touch my pulse (nor Lilian's either, rather to my surprise), but it might do both for my purse (though I fear making shop, hotel and other expenses more?). Thus consider any ideas which come to you after sleeping over this, and talking it over with Frank and Arthur too, since each may have ideas, for or against.

(1) As to helping Frank—with Palestine perhaps

(2) other jobs, e.g. London University Hostels, etc.

(3) or you, if you resume School.
(4) Outlook Tower? and Halls, Town and Gardens, etc.
(5) Even publishing—help to find Partner of business value?
(6) Scots College. Impression with Scots Universities and students or English, etc. too.
(7) Indian College. With Princes and other friends of Britain?
(8) Scots opinion generally?
(9) and possibly Highlands?
(10) (Scots Nationalists?—British Regionalists?)
(11) Sociological society and others here I have to help.
(12) Opinion abroad, e.g. would it help with wretched Scots and Highland Societies over Empire and U.S.A. which have done nothing for Marjory Kennedy Fraser Memorial practically!
(13) Pilgrim Trust?
(14) Iona University Scheme, N.Y. City,
(15) or anything else? like help of books, and demand from Press, etc. for articles.
(16) In short, if I must take it—which uses can be made of it? as to above or in other ways? for this little boom!
Write say on Sunday—or later.
(But if you feel strongly No, wire me that, tomorrow Sat.)
Love to all, Daddy P.

One can only surmise what a forty-four-year-old daughter feels on receiving such a letter from her seventy-seven-year-old father.

He accepted the knighthood and remained in London for the investiture. On New Year's Day, when the Honours List was publicly announced, Arthur Thomson, who had himself received a knighthood in 1930, wrote: "My dear Sir Patrick (I must be allowed this once). . . ." The investiture was delayed owing to the King's illness, and finally took place on 25th February. The extended stay in London's "hellish atmosphere", plus the inevitable hours of non-stop talk with friends who called at Netherton Grove, brought on attacks of what seemed like asthma, leaving Geddes gasping for breath and unable to speak.

In March he was able to return to Montpellier, and was

accompanied by Norah's eldest son, Kenneth, now aged fifteen, and Philip Mairet. In the latter's biography of Geddes he writes:

P.G. supported the twenty-four hour journey well, as keenly observant as ever of the country, pointing out the effects of the drought as the train passed through Normandy and, in the early hours of the next morning, commenting upon various features of the Provençal landscape . . .

Reinstated at the Collège, he carried out his usual programme of talking, working, and walking through the gardens and out on to the *garrigue*. But after three weeks he felt ill enough to stay in bed, and in the night of 17th April his condition suddenly worsened. By the time the doctor arrived from Montpellier, Geddes was dead.

His funeral was his final pageant. On the terrace of the Collège, which he had helped to blast out of the hillside seven years before, friends and students gathered. The Indian students chanted a lament for a departed *guru*. French and English students sang the traditional folk songs which he had enjoyed. Charles Flahault recalled the days when they had both worked as students at Roscoff—an experience that had helped to teach Geddes to value international, co-operative work so highly.

His body was carried down the hill between the banks of spring flowers and spicy, Mediterranean shrubs, while everybody sang his favourite song, *Gaudeamus Igitur*. Then it was driven to the crematorium in Marseilles, accompanied only by Lilian. John Tandy and his wife, who were living in Aix en Provence, joined her at the crematorium.

As his uncoffined corpse was placed on the furnace fire, his beard and hair instantly flared alight and for an evanescent moment his whole outworn body became pure flame.

APPENDICES

APPENDIX I
(See pp. 63–67)

(See pp. 63–67)

THE NOTATION OF LIFE (diagram overleaf)

Take this double sheet of paper for our ledger of life; the left side is for the more passive aspects, or man shaped by place and his work, while the right side is for action; man guiding his daily life and remaking place. Now fold this ledger in half horizontally; we thus get four quarters, one for each of the main chambers of human life; the out-world both active and passive, and the in-world both passive and active. In each of these quarters belongs a nine-squared thinking machine, but before introducing them let us make clear the general structure and relationships of the chart. Here it is:

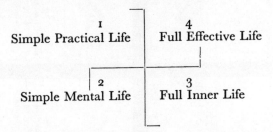

1 Simple Practical Life	4 Full Effective Life
2 Simple Mental Life	3 Full Inner Life

The movement from one quarter to another corresponds to facts easily verifiable, for everyone in some degree goes through these four steps of life. How full and rich each step might be and ought to be will become apparent as we fill in the sub-divisions of the main squares. But one further general observation. Where does the fourth quarter lead? To the first again, or a fifth if you prefer. That is, the world as remade by effective men of action becomes in turn the environment that shapes other men, stimulates their mental life, which in turn leads them on to change the world still further. Thus we may diagram the whole process of history, the succession of human generations by means of lines symbolising this unending interplay of the four parts of life. Thus also is it vividly shown how history both ever and never repeats itself.

1. *Now let us start with the passive objective life of the upper left hand group of nine squares*

Here the study of Place grows into Geography; that of Work into Economics; that of Folk into Anthropology. But these are commonly studied apart, or in separate squares, touching only at a point.

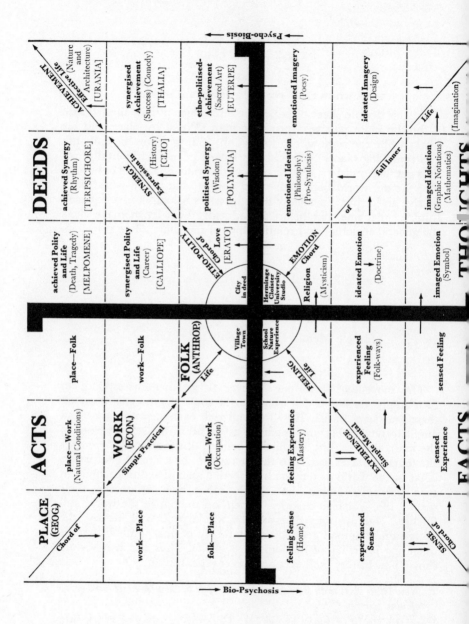

Witness the separate Chairs and Institutes and Learned Societies of each name. But here we have to bring them into a living unison. Place studied without Work or Folk is a matter of atlases and maps. Folk without Place and Work are dead—hence anthropological collections and books contain too much of mere skulls and weapons. So too for economics, the study of Work, when apart from definite Folk, comes down to mere abstractions.

But what do these side squares mean? Below our maps of Place we can now add pictures of the human Work-places, i.e., of field or factory: next of Folk-places of all kinds, from farmhouse or cottage in the country to homes or slums in the modern manufacturing town. Our geography is now fuller and our town planning of better Work-places, better Folk-places, can begin.

So again for Folk. Place-folk are natives or neighbours; and Work-folk are too familiar at all levels to need explanation. Our anthropology thus becomes living and humanised and surveys the living town.

Work too becomes clearer. For Place-work is a name for the "natural advantages" which determine work of each kind at the right place for it; and Folk-work is our occupation, often tending to accumulate into a caste, not only in India.

Our geography, economics and anthropology are thus not simply enlarged and vivified; they are now united into a compact outline of Sociology.

From these three separate notes of life we thus get a central unified Chord of Life, with its minor chords as well.

We so far understand the simple village, the modern working town. But thus to unify geography, economics and anthropology is not enough. Social life has its mental side; so we must here call in the psychologist.

2. *Let us turn to the lower subjective group of squares*

Sense, Experience, Feeling. Can we not relate these to Place, Work and Folk? Plainly enough. It is with our Senses that we come to know our environment, perceiving it and observing it. Our Feelings are obviously developed from our folk in earliest infancy by our mother's love and care. And our Experiences are primarily from our activities, of which our work is the predominant one.

Thus to the Chord of Elemental and Objective Life in village and town, there now also exactly corresponds the Elemental Chord of Subjective Life, and with this chord we must evidently play the same game of making nine squares as before.

How can we go further? Can we penetrate into the world of imagination in which the simple natural sense impressions and activities, which all observers can agree on, are transmuted in each separate mind into its own imagining?

3. *Let us turn to the lower group of squares on the right hand side*

How indeed has it come, as it so often has done, through individual (and even social) history, to seek for the transcendant and divine, to reach all manner of mystic ecstasy? Without asking why, or even here considering exactly how, we must agree that all these three transmutations are desirable. From the present viewpoint, let us call them the three conversions, or, in more recent phrase, three sublimations: Emotion, Ideation, Imagination—the essential Chord of the Inner Life.

Ideation of Emotion—thought applied to the mystic ecstasy, to the deepest and most fully human emotions—from that process comes the Doctrine of each Faith, its Theology, its Idealism. But Ideation calls for Imagery, and this in every science, from geometry onwards. Mathematics, Physics, Chemistry have long had these notations and the historian condenses his annals into graphic "rivers of time". Thought of all kinds was first written in pictorial hieroglyphics, and it is from these that have come even the printed letters of this modern page.

So far then this cloister of thought with its ninefold quadrangles: and here for many, indeed most who enter it, the possibilities of human life seem to end. Yet from this varied cloister there are further doors; and these open out once more into the objective world; though not back into the too simple everyday town-life we have long left. For though we have out-lived these everyday Acts and Facts, and shaped our lives according to our highest Dreams, there comes at times the impulse to realise them in the world anew, as Deeds.

4. *So we turn to the last upper group of squares*

Not every thought takes a form in action; but the psychologist is ever more assured that it at least points thither. With increasing syntheses with other thoughts, ideas become emotionalised towards action. Synthesis in thought thus tends to collective action—to Synergy in deed: and Imagination concentrates itself to pre-figure, for this Etho-Polity in Synergy, the corresponding Achievement which it may realise.

Here then is a new Chord of Life—that in which the subjective creates its objective counterpart. We thus leave the cloister. We are now out to re-shape the world anew, more near the heart's desire. Here then is the supreme Chord of Life and its resultant in Deed— that is in fullest Life.

This is no small conclusion; that from the simplest chord of the Acts of everyday life, from the Facts of its ordinary experience, there may develop not only the deep chord of the inward life and Thought, but that also of life in Deed. And is it not now a strange—indeed a wholly unsought for but now evident—coincidence that, in this continuously reasoned presentment of life in everyday, modern, scientific terms; first as geographic, economic, anthropological, next as psychological, elemental and developed; there should emerge this unexpected conclusion—that the Greeks of old knew all this before, and had thought it out to the same conclusions, albeit in their own nobler, more intuitive way. For our diagram next turns out to be that of Parnassus, the home of the nine Muses; and their very names and their symbolisms will be found to answer to the nine squares above, and to connect them with those below, and this more and more precisely as the scheme is studied. Not indeed that there are not one or two difficulties at first sight, but these can easily be cleared away by a little psychological and social reflection.

Condensed from notes and a paper written by Geddes when in India and quoted in *The Interpreter Geddes* by Amelia Defries, and in the 1949 edition of *Cities in Evolution.*

APPENDIX II
Geddes's Scientific Writings up to 1888

GENERAL BOTANY

Insectivorous Plants. *Encyc. Brit.*, xiii.

Numerous minor articles on Botanical detail, e.g., Mangrove, Millet, Manioc, Mimosa, etc., *Encyc. Brit.;* and Agave, Aloe, Aquatic Plants, Amentiferae, etc., etc., *Chambers's Encyc.*, 1881, and New Edition, 1888.

A Type Botanic Garden. *Trans. Bot. Soc.*, 1884.

A Text Book of Botany. By W. J. Behrens, translated by B. Harris Smith. Revised by P. Geddes. 1 vol., 8vo., Edinburgh, 1885.

Botany. *Chambers's Encyc.*, New Edition, 1888.

Outlines of Modern Botany. 100 original illustrations (coloured). *In preparation.*

ALGAE AND FUNGI

On the Life History of Spirillum. 2 plates. *Proc. Roy. Soc. Lond.*, 1878. In conjunction with Dr Ewart.

On the Phenomena of Variegation and Cell-Multiplication in a Species of Enteromorpha. 1 plate (coloured). *Trans. Roy. Soc. Edin.*, 1880.

On Chlamydomyxa Labyrinthuloides (Archer). 1 plate (coloured). *Bot. Soc. Edin.*, June 1881; and *Quart. Journ. Micro. Sci.*, Jan. 1882.

Algae. *Chambers's Encyc.*, New Edition.

CHLOROPHYLL (Vegetable and Animal)

Sur la Fonction de la Chlorophylle chez les Planaires vertes. *Comptes Rendus de l'Acad. d. Sci.*, 1878.

Sur la Chlorophylle Animale et sur la Physiologie des Planaires vertes. *Archives de Zool. Exp. et Gén.*, t. viii.

On the Nature and Functions of the "Yellow Cells" of Radiolarians and Coelenterates. *Proc. Roy. Soc. Edin.*, 1882.

On the Relations between Plants and Animals and the Gases of the Atmosphere. *Ellis Physiology Prize* for 1876–81.

PROTOPLASM AND CELL

Observations sur le Fluide Perivisceral des Oursins. 2 plates (coloured). *Archives de Zool. Exp. et Gén.*, t. viii.

On the Coalescence of Amoeboid Cells into Plasmodia, and on the So-called Coagulation of Invertebrate Perivisceral Fluids. 1 plate. *Proc. Roy. Soc. Lond.*, 1880.

On the Morphology of the Cell. *Roy. Phys. Soc. Edin.*, 1881.
Cell: Cell Theory. *Chambers's Encyc.*, 1883, and New Edition.
Protoplasm. *Encyc. Brit.*, xix.
A Re-statement of the Cell Theory, with Applications to the
Morphology, Physiology, and Classification of Protists, Plants,
and Animals. *Proc. Roy. Soc. Edin.*, 1883.

GENERAL MORPHOLOGY (Vegetable and Animal)

Morphology. *Encyc. Brit.*, xvi. Translated under the supervision of
Prof. Haeckel, as:
Ueber die Stellung und Bedeutung der Morphologie. *Jena. Zeitschr.*,
1884.

GENERAL PHYSIOLOGY (Vegetable and Animal)

Parasitism. *Encyc. Brit.*, xviii.
Reproduction. *Ibid.*, xx.
Sex. *Ibid.*, xxi.
Theory of Growth, Reproduction, Sex, and Heredity. *Proc. Roy.
Soc. Edin.*, 1886; and *Brit. Assoc.*, 1886.

EVOLUTION (Vegetable and Animal)

Darwinian Theory. *Chambers's Encyc.*, 1883, and New Edition.
On Variation in Plants. *Trans. Bot. Soc. Edin.*, 1886; and *Brit.
Assoc.*, 1886.
On the Nature and Causes of Variation in Plants and Animals.
Linnean Society, April 1887; and *Brit. Assoc.*, 1887. (Preliminary
to the following.)
On the Factors of Variation in Plants and Animals. Part 1.—
Plants. *Linnean Society*, November 1887.
On the Origin of Thorns and Prickles. *Bot. Soc. Edin.*, 1887.
On the Origin of Evergreens. *Bot. Soc. Edin.*, 1888.
Variation and Selection. *Encyc. Brit.*, xxiv.
A Re-statement of the Theory of Organic Evolution. *In preparation.*

GENERAL OUTLINES OF BIOLOGY

A Synthetic Outline of the History of Biology. *Proc. Roy. Soc. Edin.*
1886.
Biology. *Chambers's Encyc.*, New Edition.

ZOOLOGY AND COMPARATIVE ANATOMY, ETC.

On the Mechanism of the Odontophore in certain Mollusca. 3
plates (coloured). *Trans. Zool. Soc. Lond.*, Vol. X.
On the Anatomy and Physiology of Convoluta Schultzii (O. Schm.).
Proc. Roy. Soc. Lond., 1879.

Report to Committee of British Association on Researches in Mexico. *Report Brit. Assoc.*, 1880; and *Roy. Phys. Soc. Edin.*, 1880.

Sur l'Histologie des Pedicellaires et des Muscles de l'Oursin. In conjunction with Mr Beddard. *Comptes Rendus*, 1881.

On the Histology of the Pedicellariae and the Muscles of Echinus sphaera (Forbes). In conjunction with Mr Beddard. *Trans. Roy. Soc. Edin.*, 1881.

Sur une Nouvelle Sous-classe d'Infusoires. *Comptes Rendus*, 1881.

Numerous Reviews, Abstracts, and Translations. *Archives de Zool. Exp. et Gén.*, 1878–80.

History and Theory of Spermatogenesis. In conjunction with Mr J. A. Thomson. *Proc. Roy. Soc. Edin.*, 1886.

APPENDIX III

(see p. 242)

WHAT TO DO

Our faith is in moral Renewal, next in Re-education, and therewith Reconstruction. For fulfilment there must be a Resorption of Government into the body of the community. How? By cultivating the habit of direct action instead of waiting upon representative agencies. Hence these social imperatives:

1. Cease to feel Labour personally as a "burden", or see it socially as a "problem"; practise it as a function of life.

2. Raise the life-standard of the people and the thought-standard of schools and universities; so may the workman and his family receive due mead of *real* wages; the leisure of all become dignified; and for our money-economy be substituted a life-economy.

3. Stimulate sympathetic understanding between all sections of the community by co-operation in local initiative; so may European statesmen be no longer driven to avoid revolution by making war.

4. Let cities, towns, villages, groups, associations, work out their own regional salvation; for that they must have freedom, ideas, vision to plan, and means to carry out, (a) betterments of environment (such as housing fit for family life and land for a renewed peasantry), (b) enlargements of mental horizon (such as forelooking universities quick with local life and interests), (c) communitary festivals and other enrichments of life. All these must be parts of one ever-growing Design for the coming years to realize.

5. Make free use of the public credit for these social investments; but don't pay the tribute called "market rate of interest"; create the credit against the new social assets, charge it with an insurance rate and a redemption rate, and pay the bankers a moderate commission to administer it through their system of interlocking banks and clearing-houses; the present unacknowledged use of the public credit by bankers must be recognized and regulated, and being for private profit must be subordinated to the new communitary uses.

6. Fill the public purse from a steeply gradated income-tax (proceeds being shared by the local with the central authority); discriminate in favour of investments that improve the environment

and develop the individual. Let the tax-gatherer take heavy toll of "unearned increments", such as the "bonus" to shareholders, the appreciation of speculative securities, the rise in land values from growth of population.

7. Eschew the despotic habit of regimentation, whether by Governments, Trusts, Companies, tyrants, pedants or police; try the better and older way of co-ordination expanding from local centres through city, region, nation, and beyond; so may the spirit of fellowship express itself, instead of being sterilised by fear, crushed by administrative machinery or perverted by repression.

8. Resist the political temptation to centralise all things in one metropolitan city; seek to renew the ancient tradition of Federation between free cities, regions, dominions.

9. Encourage the linkages of labour and professional associations across international frontiers; it is these that can quicken the unity of western civilisation and bring forth its fruits of concord. Further, let our imperial bureaucrats cease from their superior habit of instructing the orientals and try to learn from them.

10. In general, aim at making individuals more socialized and communities more individualised. To that end, let schools subordinate books to out-door observation and handicrafts; let teachers draw the matter and the method of education from the life and tradition of their pupils' own region, as well as from the history and culture of mankind at large. Let universities seek first for synthesis in the civic life around them; and only thereafter in the pages of philosophy. Above all let governing bodies learn, if not from the Churches, at least from the psychological and social sciences, the distinction between temporal and spiritual powers, and cease to play the double role of Pope and Caesar. As for the chemical and mechanical sciences let them repent of making hell-upon-earth under war-lord and money-lord, and take service in the kingdom of heaven on earth. Then may the machine industry learn from artist-craftsman and town-planner the social significance of Design in all human things, including the city itself; that way lies the guild ideal and hope of its expressing the civic spirit. Let civic designers give rustics access to the city as well as townsmen access to nature; that way lies the regional ideal; and some day men will enter through this portal into paradise regained.

Along all these lines there is movement; but lacking in volume and unity. A crusade of Direct Action has long been afoot; but with many halts and in sparse and isolated companies. The Spirit

Creative is liberated and in flight; but too timidly and on dissevered quests. It is time for clearer understanding, closer co-operation, deeper unison between all men and women of goodwill and high endeavour. So may be prepared definitely planned campaigns for the making and maintenance of worthy homes, smiling villages, noble cities. To engage the militant energies of the race in these adventures of constructive peace and heroically to salve the perennial wreckages of humanity would be the moral equivalent of war.

REFERENCES

Chapter One

1. *Cities in Evolution* by Patrick Geddes. Originally published 1915, Williams & Norgate, London. Revised edition with editorial contributions, 1949; general editor: Jaqueline Tyrwhitt. Reprinted 1968 by Ernest Benn, London, with an introduction by Percy Johnson-Marshall.
2. "Talks from My Outlook Tower" by Patrick Geddes (first printed in issues of *Survey*, New York, during 1925). Reprinted *Patrick Geddes, Spokesman for Man and the Environment*, an anthology edited and with an introduction by Marshall Stalley (New Jersey: Rutgers University Press, 1972).

Chapter Two

1. *London of Today* by Charles Eyre Pascoe (London: Sampson Low, Marston, Searle, and Rivington, Ltd., 1888).
2. "Huxley as Teacher" by Patrick Geddes. Supplement to *Nature*, 9th May 1925, to commemorate centenary of Huxley's birth.
3. *Apes, Angels and Victorians* by William Irvine (London: Weidenfeld and Nicolson, 1955).
4. *Ibid.*
5. "Huxley as Teacher", *op. cit.*
6. *Life: Outlines of Biology* by J. A. Thomson and Patrick Geddes (London: Williams & Norgate, 1931).
7. *Le Play: engineer and social scientist, the life and work of Frédéric Le Play* by Michael Z. Brooke (London: Longman, 1970).
8. *Ibid.*

Chapter Three

1. *Humboldt and the Cosmos* by Douglas Botting (London: Sphere, 1973).
2. Report of the British Association, 1880. (Extract from Report of Committee for conducting Palaeontological and Zoological Researches in Mexico drawn up by Patrick Geddes, and consisting of himself, Dr Gamage, Professor Schäfer, and Professor Allman.)
3. Botting, *op. cit.*
4. *Chance and Necessity* by Jacques Monod (London: Fontana, 1974).

5. *An Introduction to Jung's Psychology* by Frieda Fordham (Harmondsworth: Penguin, 1953).
6. *The World Without and The World Within, Sunday Talks with my Children* by Patrick Geddes (the Saint George library, 1905).
7. *Scottish Eccentrics* by Hugh MacDiarmid (London: Routledge, 1936). The quotation refers to Thomas Davidson.

Chapter Four

1. *Architecture: City Sense* by Theo Crosby (London: Studio Vista, 1965).

Chapter Five

1. "On the Conditions of Progress of the Capitalist & of the Labourer" by Patrick Geddes (1885).
2. "Co-operation versus Socialism" by Patrick Geddes (1888).
3. *My Life* by Havelock Ellis (London: Neville Spearman, 1967).

Chapter Seven

1. *The Student*, 18th January 1888.
2. Exact details concerning the dates and locations of all conservation work connected with Geddes along the Royal Mile are contained in a very useful thesis by Paul Green. This is called *The Life and Work of Sir Patrick Geddes* and was written in connection with the post-graduate course in Environmental Conservation at Edinburgh College of Art and Heriot-Watt University.
3. *Pioneer of Sociology* by Philip Mairet.
4. *American Journal of Sociology.*

Chapter Eight

1. *Cities in Evolution, op. cit.*
2. *The Anarchists* by James Joll (London: Eyre & Spottiswoode, 1964).

Chapter Nine

1. *The New Republic*, 27th August 1930.

Chapter Twelve

1. *Cities in Evolution.*
2. *Ibid.*
3. *Ibid.*

Chapter Thirteen

1. Papers for the Present, second series No. 5: *A Citizen Soldier: His*

Education for War and Peace, being a Memoir of Alasdair Geddes by Victor Branford (London: Headley Bros., 1917).
2. *Talks from my Outlook Tower* by Patrick Geddes, *op. cit.*
3. *Ibid.*
4. Published in the Scottish Geographical Magazine, March 1902.

Chapter Fourteen

1. *City Development, op. cit.*
2. *Ibid.*

Chapter Fifteen

1. *Civics: as Applied Sociology*, Sociological Papers, 1904 (London); *Civics: as Concrete and Applied Sociology, Part II*, Sociological Papers, 1905 (London); *A Suggested Plan for a Civic Museum (or Civic Exhibition) and its Associated Studies*, Sociological Papers, 1906 (London). (For an illuminating article on Geddes's contribution to sociology centred around these papers, see "Patrick Geddes, Analysis of his Theory of Civics: 1880–1904", by E. M. Meller, in *Victorian Studies*, March 1973, Vol. XVI, no. 3 [Indiana University].)

Chapter Sixteen

1. *Town Planning Review*, April 1910.
2. Sir Patrick Geddes Centenary Celebrations, Report of a Symposium held in the Edinburgh College of Art on Friday, 1st October 1954.

Chapter Seventeen

1. *The Life of Sir Edwin Lutyens* by Christopher Hussey (Country Life, 1950).
2. Extracts from these reports may be found in *Patrick Geddes in India* edited by Jaqueline Tyrwhitt (London: Lund Humphries, 1947).
   The places covered by the reports included: Ahmadabad, Amoritsar, Balrampur, Baroda, Bellary, Benares, Bezwada, Bombay, Calcutta, Coimbatore, Colombo, Concanada, Conjeeveram, Dacca, Guntur, Indore, Jabalpur, Kapurthala, Lahore, Lucknow, Madura, Nagpur, Nellore, New Delhi, Patiala, Salem, Tanjore, Tiruvattiswarenpet, Trichinopoly, Vizagapatam.

Chapter Nineteen

1. *An Indian Pioneer: the Life and Work of Sir Jagadis Chandra Bose* by Patrick Geddes (London and New York: Longman, 1920).
2. *Town Planning toward City Development: A Report to the Durbar of Indore.* 2 vols. (Indore: Holkar State Press, 1918).

3. "The Epic of Rama" translated by Romesh Dutt, included in *The Wisdom of India* edited by Lin Yutang (London: Michael Joseph, 1949).
4. *The Interpreter Geddes* by Amelia Defries (London: Routledge, 1927).

Chapter Twenty
1. *The letters of Lewis Mumford and Frederic J. Osborn* edited by Michael Hughes (Bath: Adams & Dart, 1971).

Chapter Twenty-one
1. *The Disciple's Rebellion, op. cit.*
2. *My Father's Son* by Giles Playfair (London: Bles, 1937).

SHORT BIBLIOGRAPHY

(For a detailed bibliography, see Philip Boardman's *Patrick Geddes, Maker of the Future*.)

BOOKS BY PATRICK GEDDES

The Evolution of Sex (with J. Arthur Thomson). London: Scott, 1889; New York: Humboldt Publishing Co., 1890.

Chapters in Modern Botany. London: John Murray, 1893; New York: Charles Scribner, 1893. (University Extension Manuals.)

City Development: A Study of Parks, Gardens, and Culture-Institutes. Edinburgh: Geddes and Co., 1904. Reprinted by the Irish University Press, with an introduction by Dr Peter Green, 1974.

The Masque of Learning and Its Many Meanings. Edinburgh: Patrick Geddes & Colleagues, 1912.

Sex (with J. Arthur Thomson). London: Williams & Norgate, 1914; New York: Henry Holt & Co., 1914. (Home University Library.)

Cities in Evolution. London: Williams & Norgate, 1915. Reprinted 1949 with an introduction by Jaqueline Tyrwhitt and other additions. Reprinted 1968 by Ernest Benn, London, with an introduction by Percy Johnson-Marshall.

The Coming Polity (with Victor Branford). London: Williams & Norgate, 1917.

Ideas at War (with G. Slater). London: Williams & Norgate, 1917.

Our Social Inheritance (with Victor Branford). London: Williams & Norgate, 1919.

An Indian Pioneer: The Life and Work of Sir Jagadis Chandra Bose. London and New York: Longmans, Green and Co., 1920.

Biology (with J. Arthur Thomson). London: Williams & Norgate, 1925; New York: Henry Holt and Co., 1925. (Home University Library.)

Life: Outlines of Biology (with J. Arthur Thomson). 2 vols. London: Williams & Norgate, 1931; New York: Harper & Bros., 1931.

EDITED BOOKS OF WRITINGS BY PATRICK GEDDES

Patrick Geddes in India, edited by Jaqueline Tyrwhitt. London: Lund Humphries, 1947.

Patrick Geddes: Spokesman for Man and Environment, an anthology edited and with a biographical introduction by Marshall Stalley. New Jersey: Rutgers University Press, 1973.

Books about Patrick Geddes

The Interpreter Geddes: the Man and his Gospel, by Amelia Defries with contributions by Rabindranath Tagore, Israel Zangwill, Lewis Mumford, J. Arthur Thomson, Patrick Abercrombie and C. Setalvad. London: Routledge, 1927; New York: Boni & Liveright, 1928.

Patrick Geddes, Maker of the Future, by Philip Boardman. Chapel Hill: the University of North Carolina Press, 1944.

Pioneer of Sociology, the Life and Letters of Patrick Geddes, by Philip Mairet. London: Lund Humphries, 1957.

INDEX
by Michael Gordon